Praise for Final Flight

"Stekel has breathed warm life into these long-lost World War II airmen who disappeared while on a training mission in 1942 . . . [he] skillfully weaves the crew's fate in these rugged mountains with his own quest to unravel the mystery."

> —Eric Blehm, bestselling author of *The Last Season*, *The Only Thing Worth Dying For* and *Molly the Owl*

"Peter Stekel has captured the history, geography, and the mystery surrounding this inspiring tale of the High Sierra."

> —G. Pat Macha, author of *Aircraft Wrecks in the Mountains and Deserts of California*

"This book will make you proud of America and proud of mountaineers."

> —William Alsup, author of *Missing in the Minarets* and *Such a Landscape!*

"*Final Flight* is a thoroughly enjoyable read, a detective story [that] combines classic investigative reporting with a personal love of the mountains . . ."

> —Douglas H. Clark, Ph.D. Associate Professor, Geology Department, Western Washington University

"Peter Stekel's search for the cause of the crash of four ill-fated WWII airmen leads to . . . [an] invigorated appreciation of the dedication of the men and women of the Greatest Generation and . . . those who gave their life in service of their country."

> —Michael Sledge, author of *Soldier Dead: How We Recover, Identify, Bury, and Honor Our Military Fallen*

"Among the wildest places on earth, the remote and isolated Sierra Nevadas hold secrets from the past that only now are being discovered."

> —Karen F. Taylor-Goodrich, Superintendent, *Sequoia & Kings Canyon National Parks*

"Those who love the high country will find this a fascinating read."

> —William Tweed, coauthor of *Challenge of the Big Trees: A Resource History of Sequoia and Kings Canyon National Parks*

FINAL FLIGHT

The Mystery of a WWII Plane Crash
and the Frozen Airmen
in the High Sierra

PETER STEKEL

 WILDERNESS PRESS ... *on the trail since 1967*
BERKELEY, CA

FINAL FLIGHT: The Mystery of a WWII Plane Crash and the Frozen Airmen in the High Sierra

1st EDITION 2010

Copyright © 2010 by Peter Stekel

Front cover photo and frontispiece copyright © 2010 by Peter Stekel
Maps: Lohnes + Wright
Cover design: Steve Sullivan, STEVECO International; Larry B. Van Dyke
Book design: Larry B. Van Dyke
Book editor: Julie Van Pelt

ISBN 978-0-89997-475-0

Manufactured in United States of America

Published by: **Wilderness Press**
1345 8th Street
Berkeley, CA 94710
(800) 443-7227; FAX (510) 558-1696
info@wildernesspress.com
www.wildernesspress.com

Visit our website for a complete listing of our books
and for ordering information.

Distributed by Publishers Group West

Main cover photo: Aerial view from about 15,000 feet of Mount Darwin and Mount Mendel, from the northeast.
Frontispiece: Mendel Glacier.

Library of Congress Cataloging-in-Publication Data

Stekel, Peter.
    Final flight : the mystery of a WWII plane crash and the frozen airmen in the High Sierra / Peter Stekel. -- 1st ed.
        p. cm.
    Includes bibliographical references and index.
    ISBN 978-0-89997-475-0 (pbk.)
    1. Aircraft accidents--Investigation--Sierra Nevada (Calif. and Nev.)
2. World War, 1939-1945--Missing in action--United States. 3. Missing
persons--Investigation--Sierra Nevada (Calif. and Nev.) 4. Airmen--
United States--History--20th century. 5. Beechcraft 18 (Airplanes) I. Title.
    TL553.525.C2S74 2010
    363.12'4650979487--dc22

                                    2010007775

When I was twelve years old I went away
to summer camp in the High Sierra.
My mother was fond of saying
that I never came back.

This book is dedicated to her.

For Mary —
Merry Christmas
Seattle   2010

Peter Stekel

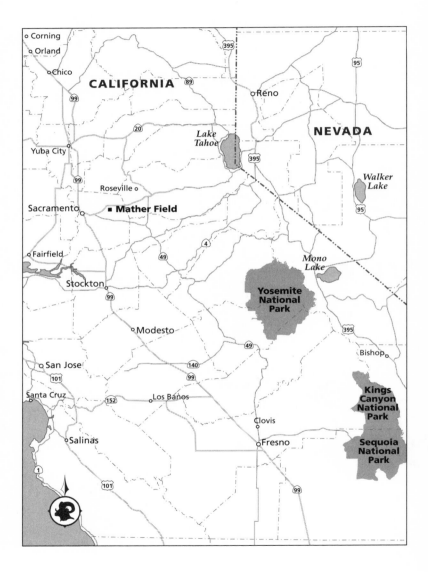

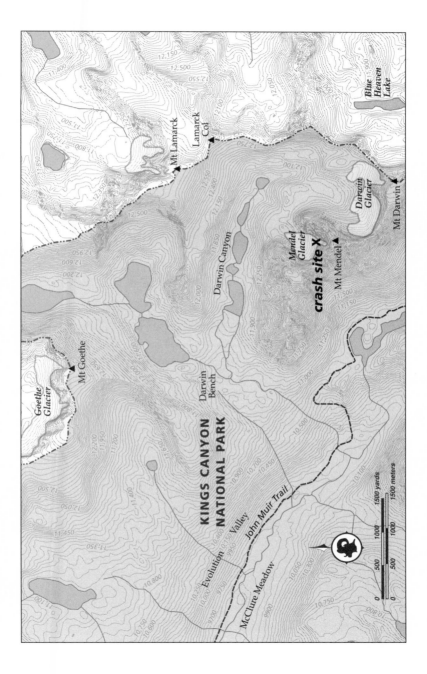

Contents

Prologue

We are the only life here. There are no trees or shrubs, no grasses or sedges. No pretty wildflowers. There are no lichens, no animals or insects. Only granite and ice. The Mendel Glacier sits in a cirque at about 12,000 feet, a coliseum of rock in the Sierra Nevada with cracked walls rising nearly another 2,000 feet. At our boots is a section of airplane engine—twisted, broken metal, oil bleeding into ice.

From the engine wreckage, my climbing partner Michele works her way down the steep slope of the glacier. She has to be careful; the surface is slick. One slip would hurt, though she wouldn't slide far. Large rocks jut out everywhere. I kick at one but it's embedded in the glacier and doesn't budge. Meltwater creates model luge courses in the expanse of ice.

Two years ago, in 2005, climbers discovered a body melting out of this glacier and I'm certain the remains are linked to the aircraft wreckage Michele and I have discovered. I want to stand on the spot where this Frozen Airman was found and think about the person who died here on November 18, 1942. Holding my GPS unit like a divining rod, I traverse west. I'm not paying close attention to anything except where to put my feet. Raising my eyes to check my bearing, I'm surprised to see a short tree, bent over and blackened, killed by the frost. Something shines in the sun: a ring hanging on a tiny branch. I stop to think about that. It couldn't be a tree. There are no trees up here. It is a man.

He is hunched over a rock, his left arm curled under him as if hugging something tightly to his chest or favoring a sore shoulder. His body is desiccated, the skin dark and rough. Shreds of a rough-woven wool, olive-drab sweater are wrapped around him. He has blond, wavy hair. Beside him is an undeployed parachute, the cotton canvas pack long ago rotted away. The parachute shrouds appear new and are still tightly arranged.

CHAPTER 1

A Body in the Glacier

It is first light, October 15, 2005. Michael Nozel and Mark Postle labor across Mendel Glacier. Step, stop, rest. Hearts pound blood. Lungs struggle for air. Muscles strain to carry heavy loads. All they see is ice, rock, and sky. All human sounds across the desolate land-scape are held master by the wind.

Pack straps chafe shoulders accustomed to this hard work. The two men move robotically. Step, stop, rest. Step, stop, rest. At 12,600 feet above sea level, the climbers are nearing a point where a third of the earth's atmosphere is below them. Do this one thing perfect-ly—one foot and then the other, upward to the objective—that is all that matters. Proper conditioning is critical, but even conditioning may fail at this elevation, making the simplest task an exercise in agony.

Linear travel is challenging. The ice underfoot is hard, like city sidewalks, but carved by tiny rivers of meltwater. Sharp granite, rocks and boulders, poke out of the frozen water. A long summer of sun has melted deep divots into the ice called "sun cups." It's like walking across overlapping potholes. Nothing grows here but time. The sky is blue, an amazing shade of blue.

The two men are here to attempt a widely known ice climb. Above the glacier, there it is—a narrow gully filled with ice and rock, rising nearly vertically in front of them. They have hiked miles over trail and cross-country into the bright sun and frozen, canine wind to this point thousands of vertical feet up in the southern Sierra Nevada.

"My body was fully engaged," Nozel says of that day, "and my mind was fully functioning. But it was idling." At these elevations, with not enough oxygen to carry on the important business of life, the body is easily fatigued and the brain becomes weak and confused. That may be why it took so long for Nozel to understand what he saw. "Far up the glacier, a brief flicker interrupted my mantra. It was almost a subconscious awareness—a fleeting thought—momentarily there, then gone. Another dozen steps ahead, and I noticed it again"—an object fluttering in the wind, like Tibetan prayer flags. Odd. Prayer flags in a national park on a glacier that rarely sees a visitor?

Nozel takes a few more steps upward. "There it is again," he says to the wind. "I am absolutely not imagining that!" His breathing is rapid, almost panting—not from altitude and lack of oxygen, but from involuntary hyperventilation, as if Nozel had narrowly avoided a head-on collision with a cement truck.

Nozel finds his voice as his eyes wake up his mind. "Holy ..." and the wind cuts off his voice. He sees nylon cords, wound tightly in long streamers. A canvas container. Silk, yellowed with age, flapping in the wind. Emotion washes over Nozel as he contemplates the scene. "Good Lord. His parachute never deployed."

● ● ●

"Mark!" Nozel yells, raising his voice over the wind. "Mark! You have to see this!"

In the ice is a frozen man, looking like a swimmer emerging from water, though he's nearly completely buried in the glacier. A portion of torso, a head, a shoulder, an arm. Fair hair. An olive-drab sweater in tatters. A canvas pack of nylon cord. Here is a man trying to wrest himself from the cold glacier's sting. Set me free.

But what would a body be doing in a glacier in Southern California?

Lost in his own reverie of wind and cold, sun and lack of oxygen, Mark Postle at first doesn't lift his head. But something in the urgency of his friend's voice makes him stop and look around. "What is it?"

"You need to see this for yourself!"

The two friends examine the parachute. The thing blends into the surrounding granite with only flowing motion differentiating silk from ground. Nozel can't believe he spotted it; Postle had passed right by—maybe fifteen feet away—without a glance because his peripheral vision was blocked by his parka hood. Right place, right time. How many other climbers have passed this point?

Wordlessly they move their attention from the parachute to the man. His right arm extends straight out from the shoulder, and at the elbow the forearm plunges downward into the ice. The left arm also extends straight out from the shoulder but without as acute a bend at the elbow before disappearing. Only a portion of the man's chest and his head are exposed. There are no facial features. There is blond hair on the skull and blond hair frozen into the ground. A D-ring for the parachute ripcord lies detached and adjacent to the body.

The wind is relentless, but neither Nozel nor Postle are aware of it. Each is trying to understand what may have brought this man here. Independently they have decided this could only be someone from the military. Sweater, parachute ... it's a feeling.

Neither of them know it, but there are still 88,000 American soldiers missing from past wars—90 percent of them from World War II. Even had they known these statistics, the climbers would not have been sure if this person was one of those lost soldiers.

Nozel and Postle aren't ready to accept that there are human remains in the ice beside them. Climbers, through life and experience, are logical, thoughtful beings. They read. They study. They learn. But this is outside their experience. "Could it have been that the military did some testing of parachutes with animals?" one asks.

"Perhaps. But why the ripcord? Wouldn't they use static line deployments then?" the other answers.

"Yeah. More than likely." A static line is employed when a team of paratroopers jumps over a site and deploys their parachutes automatically. It would also be used when dropping equipment or animals unable to pull a ripcord.

"Maybe there was some jump testing done with mannequins?"

"But why would they have bothered to clothe a mannequin?"

"Right. Good point."

What Nozel and Postle are seeing is simply too incongruous to understand. Maybe it's the altitude. Maybe it's their fatigue. How could a body end up on this glacier? "It just seems unlikely there would have been paratrooper training so far from civilization. It's pretty remote around here right now. Think about back then."

"Maybe some elite squad was preparing for European-theater mountain climbing?" *European* means World War II. This person may have waited over sixty years in this ice. They have no answers, only more questions. The first and most cogent of which is, "What should we do now?"

Standing over the body, they scan the immediate area, searching for identification. Neither feels comfortable in close proximity to this man. It's like they have stumbled across a burial site. Nozel pokes around the parachute, carefully exposing some interior folds and comes upon "US Army" in faded blue letters, with "AC41-1984" stenciled below. He cuts out the material with the number on it, hoping that investigators will be able to correlate the numbers to an owner. He takes some photos.

Postle pulls out his GPS unit and marks a waypoint directly over the body. They stand in silence. This soldier is done waiting. It's time for Michael Nozel and Mark Postle to hike out and report that somebody, missing for a very long time, has been found.

A soldier is about to come home.

CHAPTER 2

Home from the Mountain

Leaving the glacier is no easier than getting there. The two climbers must pay close attention to what they're doing. The ice is still slick. And off the ice the terrain is still steep, the talus still large, loose, and it moves unpredictably underfoot. The afternoon Sierra sun is warm, but a bitter wind still blows "with the authority of a drill sergeant," as Nozel remembers it. They aren't out of the wilderness yet.

Despite the inherent dangers of moving across talus, descent back to camp in upper Darwin Canyon goes without a hitch. All it takes is time, a wilderness staple. Michael Nozel and Mark Postle move using well-developed habits. Their eyes scan the rock, assess the safest route, and pick a trail automatically. The essence of boulder hopping has been likened to the rhythm of dance. As Doug Robinson wrote in *A Night on the Ground, A Day in the Open*, "The secret is to relax and let yourself learn without thinking of what you're doing." This is what poet and essayist Gary Snyder calls "emptying yourself," and Morihei Ueshiba, the founder of Aikido, called "No Mind," voiding oneself of all conscious thought.

Still, back at camp, among the rocks, beside the barren upper lake of Darwin Canyon, beneath the summit of Mount Mendel, thought floods in. The climbers are stunned by their discovery, fatigued by emotional turmoil, lack of sleep, and two days of hard physical exertion. And, there is still an exhausting hike out to consider, along with telling their story to the authorities.

There is no defined route for the arduous 1,300-foot straight-up climb out of Darwin Canyon to Lamarck Col. Snow lightly falls on the east side of the col and continues on and off as Nozel and Postle make their way through the miles and hours to the trailhead. Later, as Postle parks his Honda across from the Bishop Police Station, rain falls steadily and Bishop has developed that wonderfully pungent fragrance of wet high desert towns—a mix of pasture, earth, and sagebrush you can wrap around yourself like a shawl. The undistinguished cream-colored, cinder-block police station occupies the corner of West Line Street and North Warren Street, one block west of U.S. Highway 395 and next door to the Bishop Fire Department. A sign, dimly illuminated from within, juts out from the building, announcing in yellow capital letters on a blue background, POLICE.

It's not yet 5:00 P.M. and the station is shut up tight. Nozel and Postle are a bit dumbfounded by this. Neither live in a big city, but it seems odd that this small-town police station is actually closed. They don't realize that autumn weekends in Bishop are slow days for crime fighters.

Nozel works his way to the back of the station and spots an officer about to drive off in a private car. He flags the man down and comes straight to the point. "I believe I discovered a body on the Mendel Glacier earlier today. Do you know whether someone could take a statement?"

The officer's initial response is dubious. "A body? Today?" And he's slightly confused. "You're just getting into town?"

"Yes. A frozen body. I discovered it this morning. My partner and I have a section of the parachute with an ID number as well as GPS coordinates of the location."

Nozel speaks with authority, and authority knows how to respond. Gone is any indication of doubt or uncertainty as the officer responds, "Go around to the front. I'll let you in. There's definitely someone who will take your statement." The police station isn't empty after all.

Once inside, Nozel and Postle are told by Officer Brian Brossy that the Inyo County Sheriff's Department holds jurisdiction for search and rescue operations and anything else occurring outside of Bishop's boundaries. A deputy will arrive in fifteen minutes to take their statements. While they wait, Brossy quizzes the climbers. Each question he asks demonstrates a higher level of interest and Nozel, in particular, enjoys the officer's candidly appreciative responses as the story unfolds.

"Really?" Officer Brossy enthuses. "Buried to the armpits?" An avid hiker and hunter with extensive backcountry experience, Brossy knows firsthand how rare this discovery is. "Parachute still attached?" he wags his head in disbelief.

When I spoke with Brossy three years after the fact, he was still overwhelmed by the climbers' story. "It made the hair on the back of my neck stand up. I was excited. I wanted to go up there."

When the sheriff deputy Paul Baldwin arrives, he's efficient and methodical. All business, he allows Nozel and Postle to speak uninterrupted. Even Baldwin's report is brusque: three short paragraphs, just the facts. He attaches a sheet of paper with the climbers' hastily scrawled note, giving the elevation and coordinates of their find.

Ending the interview, Deputy Baldwin records addresses and phone numbers for Nozel and Postle and instructs them to contact him in the future should they remember anything else of importance. Not long after, the friends are driving north through a humongous rain storm as heavy snow falls in the mountains. They travel mostly in silence, punctuated by long and disjointed discussions of what they saw, or think they saw. They still don't know for sure, or can't really believe, what their eyes told them up there on the glacier.

By the time they arrive home, a media storm has begun and their phones are ringing with interview requests. Nozel and Postle do their best to keep a low profile, standing by a pact made during their drive home to not be drawn into the story. Several years later Nozel explained it like this: "We had been there for a recreational purpose and now we find something altogether different—possibly the remains of someone who had been entombed in Mendel

Glacier for a long time. This was a situation where someone had, or at least appeared to have, lost his life in service to our country. And because of that, it put a whole different meaning to our activity there. A lot of things start to come to your mind. Certainly, thinking that if this is the first time this discovery had been made and this person had been there for a long, long time ... What ramifications is this going to have for the family members?"

Over the next few days, the climbers experience only one mentionable negative event involving the media. Actually, they find it more humorous than negative. A representative from *Good Morning America* contacts the climbers and insists they appear on the show. "He just couldn't believe we weren't interested!" said Nozel, laughing over the incident. "Then, this individual had the audacity to get surly and tell us this was bigger than the two of us. And we had some kind of *obligation*. That we *had* to go with the news. And the news is bigger than you and you can't ignore the news!"

Nozel told me the TV show rep did get one thing right: "Indeed, it [the story] was bigger than us. And that was why we weren't interested in being on the news."

• • •

While the two climbers drove home, plans were being laid at Sequoia and Kings Canyon National Parks headquarters to bring the Frozen Airman home from the mountain. Hampering the project at first was remoteness of the site, bad weather, and the problem of ascertaining the identity of the human remains and whether they were historical or contemporary.

Mendel Glacier lies at an elevation around 12,600 feet and is situated below Mount Mendel (13,710 feet). It's located in Darwin Canyon at the northeastern tip of Sequoia and Kings Canyon National Parks. A half mile south is the much larger Darwin Glacier beneath Mount Darwin (13,831 feet). Both glaciers feed the five-lake chain of lakes that occupy Darwin Canyon. Water from the lakes flows through Darwin Bench, a broad and gently sloping area, before joining Evolution Creek in Evolution Valley. The National Park Service maintains a summer ranger station along the John Muir

Trail at McClure Meadow in the lower reaches of the valley. Access to Darwin Canyon is restricted by geography to either a way trail across Darwin Bench from Evolution Valley or a cross-country route over Lamarck Col (12,880 feet) from a trailhead at North Lake on the east side of the Sierra. Park headquarters are a long day's drive away from any trailhead at Ash Mountain, near the small gateway town of Three Rivers in the western-slope foothills of the Sierra Nevada near Visalia.

It was Sunday and already late in the day of October 15, 2005 when the Inyo County Sheriff's Department took Nozel and Postle's statements, and the sheriff waited until the following morning to contact park rangers. Ranger Edward "Ned" Kelleher was dispatched by helicopter from his station at Cedar Grove the afternoon of October 16 to investigate. "We got a report that remains with a parachute had been found," he recalled in late 2008. "It wasn't clear at the time if they were historic or not." At this point the case was being handled in the same manner as any other accidental death or search and rescue in the parks.

The weather forecast was not good, and Kelleher's immediate assignment was to locate the remains before they were completely covered by snow. His initial assessment was based on news about the parachute. "The first thing I did when I got the report was to check and see if it was a hang glider or paraglider accident." There were no recent reports of missing fliers, or of other recreationists for that matter.

Erratic, high-velocity winds precluded any sort of effective search or locating a suitable landing zone at the glacier, so Kelleher aborted the mission and returned to Cedar Grove. Continued strong winds and snow were in the forecast for the next two days before the sun was expected once again. Autumn is like that in the Sierra—startlingly nice days are quickly usurped by equally amazing stormy ones.

While Kelleher waited, further news clarified his mission. "It became clear that the remains were historic. We were able to make contact with the climbers. They had a photo of the parachute that clearly showed the historic nature and that it was military."

On October 18 the weather cleared enough for a safe flight into the backcountry. Kelleher, assisted by helitack crewmember Fred Mason and Ranger Chris Waldschmidt, flew to Mendel Glacier. They surveyed the snowy scene from the air and could spot the Frozen Airman. The helicopter set down about a tenth of a mile southwest of the remains, below the glacier's bergschrund. Kelleher and Waldschmidt unloaded tools and camping gear and then traversed the glacier and began photo-documenting the scene with a digital camera. They didn't disturb anything and awaited arrival of park archeologist Keith Hamm, a team of search-and-rescue rangers, and a videographer.

Kelleher's written report outlined what they saw. The remains appeared to be the head and upper torso of a person, lying face down in the ice, the body contorted and twisted into an unnatural pose. "The remains were not well preserved," Kelleher told me. "The visible skin was darkened, the clothing torn and ragged and there were no visible facial features. The skull appeared to be deformed but there were still portions of blondish hair visible on the head." His GPS unit recorded the elevation as 12,600 feet.

Back at Ash Mountain, park rangers assembled what little they knew about the Frozen Airman and airplane crashes in the vicinity. A media release was sent out, explaining that something had been found in Darwin Canyon and that park records suggested it could be the body of a military aviator lost, maybe, just maybe, in 1942.

Elsewhere at park headquarters on October 18, Gregg Fauth, the Sequoia and Kings Canyon National Parks wilderness coordinator, sent an e-mail to the Joint POW/MIA Accounting Command (JPAC), the branch of the U.S. military charged with recovering and identifying soldiers missing in action. JPAC currently spends more than $100 million a year in their effort to find and identify soldiers still missing from World War II, Korea, and Vietnam, and achieve the fullest possible accounting of all Americans missing as a result of the nation's past conflicts. That makes the work of JPAC an important component in bringing home the finality of death to families—JPAC delivers the remains, when possible, and provides final proof.

Fauth informed JPAC that hikers had found a body in Sequoia and Kings Canyon National Parks. Based on park archives, the remains were believed to be military in nature and historic in origin. Fauth inquired if JPAC wanted to participate in the body recovery. From its base at Hickam Field near Pearl Harbor in Hawaii, JPAC responded by dispatching Paul Emanovsky, a forensic anthropologist, to Fresno, California. He arrived the following morning.

Late afternoon of October 18 rolled around and the sun dipped below the high rock walls of the cirque enclosing Mendel Glacier. The weather hadn't improved enough to allow a helicopter to return with the videographer, archeologist, and other rangers, so Kelleher and Waldschmidt picked up their gear, hiked down to the upper lake in Darwin Canyon, and hunkered down in their tents for a cold and snowy night.

• • •

Visibility in California the following morning, October 19, 2005, was somewhere between infinity and forever. It was one of those beautiful fall days that make it easy to understand why so many people who moved to California for defense-industry jobs during World War II stayed even when all the jobs dried up. There was clear blue sky at park headquarters in Ash Mountain, without any trace of the air pollution that plagues the area most of the year.

For Kelleher and Waldschmidt, though, the morning was a dark and frosty one. High ridges in Darwin Canyon do an excellent job of keeping the sun away, and cold air from higher elevations flows down-canyon like a river. The rangers were grateful when the helicopter returned to pick them up for a ride to the glacier landing zone scoped out the previous day. They landed around 10:00 A.M., about the same time JPAC anthropologist Paul Emanovsky arrived from Fresno for a briefing session at the Grant Grove Ranger Station on the park's northwestern boundary. The helicopter shuttled Keith Hamm, park archeologist; Steve Bumgardner, videographer and photographer; and Jim Gould, park ranger, to the glacier.

Because of the previous day's snow, Gould remembered, "flying in to the glacier you couldn't really see the body." Fortunately, yellow flagging marking the spot was still visible. Gould also remembered that "it was extremely cold ... We had to land at the top of the glacier slope, at the base of the bergschrund, and then hike down to where he was located. There was no sun and because it was late October, the days were shorter than in summer. We were working in the shadows almost all day."

As the archeologist on site, Keith Hamm supervised the digging. Hamm has excavated a lot of human remains, mostly Native American, and it was his idea to dig around the body, leaving it on a pedestal just as if they were isolating a ground burial. This enabled the crew to examine below the Frozen Airman and guarantee that nothing was left behind in the ice. Hamm recognized that "you can only damage stuff in the field," so the team took care to do everything right the first time. Using hammers, chisels, and ice axes they chipped away all day, working mostly on their hands and knees and clearing a ring-shaped pit around the Frozen Airman. Everything they found, including three fingernails and pieces of bone, was placed in plastic bags.

It was cold work, but hot, sweaty, and aerobic too because the rangers were dressed for subfreezing temperatures. As the hours passed they began to slow down, fatigued by the hard labor and high elevation. Paul Emanovsky arrived at 2:30 P.M. by helicopter to find the Frozen Airman sitting atop a four-by-four by three-foot-tall pedestal that weighed nearly 500 pounds. The pit itself was nine feet long and six feet deep. To appreciate the difficulty of the excavation, imagine breaking apart an equivalent-sized concrete driveway with a hammer while taking a breath only every thirty seconds. Under Keith Hamm's experienced eye, the removal of the airman from Mendel Glacier was handled as sensitively and respectfully as could be done while working at over 12,000 feet in below-freezing temperatures with the threat of a winter snowstorm always on the horizon. Finally freed from the glacier, the remains were flown to the Fresno County coroner's office, where wilderness coordinator Gregg Fauth waited with two other park rangers.

Working with the Frozen Airman had a profound affect on everyone associated with his recovery. Ned Kelleher later described the difference between a routine search and rescue or body recovery and what he did that cold October day. "For a crime scene or accident," he told me, "—you take lots of photos. It's important for the family that you collect as much of the remains as you can. When there is major trauma, like from a long fall, or long past as in this case, the remains become more scattered," and the job of recovery becomes more difficult. The significance of what the team found on Mendel Glacier and the impact that developed in the public's consciousness are what Kelleher has never forgotten. Bringing the airman back from the glacier provided a direct link to the past: "Why did the plane crash? What was it doing there? There's a mystery that exists with it ... Here is a slice of history that has been preserved for over sixty years." For Kelleher, the Frozen Airman embodied everything the Park Service was designed to protect: the nation's history and heritage. And there was something else that made the experience even deeper. "He was a regular guy, just like us."

Removing the remains proved to be a poignant, yet uplifting, experience for Ranger Jim Gould. He began working for the Park Service in 1991 and served eight years in the U.S. Coast Guard before that. His work had always involved search and rescue, structural and wildland fire suppression, and swift-water rescue. He was medically trained as well. With such a career, Gould recognized this body recovery was different from anything he had ever done. It had archeological significance. He knew well the story of Ötzi, a paleolithic man whose body was found in a glacier on the border between Italy and Austria in 1991. Treated first as a possible modern homicide, Ötzi's recovery was a textbook study in bungling. Not only was his recovery an embarrassing mistake by authorities and experts, his remains were then subjected to disrespect and exhibition. To bring the Frozen Airman home correctly, professionally, and be able to provide closure to surviving family after all this time made Gould proud to be associated with the Park Service.

Keith Hamm was also deeply moved by the experience. Most of Hamm's work involves removing Native American remains uncovered during construction projects. "Unfortunately, when we reach that point of discovery there is no turning back. They're coming out. Nobody likes to do that. It's like moving a cemetery—and nobody likes to do that either." The Frozen Airman was all that and a whole lot more. "This is a person with relatives," Hamm emphasized. "They knew about him." And presumably still cared.

Why the Frozen Airman was so important to the public is something touched on by Michael Sledge in his book, *Soldier Dead*: "While the soldiers who die have brothers-in-arms who look after them, back home are brothers and sisters, uncles and aunts, nephews, nieces, cousins, wives, sons, daughters, fathers, and mothers who may have nothing at all." Everyone concerned cares about this person. They make him their own. He didn't die for his country; he died for them.

The Frozen Airman shared something else with those killed in action. His death was sudden, violent, premature—a young man who died in the prime of physical life. And for over six decades his family had no body to mourn over and grieve. Sledge says, "While it is doubtful that proper burial is necessary for the dead themselves, abundant evidence demonstrates its importance to the living." Funerals, especially in the face of death in battle, help us face death's randomness. Without this ceremony there exists faint hope for closure.

• • •

While Keith Hamm, Jim Gould, and the others chipped away at the Mendel Glacier, trying to dislodge the airman, frontcountry rangers at Ash Mountain worked to supply the backstory to what was developing into a media phenomenon. Since the press release was distributed that morning, interest in the Frozen Airman had mounted.

Despite their hard work, the rangers didn't know much for sure except that a military aircraft crashed in Sequoia and Kings National Parks at the onset of World War II. They knew this because Ward Eldredge, the park's museum technician, found a list of forty-eight plane crashes in the parks, both civil and military, with UTM coordinates keyed to fifteen-minute topographic maps. The list mentioned an AT-7 number 41-21079, along with the terse remark, "D.9/24/47/MELTING FR GLC." *AT-7* referred to an Advanced Trainer, Beech 18, twin-engine aircraft used for navigation training during World War II. The AT-7 entry in the list of airplane crashes also cross-referenced a four-by-four-inch piece of aluminum in the park archives. On the metal, a white, mostly typewritten label said, "U.S. ARMY AT-7 #41-21079 Missing 18 November 1942 Found 24 September 1947 in Mendel Glacier (Darwin Canyon). Based at Mather Field. 4 on board. All buried at National Cemetery-San Bruno, California."

Nobody at Ash Mountain knew how the burnished piece of aluminum came to be in the archives. And if it referred to the Frozen Airman's airplane, could he be a *fifth* crewmember or maybe a stowaway? How could all of the airmen of that plane have been buried in San Bruno if there was an apparent crewmember still buried in the ice? Confusion over the number of men on that November 18 flight would not be conclusively resolved for several months.

CHAPTER 3

Who Is the Frozen Airman?

Keith Hamm and JPAC anthropolgist Paul Emanovsky step off the Park Service helicopter at Ash Mountain. In the balmy Sierra foothills, at 1,700 feet, they are less than thirty minutes air time from the icy, 12,600-foot glacier and removal of the Frozen Airman. They are tired and hungry and in need of hot showers, but there is still work to be done.

From the landing zone they find their way to a makeshift media center set up in the park headquarters library. Hamm surveys the dozen or so expectant reporters with shy discomfort as he sits down at a desk with a microphone. Hamm is tired. You can see it in his face and hear it in his voice. What you don't see is his headache, fallout from altitude sickness. His long hair is tied in a pony tail but wisps of it escape and move across his sunburned and bearded face. He glances at the lone television camera in the room. The camera stares back.

Behind Hamm, in inexpensive wooden bookcases, are books, loosely bound reports, graduate studies, theses and dissertations, scientific papers, and assorted other publications about the Sierra. These precious resources make the library one of a kind and well suited for the unusual task at hand.

A newsperson asks for a sound check and Hamm laughs uncomfortably, mumbles "hello," adding apologetically, "It's been a long day."

Unseen, offstage, a very television-newscaster voice prompts, "Well, what did you find?"

Haltingly, Hamm takes it from the top: the report of a body, the glacier, cutting away the ice, showing respect for this great unknown.

• • •

As an archeologist, Hamm is familiar with the points Michael Parker Pearson raises in *The Archeology of Death and Burial*: "Reburial, restitution, repatriation and non-disturbance of human remains have become key issues in North America." Pearson's book is about Native Americans reclaiming their ancestors, but people like Hamm, from the National Park Service, and Paul Emanovsky, from JPAC, work under the assumption that all human remains deserve honor and respect.

Because of several state and federal laws, including the National Museum of the American Indian Act of 1989 and Native American Graves Protection and Repatriation Act of 1990, how we view the recovery of remains has changed. This change is a direct outgrowth of concerns raised by Native Americans during the 1970s and 1980s. The days of archeologists acting with impunity when excavating a burial site are long gone, relegated to pulp fiction and motion pictures. The "politics of the dead," as Pearson calls it, is a recognition that if the dead don't care, "the living most certainly do."

For the Frozen Airman, Hamm and Emanovsky worked under the same rules and ethical considerations as if they were recovering the remains of a 10,000-year-old body. This code of ethics was developed in 1986 by the International Council on Museums and was expanded by the Vermillion Accord in 1989 when the World Archeological Congress held its first meeting at the University of South Dakota in Vermillion. There are other ethics codes, including Historic Scotland's policy document, *The Treatment of Human Remains in Archeology*. All these approaches might best be summed up as simply following the Golden Rule.

Whether working with the removal of ancient or contemporary remains, or gathering evidence to authenticate mass murder by exhuming recent massacre victims, the archeology of excavating grave sites is more than digging up bones. It is about death. To an archeologist, how a person dies is not so important as how they came to be buried.

And how a person came to be buried supplies a huge amount of data for archeologists when they come across remains. Bones and tissue are historical artifacts of life. They store information and transmit to the scientist the ability to determine age, sex, presence and/or absence of disease or trauma, and physical characteristics. All had the potential to contribute significantly to identifying the Frozen Airman.

• • •

Soft-spoken and given to reflection, Hamm answers the press people's excited queries, recognizing the significance of the man found in the ice. "He's a hero who died supporting his country— right here. And sixty-three years later we're going to bring some closure to the families." To repeated questions of what was found on the body in the way of dog tags or other identifying features, Hamm can only reply that they chipped the body from the ice and didn't look at anything for fear of damaging the evidence JPAC will need to make an identification. "We tried to keep as much in situ—in place—and then it will be analyzed in the lab."

For reporters in the room who don't know anything about Sequoia and Kings Canyon and national park values, Hamm contributes a low-key educational spiel. "I'm glad to work for an organization that values the cultural resources that we have here. This is news-worthy, but we also preserve other things." He cites examples from the cavalry era (the first people who guarded the park after its 1890 establishment) and also Native American historical sites and arti-facts, to which can be added the preservation of plants, mammals, birds, insects, rivers, rocks, glaciers, and entire ecosystems. Hamm says that a previously unknown Native American site was found just that morning when the helicopter set down en route to the gla-cier. Based on projectile points found on the ground, he supposes the site could be as old as 1650 BP. Clearly, national parks are more than campgrounds, interpretive signs, and tourist attractions.

Keith Hamm finishes and Paul Emanovsky addresses the camera. Emanovsky looks like he hasn't slept since leaving Hawaii less than twenty-four hours before. Like an attorney addressing the jury, he walks everyone through techniques that can be used in identifying the Frozen Airman: dental charts, methods akin to archaeological and crime-scene recovery of remains, biological profiles, and DNA. From skeletal remains can be determined age, sex, ancestry, antemortem or postmortem trauma—the kinds of things fans of *CSI*-type shows see explained and demonstrated every week. But much of what Emanovsky says focuses on differentiating between what people expect from their television entertainment and what scientists can actually deliver. There is also old-fashioned detective work such as physical, material, and circumstantial evidence. Much depends upon the body's state of preservation and what else is available to the analysts.

Anyone interested in instantaneous results receives bad news. "Once those remains are back in the lab it can take several weeks or months or several years" to make a positive determination, Emanovsky tells the room. The people at JPAC make absolutely 100 percent certain they know what they are talking about before releasing results to the press and to families.

Emanovsky patiently explains some of the difficulties anticipated once the Frozen Airman gets to the JPAC Central Identification Laboratory in Hawaii. When it comes to making an identification, how much is already known about a site is crucial. "A normal JPAC mission would involve a lot of research [about] where we're going [i.e., where the remains are]," Emanovsky says. "There will already be investigations into who, or what, is there." For the Frozen Airman, JPAC must start in the dark and at the absolute beginning.

Detailed research and highly organized search missions throughout Southeast Asia, Europe, and other places is ongoing at JPAC. The work is accomplished by civilians and military personnel under the auspices of the U.S. government and with the cooperation of foreign governments, many of which were former enemies and others that still are. "The obligation of the state to account for and return—either dead or alive—every soldier in its service" is un-questioned today, writes Drew Gilpin Faust in *This Republic of Suffering*. Yet soldiers only began to wear some form of official identity badge during World War I, and they had to wait until the Korean War before the United States established a policy of identification and repatriation of every dead soldier.

Though what is known about the Frozen Airman's burial site is slight, JPAC is fortunate, Emanovsky says, because the remains were in good condition. It turns out that being embedded in ice for over sixty years is a good thing. "The skeletal preservation was really good," he continues, "but what is also an influencing factor here is that the ice, the altitude, and the temperature preserved the soft tissue too," including the skin, which is desiccated and "basically mummified."

The JPAC archeologist explains that skeletal preservation can be hit or miss depending on what kind of material the remains are embedded in as well as where the site is geographically. At most recovery sites, JPAC scientists consider themselves fortunate to find a few pieces of bullet-sized bone fragments and tattered bits of cloth. Uncovering personal effects is considered a bonanza. This is because it doesn't take long for nature to do her work. Left exposed, on and in the ground, bodies decay rapidly. They become food for scavengers and in short order don't leave much trace of their physical existence.

But nobody in the room seems to hear Emanovsky's thumbnail discourse on skeletal preservation. All they hear is "mummified." Speaking of mummies has temporarily led some in the room to visualize Boris Karloff and 1930s horror movies. A reporter asks, "Could this be a short-term, contemporary mummy?"

Emanovsky explains that *mummification* refers to tissues becoming desiccated in cold or hot but arid environments. It can happen naturally (as in this case) or intentionally (as in Egypt, where embalming chemicals and wraps were used). "I wouldn't go so far as to say it's a mummy," Emanovsky says of the Frozen Airman, "but it definitely is mummified or desiccated tissue."

• • •

While representatives from the media are in Ash Mountain, the Fresno County Coroner has begun the process of separating the frozen body of John Doe number 10-2-05 from within his 500-pound block of glacier. The chain of command, from recovery to identification, from informing next of kin to burial, continues to be important. As the Frozen Airman moves geographically he is also moving through governmental and legal jurisdictions. Even though everyone assumes that the remains are those of a World War II–era aviator killed in the line of duty, until there is a legal determination as to the cause of death, the body is treated no differently than the victim of an automobile wreck, a heart attack, a violent crime, or any unknown cause. In all such cases, it's the responsibility of the county coroner to make the initial cause-of-death determination.

Senior pathologist Dr. Venu Gopal supervises the process of thawing out the body. Very slowly, to avoid damaging tissue or artifacts, the body is brought to room temperature by carefully pouring water over the remains. Once the Frozen Airman is thawed and a cause of death recorded, he will be sent to JPAC's laboratory in Hawaii.

Granite rock and ice are embedded between the body's extremities. To the practiced eye that has witnessed every imaginable, and some not, kind of death, it's obvious that the Frozen Airman was heavily traumatized. Every bone in the aviator's body is broken—some several times. After all the ice is gone, he weighs sixty-one pounds. In keeping with mummified bodies, all the internal organs are shrunken.

The autopsy, attended by Paul Emanovsky, is performed by Dr. Gopal. They inventory the Frozen Airman's body and garments. He is clothed in an army-style cable-knit full-sleeved sweater and an army-style full-sleeved shirt with a front pocket. There are disintegrated white boxer shorts and a yellow parachute, undeployed. The parachute is either a backpack type, a front pack, or a seat style. This last kind ensured that you always had something to sit on—sort of like carrying around a stadium chair wherever you went except for weighing around fifty pounds. The attached parachute canvas material has the number "1984" stenciled on it.

There is no trace of an aviator's G-1 leather flight jacket with its fleece-lined collar that populates World War II airplane movies. The doctor does not mention either the military collar insignia, woolen trousers, or undershirt that JPAC will detail later in its official report.

The Frozen Airman's personal effects include fifty-one cents in change (including Indian-head pennies, Mercury dimes, and Buffalo nickels), a Parker fountain pen, and some sort of metal identification tag. There is also a leather identification tag with an embossed Sacramento address—not terribly unusual, since the assumption is that the Frozen Airman flew out of Mather Field just east of Sacramento.

The presumption continues that the airman comes from the AT-7 missing since 1942. Ward Eldredge, Sequoia and Kings Canyon's museum technician, can find records of only two other aircraft wrecks in the area. One, a Hughes 500C helicopter, crashed at the summit of Mount Darwin on July 4, 1977. The other record is for an OV-10 Bronco from October 23, 1983, that collided with the north side of Mount Darwin. No physical or material evidence exists tying the Frozen Airman to either of these accidents.

Dr. Gopal registers the cause of death: "multiple skeletal and visceral injuries." Gopal notes that, "in consultation with the forensic anthropologist [Emanovsky], most of the fractures were found to be perimortem [i.e., occurring at the time of death]." The injuries are consistent with death by a fast airplane colliding with a slow mountain and are so severe that the airman couldn't have known what hit him.

CHAPTER 4

The More I Know, the Less I Know

Media accounts of the Frozen Airman's story drew me in, as it did many others. I couldn't get over the resemblance to a great mystery book: a forgotten World War II aviator discovered, by chance, in a remote location; uncertainty about how the body got there and where it came from; uncertainty, even, of where his airplane was since none was found with the body; scant historical records that raised more questions than they answered. Mostly, I was drawn in because I've been exploring the Sierra Nevada since I was twelve years old—these mountains are my home. When something important like this happens in your neighborhood, a curious person wants to know about it. What are the reasons, causes, the how and why? I wanted to know everything about this Frozen Airman. But that would prove more difficult than I expected.

JPAC released what little positive information it possessed after examining the Frozen Airman's body. October 2005 had rolled into November and Veteran's Day, which had the effect of keeping the public's attention focused on all things war related, including the Frozen Airman. JPAC suspected he was in his early twenties, blond, around six feet tall, and with a slight gap between his front teeth. Nothing else for certain would come from JPAC until its scientists performed complete genetic testing.

Dr. Thomas Holland, at the JPAC Central Identification Laboratory, told CNN that it was "not necessarily the preservation of the remains as much as ... the preservation of the records that we're going to have to compare it to" that would help determine the young man's identity. Finding clues based on dental records, or any other records, was unlikely because a 1973 warehouse fire in St. Louis had destroyed most military personnel files. "We don't have a lot of those original records anymore," Holland explained. The most concrete clue JPAC had came from the Frozen Airman's possessions. On his sweater the lab found a round, corroded metal name badge. If it was readable, they might know the Frozen Airman's name. But that would only be circumstantial evidence because soldiers then, as now, are known to borrow each other's clothing.

• • •

Based on earlier archival research at Sequoia and Kings Canyon National Parks, JPAC assumed the Frozen Airman came from a Beech 18 AT-7 aircraft missing since November 18, 1942. The main source of official historical information available to the public and the press about the missing AT-7 came from Mike Stowe's Web site devoted to military aircraft wrecks, with the appropriate address of www.accidentreports.com. In response to interest generated by the Frozen Airman, Stowe posted low-resolution excerpts from a 1942 U.S. Army Air Forces "Report of Aircraft Accident" and a follow-up 1947 "Report of Major Accident."

The 1942 "Report of Aircraft Accident" lists the crew, their serial numbers, and rank: William A. Gamber, second lieutenant and pilot; John M. Mortenson, aviation cadet; Ernest G. Munn, aviation cadet; and Leo A. Mustonen, aviation cadet. Aviation cadets were soldiers who enlisted to become pilots, navigators, or bombardiers. The report lists the pilot's mission as "Navigation Training Flight." Lieutenant Gamber had a total of 709 hours 9 minutes of flight experience, including 255:40 hours over the ninety days prior to the accident and 505:50 hours in the same type of airplane as the missing AT-7.

In the report, investigating officer Captain Leroy G. Heston describes the accident: "The airplane left this field [Mather Field] on an authorized navigation mission at 0830, November 18, 1942, with about five hours of fuel on board. Since no word was received from the airplane during its flight, a search was started at 1330, November 18, 1942, and was abandoned at 1630, December 14, 1942 when all clues had been thoroughly investigated." No route is given, but Captain Heston does explain that the search area included ground and aerial parties from Chico, Stockton, Merced, and Lemoore, "thoroughly covering the area over which the missing airplane was to have passed on its mission and an extensive mountainous area where it most probably would have gone had it deviated from its course." Captain Heston's description ends with, "All further clues will be diligently investigated."

The extracted 1947 "Report of Major Accident" corrects Gamber's middle initial from "A" to "R" and incorrectly changes Leo Mustonen's middle initial from "A" to "M." It also describes the presumed route of the missing AT-7 but gives the wrong date: "AT-7 #41-21079 took off from Mather Field on 8 Nov '42 on a Navigation training mission to Corning, California and return, and was not reported over Merced or since. The wreckage was not found until 24 Sept 47 on Darwin Glacier on the north side of Darwin Peak, approximately 80 miles NE of Fresno, California." The report goes on to describe wreckage on a sixty-degree slope, "strewn over a wide area and partially buried in the ice of the glacier." Identification of the wreck came from an engine date tag and "an aviation cadet name tag." The report concludes that "the cause of the accident remains undetermined." Underlined in pencil is this statement: "No bodies were recovered."

Included with the 1947 report is an interesting narrative written for the commanding officer of the Sixty-second Army Air Forces Air Rescue Service at Florida's MacDill Field. Dated October 3, 1947, the description covers the time between September 24 and October 1, detailing a mission dispatched to identify the wreckage and the failure of this mission to retrieve remains.

Apparently, William Bond and Thomas Hodges, two college students "of University of California," discovered "portions of an aircraft wreck on Darwin Glacier" during a 1947 summer pack trip. The plane, says the report, "did not burn on impact and appears to be a twin engine Beechcraft." A name tag for John M. Mortenson, some shoes, two Pratt & Whitney engines, and pieces of "frozen flesh" were found "scattered over the glacier." This glacier is identified as Darwin Glacier, which is about a half mile south of where the Frozen Airman was found in 2005. I read that and thought, could his aircraft be buried in Darwin Glacier?

The 1947 report says that with help provided by "Mr. Brower of Sierra Club," William Bond was located. Bond agreed to escort an expedition consisting of two Air Rescue Service captains, a forest ranger, and a horse packer to the crash site. The party rode to McClure Meadow in Sequoia and Kings Canyon National Parks. Camp was established, and the next day they entered Darwin Canyon and visited the accident site.

It took almost four hours to reach the wreckage, including "a very hazardous three mile climb up [the] side of Mt. Darwin." Debris was observed widely scattered across the top of the glacier, and buried in the ice were two Pratt & Whitney engines. An engine identification tag was removed. On a spur of rock they also found a small piece of "frozen flesh," along with small pieces of clothing and a blank navigation log. "Insufficient remains were found for identification of bodies or to indicate the number of persons aboard," reads the description. After three hours of searching, they left. The following day the five men rode back to the trailhead at Florence Lake, returning home to the San Francisco area that evening.

Granted, the recovery team found conditions on the glacier to be "extremely dangerous," but I had difficulty understanding why after all the hard work to reach the site the Air Rescue Service was content to return home with only an engine identification tag. This tag later identified the wreckage as belonging to an AT-7 number 41-21079, piloted by Lieutenant William Gamber, with three aviation cadets onboard for a navigation training mission. Names of the crew were confirmed with the aid of an *Oakland Tribune* reporter by the name of Dubois. In the paper's morgue files, Dubois found John Mortenson's name in a November 19, 1942, newspaper story documenting the missing aircraft.

Explaining disposition of remains, the report to the Air Rescue Service commanding officer said, "The remains of deceased were not recoverable since the wreckage is several years old, is widly

[sic] scattered, and is almost entirely covered by a great amount of snow and ice." Closing out the matter, Colonel Richard T. Knight, commander of the Sixty-second Army Air Forces Base Unit at Mac-Dill Field, sent a letter of approbation to William Bond: "I wish to commend you for the splendid manner in which you assisted personnel of Air Rescue Service Squadron 'B' in the location and identification of the aircraft wreckage found atop Darwin Peak."

• • •

Following the Frozen Airman's discovery in 2005, some news reporters expressed disbelief that glaciers could be found in Southern California. More important for me was how the Frozen Airman got into the ice, not that ice was there. Why is it that no one found him before? I mean, Darwin Canyon is remote and Mendel Glacier even more so, but it's not as if nobody ever goes to either place. For one thing, anyone interested in climbing Mount Darwin, Mount Mendel, or the icy couloirs that initially brought the Frozen Airman's discoverers to Mendel Glacier, always finds Lamarck Col the quickest way in. Surely some of them, over the course of six decades would have at least found airplane wreckage. Yet this never happened.

Beyond the Frozen Airman's presence in Mendel Glacier, the next biggest question for me revolved around why an airplane would fly up Darwin Canyon in the first place. The canyon isn't on the way to any place in particular. The contemptuous presumption on the part of news media in 2005 was that the pilot must have been lost. Reporters arrived at this conclusion based on Mike Stowe's Web site. In the 1947 "Report of Major Accident" excerpted on the site, the route is described as leaving from Mather Field in Sacramento and flying to Corning—which is about 120 miles *north* of Mather, while Mendel Glacier and where the Frozen Airman's body were found are 150 miles *southeast*. How could a pilot be so lost to not know the difference between north and south? And with *three* navigators onboard? That's not being lost; that's being completely bewildered. A critical reader would think some data were missing from the 1947 report. Also, the news people never appeared to notice the description from the 1942 report explaining that search parties were dispatched to Merced—which is south of Mather Field as well.

• • •

From the outset, it was the Frozen Airman's body that generated the greatest interest. Newspapers, television programs, blogs, and Internet discussion forums all gravitated to the ice mummy, who he was, and the novelty of finding his remains. Tony Waldron, consulting physician at St. Mary's Hospital in London and author of *Shadows in the Soil* (2001), comments that "interest in human remains has probably never been so great as at present" and that "part of the interest in the dead from the past is certainly voyeuristic." Though Waldron says that "few people die at home now, and most of the population has never seen a dead body," he thinks our fascination has to do with a "sense of continuity" we lack. "We do not have extended families anymore," he writes. "Grandparents are rarely on hand to describe how things were in the past or to provide information on other branches of our families, and it is perhaps to make good this deficiency—to satisfy our curiosity of where we have come from—that we take such an interest in those who lived many generations ago."

The greatest conundrum posited by news reports in 2005 revolved around burial of the pilot and three cadets. Many times in the narrative given in the 1947 army report extract on Stowe's Web site, I read that no remains were recovered. Yet news reports and other sources, including some from the Sequoia and Kings Canyon National Parks scant historical files, said that commingled remains of the four aviators had been buried in Golden Gate National Cemetery in San Bruno, California.

The burial was confirmed, somewhat, when a *San Francisco Chronicle* reporter interviewed Barbara Adams, cousin to pilot William Gamber. Holding a photograph of the lieutenant taken during his pilot training, Mrs. Adams posed at Golden Gate National Cemetery beside a marble headstone with the names of William R. Gamber, Ernest G. Munn, John M. Mortenson, and Leo M. Mustonen inscribed upon it. Gamber is identified as a "2d Lieutenant," the other three as "Aviation Cadets" in the "Air Corps." The date of death is November 18, 1942.

On the cemetery's Web site I read the date of the crew's interment in Section F, Site 43, as October 15, 1948. I didn't understand that chronology at all, since the official records stopped in 1947 with the comments "no bodies were recovered" and "incident closed." What delayed burial for a year, assuming there was something to bury? What happened in 1948 to change everybody's mind, and why hadn't the Frozen Airman been discovered fifty-seven years previously if he was buried in 1948?

If the four crewmembers of the missing AT-7 were buried in San Bruno, as the cemetery record showed, I was now understanding why some reporters who never read the army report extracts were suggesting that the Frozen Airman must be a fifth crewmember.

• • •

I found a source for the burial mystery, along with a few other questions to puzzle over, in "The Secret of Mendel Glacier," a 1979 magazine story by R. W. Koch published in *Airplane Progress Aviation Review*. Koch, who died many years ago, spins an engaging story about a Beech 18 AT-7 Navigator number 41-21079 and its life from birth to death. He begins with the aircraft's departure from the Beech Aircraft factory on October 15, 1941, and ends with its disappearance, discovery, and crew recovery from the Mendel Glacier. What makes Koch's article so intriguing are his conclusions. His story does nothing to expose the secret of Mendel Glacier and everything to deepen the mystery. Koch had the hindsight of twenty years to help him fill in gaps, and yet he garbles, glosses over, and embellishes facts with abandon.

Details in his story point to the 1942 and 1947 army accident reports excerpts that I had read. But how did Koch know the crash was on the Mendel Glacier when all official reports placed it half a mile south on Darwin Glacier? Koch mentions that college student William Bond discovered the missing aircraft. He doesn't mention Bond's companion, Thomas Hodges—only "two of his [Bond's] stalwart hiking companions" on a trip past "four, clear, trout infested lakes" in Darwin Canyon. Koch writes that after the aircraft wreckage was discovered on Mendel Glacier, a park ranger was notified. This ranger contacted Air Rescue headquarters at Hamilton Field, and two "Air Force" officers were dispatched to investigate.

Never explained is how Bond and his "stalwart companions" notified a ranger. Backcountry rangers are all over the Sequoia and Kings Canyon wilderness today, as they were in 1979 when "The Secret of Mendel Glacier" was published. They're found mostly along the John Muir Trail but in other high-use areas as well. There is even a ranger at McClure Meadow where William Bond and his two captains, forest ranger, and horse wrangler stayed before making the three-mile cross-country hike into upper Darwin Canyon. But there was no ranger there until 1950, when Charlie Summers manned the post.

Koch describes how Bond guided army officers "ill-equipped for their stay in this wilderness region," noting that they returned to base and recommended that a second, better-equipped party hike to the glacier. This was done by a detachment of "crack army troops," but heavy early snows drove this second team away before any work could be done.

Koch goes on to write of a third recovery team coming back in 1948 via Lake Sabrina. With ice axes, the troopers chopped their way through fourteen feet of glacial ice to find the AT-7 all in one piece. Four bodies were within, "found in the forward section of the aircraft's fuselage perfectly preserved by the ice of the glacier." The bodies were removed "from the twisted wreckage," positive identification of Gamber, Mortenson, Munn, and Mustonen "was made at the site," and the four were "evacuated" to a "local mortuary." Shortly thereafter, "the remains of Lt. Gamber and his crew were transported to the Golden Gate National Cemetery at San Bruno, California, where they were given a full military burial."

In Koch's tale are traces of fact, fancy, inaccuracies, and a source of many Frozen Airman mysteries. Climbers may use ice axes for chopping footholds in glaciers, but they aren't adequate digging tools for cutting through fourteen feet of ice to uncover an airplane thirty-four feet long, ten feet high, with a wingspan of forty-eight feet. That would be a feat analogous to digging the Panama Canal with garden trowels. Koch has the soldiers working from morning to late afternoon to uncover "part of an aircraft tail section in very good condition." It took Keith Hamm and the Park Service rangers all day to dig the Frozen Airman out of the glacier, and he was smaller than either of the twin tail booms of the AT-7.

It's inconceivable that an airplane would crash and remain in one piece, even if Koch was assuming the plane missed colliding with the high granite walls of the cirque surrounding Mendel Glacier and hit the ice instead. Perhaps he assumed a glacier was as soft as a field of snow, which is also a mistake. As any skier can attest, snowfields are about as soft as the cold hard ground.

According to what I read in the extracted 1947 army report, the military trip guided by William Bond to Darwin Glacier found no fuselage wreckage or wing wreckage beyond the engines. During the college student's earlier trip when the wreckage was first discovered, the report says debris was found scattered all over the glacier. This suggests to me that the airplane broke apart on impact into a lot of little pieces. Koch's claim of finding a complete airplane buried in either glacier, Darwin or Mendel, is not supported by the facts.

Finding an inviolate airplane with the crewmembers still at their stations is also unlikely. Yet this idea persisted through the years and resurfaced the first week following the Frozen Airman's discovery. Not knowing anything about how glaciers are formed and how they work, and never thinking what could happen to an airplane that crashes, an anonymous reporter at KFSN, the ABC network affiliate in Fresno, wrote, "It's believed most of the plane is still preserved under the glacier above the spot" where the Frozen Airman was found.

Of course, there was always the possibility that the AT-7 did not break into a million pieces. George Bibel, a professor of mechanical engineering at the University of North Dakota and author of *Beyond the Black Box*, writes that, "usually, a crashed aircraft remains substantially intact and is clearly recognizable as an airplane. The fuselage sometimes breaks into two or more sections." Unlike a crashing automobile, which is traveling in one direction, when an airplane hits the ground it is traveling both forward and down. "A plane about to contact the ground," writes Bibel, "has forward kinetic energy and downward kinetic energy."

The presence of lots of tiny pieces of metal "strewn over a wide area and partially buried in the ice of the glacier" suggests damage from vertical impact. In the late 1970s, engineers at the Boeing Company termed accidental vertical impacts *controlled flight into terrain*, or CFIT. With fatalistic humor, pilots call this "the act of flying a perfectly good aircraft into the ground." CFIT can happen to anyone, despite their level of flight experience. Some of the main causes occur when pilots lose situational awareness, are fatigued, or become disoriented. CFIT incidents occur frequently in the mountains, with rising terrain, or when flying with reduced visibility such as in clouds. When CFIT occurs in mountains, pilots refer to it as making contact with "cumulo-granite."

In addition to all of the questions raised by Koch's account of the missing AT-7, the man himself was a bit of a mystery. Pat Macha, an aviation historian living in Southern California, knew Koch. According to Macha, "Koch was always a little cagey about where he got his information and how he knew this and how he knew that."

Macha has seen and investigated hundreds of military airplane crashes in the mountains and deserts of western North America and is coauthor with Don Jordan of *Aircraft Wrecks in the Mountains and Deserts of California, 1909–2002*. As for a complete airplane entombed within Mendel Glacier with its crew still inside, "I have a hard time believing the airplane was that intact," Macha told me. "How much of a plane is left after a crash depends on the angle it hits. I've seen airplanes hang remarkably together if the pilot pulled back on the stick just before hitting." How about what Koch described? "Not that kind of together," Macha replied.

CHAPTER 5

Playing Detective

My path was clear. Something happened in 1948 to cause the army to set a headstone in the Golden Gate National Cemetery. Though he garbled the message, R. W. Koch knew what it was and took that knowledge to his grave. If I were to solve the mystery of the Frozen Airman, I had to uncover Koch's secret of Mendel Glacier all over again. I could see that figuring out how the crew ended up in the glacier involved learning the actual route that Lieutenant Gamber and the three cadets took the day they crashed—assuming there were indeed three cadets and not four. I needed to know what the weather was like on November 18, 1942, and if that was a factor in the crash. And I had to figure out if the pilot's experience was an issue. Finally, I had to find William Bond and Thomas Hodges and hear their stories about discovering the wreckage in 1947. But sixty years after the students' discovery, would they still be alive?

Detectives must start somewhere, so I began with the best clues I had: Mike Stowe's 1942 and 1947 U.S. Army Air Forces accident reports. Rather than rely on the extracts posted on his Web site, I contacted Stowe and arranged to purchase the complete documents. Stowe had not intended the posted extracts to present the whole case—just enough to answer journalists' basic and immediate questions about who, what, when, where, why, and how. Close study of both full reports revealed how the excerpts provided a flavor of the event while lacking essential details.

There were more errors to find—nothing egregious—just sloppiness, like getting Gamber's and Mustonen's middle initials wrong. I also noticed in the 1947 report that Gamber, the pilot, who hailed from Fayette, Ohio, was said to come from Payette—which doesn't exist outside of Idaho. Ernest G. Munn is called Eugene. There were enough of these kinds of mistakes to shake my confidence in the complete accuracy of the reports. I mean, if I couldn't trust the details, what in the reports could I believe?

For instance, once again I saw the route description: from Mather Field in Sacramento, north to Corning. And, once again, I wondered why no one but me questioned the route's incongruity. Corning is 120 miles north of Mather Field and the airplane was found 150 miles southeast. Was the whole world geographically challenged? How could a pilot become so lost, traveling south when he is supposed to be flying north?

Digging through copies of dozens of pages of faded telegrams and teletypes sent in November and December 1942 from base commander Colonel L. R. Hewitt at Mather Field to army headquarters in Washington DC and to the aviators' families, I found what I chose to provisionally accept as the actual route. Two days after the AT-7 disappeared, Colonel Hewitt informed his superiors by teletype that the training route was from Mather Field *south* to Los Banos, then north and east of Mather to Roseville, farther north to Corning (finally), and then back to Mather Field. Los Banos is nearly due west of where the AT-7 was eventually found. Suddenly I thought that the crew hadn't been *that* lost. At least they weren't supposed to be north in Corning until the end of their mission.

Also transmitted with the route description was a weather report for the day. It sounded like good visual meteorological conditions (VMC), defined these days by the Department of Defense as "weather conditions in which visual flight rules [VFR] apply; expressed in terms of visibility, ceiling height, and aircraft clearance from clouds along the path of flight. When these criteria do not exist, instrument meteorological conditions [IMC] prevail and instrument flight rules [IFR] must be complied with." Basically, VMC means a pilot can see where he is and where he is going without using navigational aids. The forecast for November 18, 1942, was a

4,000-foot ceiling south of Mather to Stockton and a 5,000- to 7,000-foot ceiling farther on, with unlimited visibility and broken clouds. Occasional light rain was forecast in Red Bluff, north of Mather Field. I saw no mention of approaching bad weather.

This relatively benign weather forecast from Colonel Hewitt's office was supported in the 1947 "Final Mission Report" submitted by Lieutenant Edward W. Lynch, which accompanied the "Report of Major Accident" filed with the War Department on November 19, 1947 (one day longer than five years since Gamber and the three cadets disappeared). The weather synopsis given for November 18, 1942, differs somewhat, but not radically, from the 1942 report forecast: "At Fresno—Overcast at 4000 ft, lower scattered at 1000 ft, light rain. Pressure 1014, temperature 60, dew point 57, wind SE 9. Rain ended 1220." In another section of the same 1947 report, Mather Field weather officer Captain Myron E. Howe directly contradicted the official line when he wrote, "Unknown definitely but from the available weather data at Fresno, weather might have been an influencing factor in the accident. Weather data was obtained from the U.S. Weather Bureau at Fresno who reports from their experience with weather in that region, it was undoubtedly bad in the Mt. Darwin area." I had to add Captain Howe's comment to the list of Frozen Airman mysteries. What experience did the weather bureau staff in Fresno have to belie the forecast of the "Final Mission Report"?

Contributing to my growing discomfort about the weather forecast was a conversation I had with Leonard Spivey. Spivey graduated from navigator training at Mather Field a few weeks before Gamber, Mortenson, Munn, and Mustonen disappeared. His friend, William Bechter, was a cadet one class ahead of the missing navigation students, and Spivey had a copy of Bechter's diary. For November 18 the entry was, "We flew part of an interception mission this morning but had to turn back short of the goal because we ran into a bad storm and low ceilings. The war was brought close to home tonight when one AT-7 in Bill Davis' class failed to return from this morning's hop. Tomorrow we will fly a parallel search along the foothills of the Sierra range to hunt for the plane." Diary entries for the next two days mention continued searching with no results. Bechter's diary entries had me wondering. If he noted stormy weather the day that Gamber's AT-7 disappeared, why hadn't the 1942 official report done the same? And why did Lieutenant Lynch and Captain Howe contradict each other in the 1947 report?

California has a reputation for a benign climate, but fall and winter weather can be murderous on airplanes and pilots. Storms march through, bringing dangerous atmospheric conditions such as heavy snowfall and high winds in the mountains and pelting rain to the valleys. Cumulus clouds rise 35,000 feet above sea level and can bury an airplane. If it's nasty in the lowlands, it's worse in the mountains where several feet of snow can fall.

My friend Marge Carpenter volunteered to help me, and the first research she undertook involved the weather conundrum. From newspaper reports she turned up, I was surprised to learn how nasty the weather was in and around the Sierra Nevada the day the AT-7 disappeared. Placerville, in the Sierra foothills east of Sacramento, reported 3.13 inches of rain for November 18. At Rubicon Point at Lake Tahoe, 4 inches of snow fell. The *Reno Evening Gazette* reported 16 inches of snow on State Route 89 at Yuba Pass and 0.43 inch of rain in Reno, located in the high desert east of Lake Tahoe. Heavy rainfall to the south in Carson City, Nevada, threatened to flood the state capital with a "violent downpour" of 2.65 inches of rain. How could Colonel Hewitt's 1942 transmitted weather forecast be true?

Despite Lieutenant Gamber's 709 hours of flight experience, he probably hadn't spent much time flying in bad weather. The 1942 report showed that he had been instrument rated since May 2, but he had accumulated all his hours using visual flight rules. He shouldn't have been flying under instrument meteorological conditions in bad weather, through clouds, and in the mountains where experience in instrument flight rules was required.

Why would a VFR pilot be flying into bad weather? Was Gamber a "tough it out" kind of guy, too arrogant for his own good? If William Bechter's pilot turned around due to bad weather, why didn't Gamber? Did Gamber find trouble because he believed the good weather forecast, the same forecast Colonel Hewitt sent to

Washington DC after the accident? Was Gamber blown off course while flying south from Mather Field to Los Banos?

That was Leonard Spivey's hypothesis. "If the weather had them where they had loss of visibility, then they were only relying on the wind information they had before the flight began," Spivey told me. California winter storms blow counterclockwise from southwest to northeast, and the AT-7 could have been diverted without the crew even knowing. "I had that experience," said Spivey. "Suddenly you break out of the clouds and you see you're someplace you didn't figure you would be. That aircraft could have been blown east, right over the top of the Sierra and they figured all along they were still over the foothills." Trying to head back, maybe "they ran into that storm and the wind just blew them right up against the mountain."

Another idea: maybe the flight plan Colonel Hewitt sent to his superiors was as accurate as the weather forecast. In that case, Gamber might have been flying anywhere. Spivey said that training missions sometimes flew over Lake Tahoe to Salt Lake City. Could Gamber's actual route have been *east* over the mountains and in the Sierra's rainshadow and into the desert, where the weather would have been better than in the Central Valley? If this was the case, and bad weather was expected, why did anyone fly at all? Or, was bad weather—or weather not quite as bad as what developed—not expected? The more I dug into the story, the more mysteries popped up.

I trusted Spivey. He had the knowledge and the experience—but I couldn't accept the idea that Gamber had been lost. There were too many holes in the data. Donald J. Satterthwait, a retired lieutenant colonel in the U.S. Air Force who also served as a navigator in World War II, helped firm up my conviction when he told me that the AT-7 "had three navigational cadets aboard, and all of them were navigating with their own set of instruments. I don't think they all would get it wrong."

It also seemed to me that Gamber was an experienced pilot and would know what he was doing. Nevertheless, pilots can make mistakes. Pilot error is often the initial focus in crash investigations, though, as Tom Betts, retired lieutenant colonel in the U.S.

Air Force, pointed out to me, "Pilot error is rarely the cause of a mishap—no pilot intends to make an error. In modern mishaps it is usually found that there are human factors involved that, often, better engineering or supervision might have prevented." One crucial measure of a pilot's experience is his amount of flight time. I already knew what the 1942 report said about the Gamber's flight history: 709 hours since getting his pilot rating on April 24, 1942, with 70 percent of his experience in the AT-7 and 35 percent of those hours in the previous ninety days. Gamber had been doing a lot of flying.

From my initial investigations of the AT-7, the airplane itself didn't strike me as a "widow-maker," the type of aircraft prone to accidents—mostly fatal—due to design imperfections or crew inexperience. John Little, a volunteer with the Museum of Flight in Seattle, told me the Beech 18 AT-7 was a popular plane because "it had no nasty traits and that made it good for students." It was powered by two Pratt & Whitney Wasp Junior R-985 radial engines. Little reminded me that *AT* meant *Advanced Trainer*, and the numeral designation meant the plane was outfitted for navigation training. The AT-11, in comparison, was used to train bombardiers. In its factory configuration, the Beech 18 had room for eleven passenger seats. For the AT-7, they removed the passenger seats and installed tables and chairs for cadets to use while training. The AT-7 had three work stations located behind the celestial dome, where students could "shoot the stars" with their octants. Taking a fix on three stars allowed cadets to triangulate and chart their position just as shipboard navigators had been doing for centuries.

Trying to discover what I could about the lost AT-7 crewmembers, I submitted a request for their service records. Instead, I received a reminder of what Dr. Thomas Holland from JPAC had told CNN—that the preservation of records could be more important than the preservation of the Frozen Airman's remains. A letter arrived informing me that on July 12, 1973, a fire at the National Personnel Records Center in St. Louis, Missouri, destroyed approximately sixteen to eighteen million official military personnel files, including all from the period between November 1, 1912, and January 1, 1960. On the cusp of the computer age, everything had been paper, and all had been lost: "No duplicate copies of the records that were destroyed in the fire were maintained, nor was a microfilm copy ever produced. There were no indexes created prior to the fire."

Frustrated by this setback, I zeroed in on locating the college students William Bond and Thomas Hodges, identified in the 1947 army accident report as University of California students who had discovered the AT-7 wreckage on Darwin Glacier in 1947. The commendation letter of thanks had been sent to Bond at an Oakland address, and contacting the university alumni office with this scant piece of evidence I hit pay dirt. George William Bond and Thomas Hodges had graduated from UC Berkeley with majors in geology. Hodges was no longer alive but Bond was. The alumni office wouldn't give me Bond's contact information but told me if I sent them a letter they would forward it on.

A few weeks later I was speaking to Bill Bond on the telephone. The first thing he expressed to me was his surprise at getting my letter. It appears that no one else had attempted to contact him. I felt elated. I was making progress and was ready to tackle the points, errors, inconsistencies, and mysteries of R. W. Koch and his "Secret of Mendel Glacier" article. In Bond I had found my first witness.

CHAPTER 6

First Discovery: 1947

The students from UC Berkeley thought a day-long excursion from their camp at Evolution Lake into Darwin Canyon would be an ordinary fishing trip. Instead, it became the most exciting day of their summer. It also brought them a reminder. Two years after Yalta, Potsdam, and the atomic bomb attacks in Japan, the war was still not over.

Leaving their lone pack animal behind in Evolution Valley, they grabbed lunch and fishing gear. The plan was to fish up into Darwin Canyon, trying all the lakes and the streams, and then to take a look at the glacier below Mount Darwin. At least that was the plan. They moved quickly along the John Muir Trail to nearly 10,800 feet, where a narrow way trail split off north. Short and steep switchbacks danced through a thin lodgepole pine forest, bringing them to the large sloping hillside area above tree line called Darwin Bench.

Continuing their ascent through alpine meadows, they clambered across granite slabs to reach the lowermost of five lakes in Darwin Canyon. From there they began to fish up-canyon, lake to lake, casting their lines unsuccessfully into cold, deep water. Bored with their lack of success, William Bond and Thomas Hodges set aside their fishing poles and decided to climb into the cirque below Mount Mendel, not Darwin Glacier as the official reports had it, and explore that glacier instead.

And that's where they found wreckage from an airplane and partial human remains.

Summer over and home from the hills, one evening at a fraternity party, Bond and Hodges told their story. Someone in the crowd, a part-time student in the army reserves, took notice and spread the word the following weekend at Hamilton Field, across San Francisco Bay from Berkeley in Marin County.

Both UC students were contacted September 24, 1947, by Air Rescue Service Squadron B, part of the Sixty-second Army Air Forces Base Unit. In the army's subsequent report, Hodges reported by phone that the aircraft wreckage was inaccessible and half buried in ice on a sixty-degree slope. "It will require ropes and experienced personnel to reach the scene," he told the army. He suggested the best and fastest route in would be by vehicle from Fresno to Florence Lake, then twenty-seven miles by horseback up the South Fork San Joaquin River, through Goddard Canyon to Evolution Lake. From there, he said, "it is approximately a one-hour walk to the foot of the glacier."

The army asked Hodges if he would guide a mission to the location. Remains should be recovered or, at least, the wreck could be identified. Assuming the remains the students had found could be identified, next of kin would want to know—they deserved to know what happened. Hodges declined the army's request because fall semester classes were about to begin. The 1947 army report then says that William Bond was found. As he had yet to start school, Bond agreed that evening to "aid this organization on the mission."

Bond met up with army officials on September 25, 1947, at the High Sierra Pack Station in Prather, east of Fresno, and proceeded to the trailhead at Florence Lake. The ground party consisted of Captains Robert Lewis, Andrew Walton, and Robert Goulding along with U.S. Forest Service ranger Neil L. Perkins and wrangler Harvey Sauter, guided by William Bond. Leaving Captain Walton behind at the trailhead, the men rode five horses and trailed three pack mules. Sauter came along because the animals belonged to him. He probably took one look at the army captains in their loafers, standard-issue garrison caps, olive-drab flannel shirts, and neckties with a half Windsor knot, and decided to keep close tabs on his pack stock. At least Bond dressed like someone who belonged in the mountains, with his full beard and in his flannel shirt, dungarees, and Swiss alpine hat.

• • •

Memories from his discovery and guiding trip to Mendel Glacier are still fresh and vivid for Bill Bond. During several telephone conversations and an extended in-person interview at his home in Bakersfield, Bond filled me in on what the 1947 army report only hinted at. He also supplied me with the answer to the mysteries perpetrated by R. W. Koch.

The first thing Bond told me were the names of his companions that day of discovery on the glacier in 1947 when they found pieces of an airplane. Koch had mentioned two "stalwart companions," but there were actually three. Besides Tom Hodges, Wes Houseman and Kirby West were both along on the fishing trip into Darwin Canyon. Bond still kept in touch with West, but Houseman got married while still in college and Bond lost track of him after graduation. Hodges, as I've mentioned, died several years ago.

Sixty years is a long time, but the memory of this man from the Black Hills of South Dakota is keen with details. "Tom Hodges and I started up over the end of the glacier and up all that scree and boulders to get up to the ice," Bond began. "Just before we arrived at the ice, I picked up a sheet of aluminum, the idea being that we'd go up onto the ice field and make a toboggan out of it." Bond had seen two years of action in Europe with the Tenth Mountain Division and thought the piece of metal they'd found resembled an exploded fuel tank dropped off an airplane. The men really had no idea of what they had, what they were looking at, or why it could be there.

Carrying the aluminum sheet they continued climbing up the glacier and next came upon a wheel. "So we picked that up and rolled it down the glacier just for the sport of it, you know." At this point, despite any frivolity they may have demonstrated, they both knew there had to be an airplane somewhere nearby. They weren't surprised to run across two engines lying fairly close to-gether. "Having found the engines," Bond continued, "we decided they probably came from an impact up the glacier someplace, or up the peak."

They whooped and hollered to Kirby West, far away on the north side of the cirque, to come take a look. Sensing something was up, West dug out his thirty-five-millimeter camera and snapped a photo.

• • •

World War II caught up to Kirby West in October 1944, after two years spent studying engineering at UC Berkeley. With his experi-ence in the navy ROTC, he received a commission and spent two years in the Pacific. Like the others on this Sierra trip in the sum-mer of 1947, Kirby was starting school, returning from the war to long mountain trips and picking up his life from before. West knew Hodges from Theta Xi, their fraternity, and Hodges knew Bond and Houseman, and they all liked to hike.

I met West at his home in Moraga, a quiet neighborhood east of San Francisco Bay. He greeted me at the front door, a carved wood-en bear two feet tall standing guard in the entryway. Two more stood sentry within the foyer. A bit frail these days and maybe lack-ing the vigor of his Sierra days, West hasn't lost his youthful enthu-siasm. From the excitement in his face and his greeting, I knew he had been waiting eagerly for our meeting.

By way of introduction, West dropped a few pieces of paper on the table. They included copies of newspaper articles from 1947 and 1948 and a section of Tom Hodges's typewritten journal from Sunday, August 17, 1947. "As we reached the glacier we noticed evidences of an airplane wreck," it read, "namely a wheel and one engine." Higher up, "Bill discovered much more ... of the plane and there was some evidence of the occupants found... a name plate revealed that one member of the crew was John Mortinson [sic]." Hodges journal entry describes the scene of the wreck as "high on the boulders and glacier in a most inaccessible location."

Then West dropped photographs from the 1947 Sierra excursion onto the table in front of us. There is one of Bond and Hodges on the southward side of Mendel Glacier, the bergschrund a dark horizontal gash across the ice. The glacier looks like a dirty golf ball, pitted with sun cups. Another photo shows the twin couloirs where Michael Nozel and Mark Postle will be drawn in another almost sixty years. The bergschrund is shown in this picture too, as well as a snow-covered buttress of rock that climbs to the summit ridge of Mount Mendel. West pointed at the bergschrund and without a trace of drama said, "Right here on the edge of one of these rocks was a name tag that said John Mortenson. And down in there," he said, pointing into the bergschrund, "was a shoe and some other things."

West was visibly sad remembering the scene, sighing deeply at one point. "We figured the plane must have crashed there," he touched a spot on a photograph. "And there wasn't much we could do."

• • •

Bill Bond told me a similar story to that of Kirby West but with much more detail. "We came to the bergschrund, and looked around in it," he said, "and started to find debris of various kinds." Eventually, Bond cautiously crossed over onto the rock face and on the eastern edge of the ice field: "I found shreds of human flesh—I could identify that from being in action in World War II." Nearby was John Mortenson's name badge and the back of his watch.

"We started scouting around, looking for whatever we could find," Bond recalled. "We did find some log books, nothing of importance in them, and various pieces of aluminum. One of them was scrunched up like an accordion. Just incredibly tight folds." The friends gathered up what they could and created a little pile of detritus and debris on rocks beside the bergschrund.

It was a sorrowful, desolate sight. "We figured we weren't going to find much more," Bond told me, his voice barely a whisper. "We didn't have any equipment really, to go much further. No ropes, no ice axes, crampons, or anything to work on the ice with. So we were limited in what we could do. Finally we decided to retreat off the glacier."

They were on the first week of a four-week-long trip that would eventually take them south to the Palisades Glacier. Each of them figured they could pick up the stuff on their way back. Except that they never got around to returning.

• • •

Bill Bond also told me about the Air Rescue Service asking him in 1947 to guide them to the airplane wreck. "Everybody there at Theta Xi, virtually, was a veteran," he said. "Among those was a guy who was in the Air Force Reserve, flying out of Hamilton Field—Harry Bothwell was his name." Bothwell contacted Squadron B, and Squadron B called Bond. "Apparently I was the only one of the four of us who didn't have any commitments that week."

Bond flew to Fresno from Hamilton Field in a Douglas C-47 Skytrain (DC-3) along with Captain Robert Lewis and Captain Andrew Walton, radio gear, and two jeeps. It must have been a cold and uncomfortable ride, sitting on utility seats along the walls of the drafty fuselage with two jeeps rattling around the center aisle.

After a brief stop to inform the Fresno County sheriff and coroner of their plans, and receiving permission to remove any remains they might find, the three continued on in jeeps to the High Sierra Ranger Station. There they met Ranger Perkins and another army captain, paradoctor Robert Goulding. Paradoctors were medics trained as paratroopers. Goulding's job was to supervise the recovery of any bodies.

Walton stayed behind at Florence Lake with the jeeps and communication equipment to serve as a radio link between the men in the field and headquarters back at Hamilton Field. During the next few days, the C-47 flew several sorties, dropping a one-man tent and some paperwork at McClure Meadow and some light bulbs for the jeep at Florence Lake. Radio communication was never established. It was later determined that dead batteries in the walkie-talkie carried by the backcountry team was the cause.

The 1947 "Report of Major Accident" focuses extensively on communications. Bill Bond laughed when I told him that. "I have no idea why it would because none of it worked!" he shook his head. "The reason they wanted the communications was in case we did run into any bodies or anything of that nature, you know. We didn't find any at that time. Of course, there was no helicopter that would fly at that altitude so it boiled down to the fact that we were going to go in there and walk up."

"We rode horses in," Bond told me, "and we stayed in the little ranger station [at that time, a snow survey cabin] at McClure Meadow late in the afternoon the first day." The team set up camp and prepared for an early morning departure to the glacier. "I'll tell you one thing," said Bond, "there was nobody else out there!" Autumn into winter in the High Sierra is a quiet and lonely place. All the critters are gone. Brown meadows contrast sharply with white granite. The sun barely pokes over the high ridges before dipping back down. It feels like an empty place.

"The next morning we took off and rode the horses up as far as we could up into Darwin Canyon," Bond continued. "Ultimately we had to abandon the horses and get off on the glacial debris." He was surprised, and he said Captains Lewis and Goulding were dismayed, by what they found after reaching Mendel Glacier: "By the time we got back there, there was over three feet of new snow on the ground." That was devastating for finding any debris. "The main reason for the trip was to make sure they knew what airplane it was, get the engine numbers and take some of that dried flesh that I had found and determine if it was human or not."

Bond said the forest ranger and horse packer were of little help on the glacier, huddling in the sun and complaining about the cold. "I did have equipment with me, but all of them were reluctant to get involved with it. Perkins [the forest ranger] was not all that excited about trying!" Bond rigged some ropes in a self-belay kind of system so he could get out onto the ice and survey it more carefully. "Finally we realized that it was going to be difficult as hell to find anything with all that fresh snow." Given that it was late September and snow had already fallen, Bond remembered, "we didn't linger up there; we didn't really do much else."

According to Bond, Goulding and Lewis resolved that someone from the army with better training would have to come back
the next year with proper equipment, including ice-climbing gear.
When Bond told me this, I thought at first I hadn't heard correctly.
Here was positive confirmation that R. W. Koch hadn't been making
things up in his "Secret of Mendel Glacier" article when he wrote
that a military party of "crack Army troops" had journeyed to the
glacier in 1948 to recover remains. Maybe they had been successful.
Maybe the October 1948 burial at Golden Gate National Cemetery
mentioned on the little piece of metal that park museum employee
Ward Eldredge had found was correct..

I asked Bond about this. "The year after we found the aircraft
there was an Air Rescue Service group from Hamilton Field that
spent a whole week in September, looking for the wreckage," he
told me. When I showed Bond the article that Koch had written,
though, he began to chuckle. He was amused by Koch's description of the 1947 expedition extracting four complete bodies from an
airplane, buried in fourteen feet of ice, using jackhammers to do it,
and then taking them to a funeral home in Bishop before transport-
ing the aviators to San Bruno and Golden Gate National Cemetery
for burial with full military honors.

"Well, nobody ever went to Bishop, first of all," said Bond. "It
also sounds like he mixed up the 1948 trip, when they did have a
jackhammer, with the trip in 1947. We didn't take any jackhammer
in with us on that trip at all." The reason Bond knew about what
was done on the 1948 trip is that he was recruited to be on it.

"I was supposed to go with them," he told me. "Problem was,
I didn't have any transport to get down there because they had a
full crew they brought from Fort Lewis, Washington. There was no
room in their vehicles. So what I did was tell them, I'll meet you
down there." Being a resourceful college student and lacking the
resources of the U.S. Army, Bond nevertheless found a way to get
there. "I took the bus down [from Berkeley to Fresno]."

Arriving in Fresno, he discovered a problem. "All my mountain
gear was gone," he said. Where it went to was a mystery. Bond ultimately got it all back, but it never arrived in Fresno where it was
supposed to be. "In horsing around with all that," trying to find out

where it was and trying to get it back, "the military had already left by the time I hitchhiked to the High Sierra Ranger Station."

• • •

As in 1947, on this second recovery mission during 1948, the military group drove from Prather and the High Sierra Ranger Station to Florence Lake, loaded their gear onto mules, put themselves on horses, and rode to McClure Meadow. There was a lot more gear than for the 1947 trip, Bond recalled, "because they had some relatively heavy equipment they were taking with them." The idea in 1948 was to dig through the ice with gasoline-powered jackhammers and pull out the airplane that, somehow, the army had become convinced lay in one piece beneath the ice.

Though he missed meeting up with the army group at the beginning of the trip, Bond did eventually rendezvous with them in Oakland, at the end. He remembers there were nine or ten in the group. Some were experienced mountaineers. Besides the jackhammers, he recalls, "they had quite a bit of gear."

It was a disappointing trip. But with hindsight over six decades, Bond can appreciate the irony of finding the Frozen Airman in 2005: "They [the 1948 army group] didn't find anything more than what we had found, even though they looked all over the place. And that's why finding *this* body [the Frozen Airman] is so unusual." Given the lack of success in 1947 and 1948 it was natural to think nothing else would ever be found.

But Bond always held out hope that something more would be discovered. As a combat veteran he had seen not only the horrible nature of war but the randomness of battle as well. "It would not be unusual," he told me, to find bodies long after an airplane crash. "I did not think, after what that I had seen, there would be any [complete] body present," Bond said. "However, airplane crashes are funny things. It's just like explosions. There are funny things that happen from explosions and you just never can tell what's going on with them."

Bond also helped me understand the confusion about the weather in the 1942 and 1947 army accident reports. "Evidently they [the

1948 army recovery team] knew something, or thought they did, that wasn't in the official reports," he guessed. "I got the idea from the air force there was a stormy condition they [the pilot and crew] were in. I just figured they had not known where they were, they were completely off their course. But, knowing the Sierra ..." He shrugged.

Discussing the confusion between where the wreckage was found, whether on the Darwin or the Mendel glacier, Bond explained that "maps of that day and age didn't have Mendel mentioned on them." So even though the 1947 army report said the missing AT-7 was on Darwin Glacier, probably Mendel Glacier was meant, which is where the Frozen Airman was found in 2005. Mount Mendel was not identified correctly on a topographic map until 1951. Early editions had erroneously named it Mount Wallace, and later maps only gave the elevation. In fact, up to the time that Mount Mendel finally made it onto the map, a generation of climbers venturing into the region humorously referred to the peak as Mount Ex-Wallace. Also, Mount Mendel's glacier had attracted people since at least 1908, when a geologist with the U.S. Geological Survey, G. K. Gilbert, first photographed it from Darwin Canyon. Gilbert referred to the ice below Mount Mendel as the "Little Darwin Glacier," which I'm sure partially explains the misleading names used in the 1942 and 1947 reports. Finally, even the 1988 version of Delorme's *California Atlas & Gazetteer* mislables the Darwin Glacier, showing it on the northeast slope of Mt. Mendel.

Despite four score years of High Sierra exploration, even by the mid-twentieth century, the farther you traveled from a trail the more likely you were to be in unknown territory. Something like 90,000 people backpack in Sequoia and Kings Canyon each year these days. During World War II, annual visitation to both parks was far less than that. Hardly anyone backpacked in the High Sierra. Problems with this terra incognita became obvious to the college students when they tried to explain to Air Rescue Service Squadron B where they had encountered wreckage. "How do you tell somebody you found this aircraft wreckage and nobody knows a thing about the country?" Bill Bond asked me. Because the army people didn't know Sierra Nevada geography, it was easy for them to confuse one location with another. "And that is how the wreckage got to be about Mount Darwin and not Mount Mendel." By the time R. W. Koch wrote his article in 1979, all these geographic issues had been sorted out and he was able to correctly identify where the wreckage lay.

• • •

Thinking about the crash, Bond said, "My impression was these guys just flew right straight into the peak and the ice someplace up above where the debris field is. Pieces of aluminum I found were so compressed, it just looked like that airplane had folded up like an accordion. Everything was shredded, including them. The only things that came out of it, you know, would have made it just like a meat grinder as far a human body is concerned." Bond and his friends did find a shoe on the glacier. "Those guys wore things like Oxfords and the side of that shoe was ripped. And . . . well, that was it. It indicated to me that they just wrapped into it full bore—power on." The only large parts of the airplane, like the engines and wheels, were found "way down at the bottom of the glacier where they undoubtedly rolled, slid, or skidded."

Bond shook his head in disbelief that an airplane could fly right into a mountain. "If you have an inkling you're out in that country around the high peaks, you want all the elevation you can get. You know that. You want to be at 15,000 feet at the minimum. The most shocking thing, it was undoubtedly a navigation problem. Those guys were lost. Getting lost happened to a lot of aircraft in those days. They would fly over their target and then keep going." Until they hit something.

CHAPTER 7

What Was Recovered: 1948

When I drove away from Kirby West's house, I had copies of his photographs and the 1947 and 1948 newspaper articles he had kept through the years. I pulled over at a scenic spot in the springtime green hills overlooking San Francisco Bay to study the images and read the stories.

In our conversations, Bill Bond was adamant that no remains or bodies had been recovered in either 1947 or 1948, and I believed him. Yet I read a September 30, 1947, newspaper story in West's collection that told of the Fresno County Coroner "studying remains found in the wreckage to determine if they were human." And several clippings from 1948 unequivocally reported that bodies recovered from the glacier were being awaited at Sixth Army headquarters in the Presidio in San Francisco, "brought down from their icy crypt on Mount Darwin by trained Army mountain troops." Given that Bond had been at the crash site in 1947 and had spoken with the 1948 recovery team, it was comforting to conclude that articles like these had been the source of R. W. Koch's misinformation for his magazine article.

The only name mentioned in the 1948 newspaper stories was that of Captain Roy F. Sulzbacher, the 1948 party leader. Sulzbacher graduated in 1934 from the High School of Commerce in San Francisco and spent his college years at San Francisco City College, where he played football and received a degree in mortuary science. Following college and a few years in the merchant marine, Sulzbacher enlisted in the U.S. Army, entering as a twenty-four-year-old buck private on February 28, 1941. With his educational background, he was assigned to the Sixth Army Quartermaster Corps, Graves Registration Service, based in the San Francisco Presidio, and was assigned overseas where his duties centered around recovering and identifying soldiers killed in action, preparing the dead for burial, and establishing cemeteries.

In 1943, Sulzbacher met an army nurse named Julia Volpigno at a dance in New Guinea. They were married January 14, 1944, in Sydney, Australia. Discharged December 28, 1946, Roy Sulzbacher joined his wife and their daughter, Barbara, on the East Coast, intending to open his own mortuary business. When that didn't pan out the young family relocated to San Francisco, where Sulzbacher reenlisted, receiving a presidential appointment as captain, and assumed his former duties. Roy and Julia Sulzbacher found off-base housing south of the Presidio and Golden Gate Park, and their second daughter, Marjorie, was born in 1947.

With Sulzbacher's name and a search of newspaper databases, more articles about the 1948 trip turned up. Several California newspapers, including the *Long Beach Press-Telegram* and *Oakland Tribune* followed Captain Sulzbacher's September 1948 mission to the Sierra. The story was even covered as far away as Iowa in the *Council Bluffs Nonpareil* and *Iowa City Press-Citizen*. Most of the stories from outside of California were brief, and some appeared to be based on a series of *Inyo Register* articles from Bishop, in the Owens Valley. Taken together, they laid out the more or less complete—though not always coherent—story of Sulzbacher's mission to Darwin Canyon to retrieve the remains of a U.S. Army Air Forces pilot and three navigation cadets lost since November 18, 1942.

On September 9, 1948, the *Inyo Register* reported that "a detachment of army-trained mountaineers this week opened their first attack on a glacier holding the bodies of four airmen downed in the rugged Sierra-Nevada mountains in 1942." According to the *Register*, the "retrieving team" was to "jump off" for a three-mile "tedious" journey in which they would "chip around the 14-ft. ice pack until the afternoon" before making "the perilous trip back to camp." Sunshine was promised by the Fresno weather bureau for the next ten days, "the only period in which the ice-bound area is accessible at all."

The *Oakland Tribune* that same Thursday picked up and expanded on the story: "Army mountaineers were making their way down the summit of a treacherous glacier near Mount Darwin, east of here, today, but the results of their mission to locate the bodies of four Army airmen missing since 1942 remained a mystery." Ranger Fred Greene, "of the National Forestry Station at Northfork," reported that he anticipated being contacted by the "specially-trained and equipped mountain troops" from Fort Lewis, who had left the San Francisco Presidio "last Friday [September 3, 1948]," commanded by "Capt. R. F. Sulzbacher of the Sixth Army memorial division." These were the "crack Army troops" that R. W. Koch wrote about.

The *Tribune* went on to say that the team "hoped to find the plane containing perfectly preserved bodies but may have found nothing but barren ice, 15 feet thick in some places." Ranger Green speculated that the recovery crew would be "coming down on the second day of their planned 10-day expedition," indicating that "they may have met with success." Reference to William Bond was made. "They were joined here by civilian mountain climbers who were to accompany them at least part of the way to their base camp at Darwin Lake high in the Sierra Madre [sic]." The article ended by saying that "they carried with them portable pneumatic jack-hammers to cut through the ice if their quest was successful."

The *Long Beach Press-Telegram* from September 9 disagreed with any speculation of success, reporting that *Frank* (not Fred) Green told them the expedition attempting to "recover bodies of four Army pilots from Darwin Glacier, high in the Sierra northeast of here apparently has given up its task." Contacted by radio the previous night, Green said the expedition was leaving the high country and that "no explanation was given."

September 10, the following day, the *Oakland Tribune* changed its mind and wrote that "reports that the Army mountain search party which scaled Darwin Glacier near Fresno in search of the bodies of four Army fliers missing since 1942 was 'pulling out' proved false today." Apparently, reporters jumped the gun and assumed the expedition was pulling out because the journalists got wind of Captain Sulzbacher leaving the wilderness in order to place some phone calls. They may have assumed, since the captain had a twenty-seven-mile solo ride to Florence Lake, followed by a sixty-five-mile drive on a narrow two-lane road to the nearest phone, that he had found something, or found nothing, and perhaps was calling headquarters for instructions.

William Bond and Kirby West are identified by the same *Oakland Tribune* article as "two U.C. students" responsible for sighting the "twin-engined advanced Army trainer which crashed into the desolate peak with its four-man crew in November, 1942."

• • •

Because I had never contemplated such things before, I was surprised to read about the efforts of the military in 1947 and 1948 in identifying the wreckage and repatriating the remains of Lieutenant Gamber and his crew found in Darwin Canyon. Despite my familiarity with how the Park Service rangers, in conjunction with JPAC, had recovered the Frozen Airman in 2005, I had assumed that methods and intentions would have been different fifty-seven years previously. Captain Sulzbacher's 1948 mission, outlined by these newspapers, also encompassed a theme I'd first encountered in *The Iliad* and stories about the burial of Hector. How do we treat soldiers who give their lives for their country?

In the United States, military burial traditions have been in place for only a century and a half, since the Civil War. This most uncivil of wars killed more Americans than any war the country has been involved in since. People in the North and people in the South wanted to know about their menfolk. Were they alive or were they dead? If alive, were they camped out with their fellow soldiers? If wounded, at what hospital? If captured, please God, tell me where? And, if dead, when, how, and where?

Before the Civil War, these important questions went unanswered for the common soldier. The government and military were content to accept bodies, blood, and guts without considering the effects of bullets, cannonballs, bayonets, and disease. The slaughter of 1861–1865 changed all of that. In *This Republic of Suffering*, historian Drew Gilpin Faust explains how the concept of the "good death" influenced people's thoughts.

During the Civil War, the traditional idea of a good death referred to a process of readying oneself for death, not the event itself. Faust discusses how central *ars moriendi* was to mid-nineteenth century Americans: "Civil War soldiers were, in fact, better prepared to die than to kill, for they lived in a culture that offered many lessons in how life should end." These lessons taught dying as an art with "rules of conduct for the moribund and their attendants." How a person died exemplified how they lived and reflected on "the quality of life everlasting." Death was to be at home, attended by family who would gather for the soon-to-be departed's last words. "The *hors mori*, the hour of death, had therefore to be witnessed, scrutinized, interpreted, narrated—not to mention carefully prepared for by any sinner who sought to be worthy of salvation," Faust writes. Violent, sudden death in battle could not be considered a good death because it was unattended and the deceased unable to prepare himself to meet his maker.

In wars, soldiers die far from home in strange lands, far from the acceptable setting of the good death. They die in isolation or in the company of strangers, unable to fulfill the rules of the dying art. Civil War soldiers and families found ways to circumvent this problem. Prior to battle, soldiers wrote letters home that could serve as their last words. Nurses served as family surrogates to soldiers dying in hospitals. Repatriating the remains of the soldier dead helped assuage a family's feelings that their loved one had died properly. Importantly in this regard, soldiers carried some sort of identification so their graves would be marked and they would not die unknown.

Incorporated within the concept of the good death was a decent burial. During the Civil War, families would journey to battlefields searching for sons and fathers or friends to provide proper burial. The Christian Commission and the Sanitary Commission, among other organizations in the North, were established to locate the bodies of soldiers killed in action, ascertain their names (if possible), and transmit that information to families. If anything could be worse than contemplating the death of a family member, it had to be not even knowing whether they were dead or alive.

Mark Harris points out in *Grave Matters* that having a body to grieve over is an accepted part of the American way of death. Through history and custom, this is what we have come to expect. The funeral trade has helped this concept along by christening the "embalmer's creation a 'memory picture,' a pleasing illusion of a loved one who has simply slipped off to sleep," as Harris writes. Through my reading I came to understand why people consider it necessary to view the deceased's remains, soldier or not. Such witnessing is all part of the acceptance that a death has occurred, enabling "the necessary grieving and subsequent healing process," says Harris. Having a "pleasant and true-to-life" picture makes it easier to "acknowledge the death and, perhaps, let go."

In Civil War days, families learned of soldier deaths from often highly unreliable lists published in newspapers. A more reliable method was a letter home from the soldier's commanders. Even better was a letter by the soldier's companions, since these men were the ones most likely to have witnessed the death.

The pain experienced by nineteenth-century families over the loss of their loved ones must have been excruciating, made even more so by the manner in which so many of the dead were treated. The dead were buried, often hastily and not terribly deeply, by the hundreds in trenches—unmarked and unregistered. Faust writes, "In the absence of arrangements for interring and recording overwhelming numbers, hundreds of thousands of men—more than 40 percent of deceased Yankees and a far greater proportion of Confederates—perished without names," known only as *un*known.

Soldiers were understandably not happy with this arrangement, especially when considering how their own deaths would be treated. From this evolved the idea that government was obligated to not only treat the wounded but to deal with the dead as well. Faust writes that this change in attitude developed out of a commitment to individual human rights that derived from the principles soldiers on both sides fought for: "Honoring the dead became inseparable from respecting the living."

Burying the dead therefore became more important than simply disposing of the bodies. Burying the dead became a way to honor and preserve the dignity and privacy of the deceased. The United States was a very Christian country in mid-nineteenth century. Faust writes, "Redemption and restoration of the body were understood as physical, not just metaphysical, realties," so it mattered greatly to soldiers that their remains be handled with reverence and care. They believed their bodies served as a "repository of human identity" and had the "intrinsic selfhood and individuality of a particular human." If a soldier expected to rise from the dead, as promised by his faith, it was important that his body be given proper burial.

World War II experienced tremendous casualty numbers: Germany lost 5.5 million soldiers and 1.6 million civilians. Japan lost 2.1 million soldiers and 580,000 civilians. The United Kingdom lost 382,000 service personnel. France lost 217,000 plus 282,000 civilians. Poland lost 5.6 million civilians. The Soviet Union lost 10.7 million soldiers and 11.4 million civilians. How much is a million? The estimated population of Los Angeles in 2008 was 10.3 million. And in the United States, where 416,000 soldiers died, families became familiar with the War Department telegram, "The President regrets to inform you that your son ..."

During World War II, Michael Sledge writes in *Soldier Dead*, 25 percent of U.S. soldier deaths were not combat related. That translates to about 100,000 dead from disease, automobile accidents, training accidents—whatever. "On an average daily basis," writes Sledge, "the United States lost service personnel equal to the number killed in the crash of a Boeing 747 with a full complement of passengers." The period between 1944 and 1945 saw the highest casualties. "It was as though several jumbo-jet-loads of men and women went down daily."

As I began to understand the concept of *ars moriendi*, I also began to understand my developing need to tell the stories of Lieutenant Gamber and Cadets Mortenson, Munn, and Mustonen and how they died. I had felt uncomfortable since childhood, after becoming aware of the Tomb of the Unknown Soldier, knowing that a person's passing on earth could go unrecorded or that a family wouldn't know where their loved one was buried or how they died. In relating the stories of the Frozen Airman and his three compatriots, I believed I could bring them back to life—not in any physical sense, but within the memory of their families, for the children of generations the airmen had never met. If I might make them live in their descendents' eyes, they could not die unknown, even though their bodies had never been recovered.

•   •   •

Three days after Captain Sulzbacher's phone call, on September 11, 1948, the story made an impressive change. The *Press-Telegram* in Long Beach, California, reported that "climbers [were] due back with four bodies" that had been removed by "mountaineers led by Capt. Roy F. Sulzbacher" after four days digging through "14 feet of ice." The *Iowa City Press-Citizen* contributed that the remains were "brought down from their icy crypt on Mount Darwin by trained army mountain troops," who had endured "four days of perilous climbing." The remains were then shipped to Sixth Army headquarters for "positive identification." For the *Press-Citizen*, the recovery team's "success was a triumph over the elements," since "for virtually all of the year the mountain is subject to avalanches and blinding blizzards at the 13,800-foot level where the wreckage was located in August, 1947, by a skier."

Two days later, on Monday, September 13, the *Oakland Tribune* caught up with the news and expanded the topic. "Air Crash Victims, Dug From Glacier, Arrive at S.F.," the headline announced. In the *Tribune* account, the amount of time spent in the High Sierra became "two days digging in the ice of one of the Mount Darwin glaciers." This was the first written instance that the site was anywhere other than on the Mount Darwin glacier.

An army spokesman quoted in the *Tribune* said that aircraft wreckage "was scattered over the glacier, buried in the ice with their [the crew] bodies over an area half a mile wide and three-fourths of a mile high." This spokesman must have been Captain Roy Sulzbacher or, at least, someone who had debriefed the captain.

William Bond was mentioned as assisting the army mountain troops on their mission, though in reality he wasn't there.

Sealing the "facts" in print for thirty-one years until they reappeared in R. W. Koch's "Secret of the Mendel Glacier," the short *Tribune* article ended with the comment, "Word is awaited from Washington to determine the place of burial." Despite recovering no remains, word about burial came twelve days later on September 25, 1948, to the four crewmembers' families. A letter from Brigadier General Garrison H. Davidson, the army chief of staff at the Sixth Army headquarters at the Presidio in San Francisco, informed the families that "the remains of the crewmen on the plane in which your son lost his life have been located, and recovered from Mount Darwin Glacier, California." The general also wrote that individual identifications were "physically impossible, due to the manner in which the crewmen lost their lives." Location of the group burial wasn't included in General Davidson's letter.

• • •

Because all reported evidence about retrieving the remains from the AT-7 accident is countered by eyewitness and official documents, it would be convenient to say that some dissembling went on when it came to informing the families and providing reporters with the results of Captain Sulzbacher's 1948 Darwin Canyon mission. From my reading I learned that it was not unusual for families to be told less than the truth about what, exactly, was in a casket being lowered into the ground. Michael Sledge points out in *Soldier Dead* that "with World War II came the extensive use of high-speed aircraft laden with fuel and explosives. Crashes would mingle and burn remains to the extent that it was difficult to separate them. Often, no single individual body or body part could be identified and all were buried together." We know from the 1942 accident report that Lieutenant Gamber's aircraft did not burn. However, Bill Bond, whose wartime experience in Europe gave him perspective on such things, described the Mendel Glacier crash scene in 1947 as "a meat grinder." It seems reasonable to expect that six-year-old remains from such an airplane crash would consist of unrecognizable body parts—and not many of them.

Parents and relatives of the missing AT-7 crewmen never forgot their sons and brothers, but it can be difficult to accept death when there is no body to grieve over. The parents of Munn and Mustonen kept their sons' memories alive within the army by writing letters and making personal visits to Mather Field in Sacramento. In September 1943, the Munn family prevailed upon their local congressman, Earl R. Lewis, to intercede on their behalf with the War Department to encourage the army to keep searching. The result of such prodding was to push the army into changing the status of the crew from "missing" to "dead" and releasing their personal effects to the families.

What accounted for what the families saw as bureaucratic foot dragging and delay? From *Soldier Dead*, I learned of the logistical and political challenges of bringing home the over 400,000 American soldiers killed in action in World War II from Europe, Asia, and the South Pacific. Sledge writes, "Families had to wait two, three, four, or five years and longer before being able to bury their loved ones." Domestic repatriation of remains took a backseat to bringing the boys home from overseas.

So it took nearly six years for the four families to finally have what they had been waiting for: official word, not only that the airplane had been found, but that the boys inside of it were coming home. Grieving required a body to mourn over, and in the case of the AT-7 crew there had been none for too long.

At worst, not telling the truth was perpetuating a fraud. But I doubt the army people in 1948 had any other thought but to cause as little pain and distress as possible. At best, I suspect the army was simply trying to provide closure for the families. Experience was probably the guide, not expediency, when the army contacted the families from the no longer missing AT-7. Telling them there were commingled and partial remains was better than saying there were none at all. And so, as the *Inyo Register* in Bishop reported on September 16, 1948, the crew was "brought down from their icy crypt..."

• • •

I have other evidence that no remains were recovered from Captain Sulzbacher's mission because his wife Julia Sulzbacher confirmed what Bond had already told me. "Roy went with four or five men and he was gone a little over a week," she said of her husband's September 1948 trip. "He came back sunburned and tired and sweaty. I was glad he came home. He said he went up to find some bodies but he was not able to find anything."

Their daughter, Barbara Sulzbacher-LaCroix, told me the same thing: "My mom always told my sister, Marjorie, and me about dad's final trip. Just that he went and was gone for a while but came back with no remains."

The captain was gone from September 6 to September 13, though there are indications from the first newspaper reports and a September 25 letter sent by General Davidson that a longer mission was planned. Upon returning to San Francisco, Sulzbacher developed and printed the photos he took during the trip. Mrs. Sulzbacher shared those photos with me. Most are labeled September 1948, but a few are marked July, which indicated to me that the captain had made an earlier trip, possibly to reconnoiter the glacier.

Sulzbacher also wrote up a report and communicated his findings to his superiors. He made a statement to the press. I have no doubt that the letters received in late September by the families of the missing airmen were a direct result of Sulzbacher's fieldwork.

A week later, Sulzbacher was dead from bulbar poliomyelitis. Spending a physically strenuous week at high elevation where the air is thin would not have done his respiratory system any good.

Julia Sulzbacher doesn't think her husband knew he was sick. The day previous to his death he had been very ill and the next morning he fell out of bed. As an experienced nurse, Mrs. Sulzbacher knew something was seriously wrong. She called for medical help and Roy was taken to Letterman General Hospital at the Presidio in San Francisco at 10:30 A.M. "He was in quarantine. I had to wear a cap and gown before they would let me in," she told me. "He was not rational at the time. He didn't know me." She had two young children waiting for her at home, so that is where she went. "The next morning around 7:30 the hospital called me to say he had died." All these years later and her voice is still sad and sorrowful with the memory. "He was my whole world and it fell in on me."

More than most, Captain Sulzbacher knew from personal experience in the Pacific Theater during World War II the responsibility of government to locate, identify, and give decent burials to soldiers who died for their country. A basic tenet of human rights obliges governments to provide care for its veterans and its dead in order to not deny them their humanity. Or, more simply put: this is what civilized people do. In that tradition, Sulzbacher journeyed not once but twice to Mendel Glacier in 1948 to recover the crew from the wrecked AT-7. That he failed in his obligation is not because of his lack of duty, initiative, or will, but is due to climate, geology, and the captain's own imminent death.

Posthumously promoted to major, Roy Sulzbacher was buried October 4, 1948, at Golden Gate National Cemetery in San Bruno, California. A ceremony and burial service was held for the crew of the AT-7 eleven days later at 11:30 A.M. on October 15, 1948, at the same cemetery. Roy Sulzbacher's grave lies a hundred yards nearly opposite the headstone for the pilot and navigation cadets he never found.

CHAPTER 8

The Frozen Airman Is Identified

Answers to the mysteries of the Frozen Airman were coming one by one through careful reading of newspaper stories from 1942, 1947, and 1948, checked against interviews with crucial witnesses. I knew these things for certain:

- The airplane he flew in crashed into Mendel Glacier. All references to Darwin Glacier came about because of poor geographic awareness and unmarked topographic maps. Bill Bond told me how ignorant of Sierra Nevada geography the Air Rescue Service captains had been. William Tweed, chief park naturalist at Sequoia and Kings Canyon National Parks, gave me a thirty-minute Mount Goddard topographic map from 1937 that showed Darwin Canyon, Mount Darwin, and Darwin Glacier, but no mention of a Mendel Glacier. The daughters of Robert Lewis, one of the captains guided by Bond in 1947, sent me a map from their father's papers. On it, Mount Darwin and Darwin Glacier were circled, suggesting that this was where Lewis thought his recovery team had been.

- The weather on November 18, 1942, was not as mild as base commander Colonel Hewitt reported to his superiors in Washington DC. Cadet William Bechter's diary showed this, as did contemporary newspaper articles.

- The missing AT-7's route was not a simple hop from Mather Field north to Corning and back, as initially reported. Colonel Hewitt's teletype in the 1942 accident report to army headquarters in Washington DC specified that the route went from Mather Field, south to Los Banos, then north to Roseville, continuing on to Corning, and then finally turning south toward Mather.

- No airfield existed at Los Banos until the 1950s, though sixteen miles southeast of there was Eagle Field, a U.S. Army Air Forces training base opened early in 1942. There was no airfield at Corning either, though fourteen miles south of there was an army airfield in Orland.

- I knew when the AT-7 departed Mather Field and when it was expected to return, and I knew when search parties were dispatched. According to an unsigned handwritten note in the 1942 "Report of Aircraft Accident" and a typed summary prepared by Captain Leroy Heston (the investigating officer), Lieutenant Gamber departed Mather Field at 8:30 A.M. with "about five hours fuel on board." When the airplane did not return, "a search was started at 1330," or 1:30 P.M. But elsewhere in the complete file in my possession are dozens of telegrams that peg 1911Z, or "Zulu Time," as when the AT-7 officially went missing and 1511Z as the time that Gamber departed Mather Field. To avoid confusion that might result when flying between time zones, a standard based on Coordinated Universal Time (UTC) and a twenty-four-hour system is used in aviation. All local time is corrected for the UTC clock, which begins in Greenwich, England. To calculate Zulu Time in the Pacific Standard Time zone, you subtract eight hours. Therefore, 1511Z equals 0711 hours, or 7:11 A.M. and 1911Z equals 1111 hours or 11:11 A.M. This means that when the AT-7 was reported missing it was four hours into an approximately five-hour flight.

- No remains had ever been recovered, though the army tried three separate times to bring the boys home from Mendel Glacier: once in 1947 (when Bill Bond escorted Captains Lewis and Goulding) and twice in 1948 (Captain Sulzbacher's July reconnoiter and his September trip reported so well in the newspapers). They failed each time. The 1947 Army Air Forces "Report of Major Accident" established this conclusively when it said, "No bodies were recovered." Bond, who met with Sulzbacher in 1948, confirmed this. During a phone conversation with Julia Sulzbacher, she also confirmed that no remains were recovered.

• A symbolic burial took place in San Bruno on October 15, 1948 at Golden Gate National Cemetery. The families were told it would happen, without knowing the burial would be symbolic, but I did not know if any had attended. I also did not know what, if anything, the army found to fill the casket.

• Official identification of the Frozen Airman came on March 6, 2006, with a media advisory from the U.S. Army Human Resources Command: "The remains of a World War II soldier recovered from a California glacier in October 2005 have been identified as Aviation Cadet Leo Mustonen, 22, of Brainerd, Minn." Leo Mustonen had been identified using a combination of science, circumstantial evidence, and plain old detective work.

• • •

JPAC's forensic anthropology report of the Frozen Airman's remains concluded that they belonged to a six-foot-tall Caucasian male, twenty to twenty-five years of age, with light brown or blond hair and a history of poor dental care. Of the four boys from the missing AT-7, this profile best suited Leo Mustonen but was not conclusive because the evidence was anecdotal.

Next, JPAC addressed the physical evidence. The agency repeated, then expanded upon the Fresno County Coroner's report of John Doe number 10-2-05 from the previous October. Found on the body were coins dated no later than 1942. Collar insignia on his clothing, the clothing itself, as well as the unopened, undeployed, parachute (serial number 41-1984) attached to the body indicated that he was in the U.S. Army Air Forces and served as an aviation cadet. Also found on the body was a name badge, unreadable in normal light. But alternate-light-source photography was used to elucidate the lettering. The visible letters, with blanks before and after, were EO A. M. There was initial doubt about using the name badge for identifying the Frozen Airman until JPAC learned that the army's 1947 report had incorrectly stated that Leo Mustonen's middle initial was "M."

Positively placing Cadet Mustonen on scene at the glacier in 1942 was important, especially in light of finding no identifiable aircraft debris associated with the remains. In 1947, the four University of California students found a name badge for John M. Mortenson on Mendel Glacier. The 1942 army accident report says that Mortenson was with Mustonen and two others when their AT-7 number 41-21079 disappeared. Tags removed from the aircraft engines found in Mendel Glacier in 1947 confirmed that the engines came from the missing plane. This strongly places Mortenson and Mustonen together. JPAC believed this presented a compelling case that the remains of the Frozen Airman were from the missing aircraft, number 41-21079. And, despite the history of airplane crashes in Sequoia and Kings Canyon National Parks, and the proximity of two other crashes to Mendel Glacier, there was no evidence that any other U.S. Army Air Forces aircraft ever crashed in the vicinity.

Whenever possible and practical, JPAC verifies individual determinations with genetic testing. Samples of mitochondrial DNA from the maternal line were collected from living relatives of the missing crewmen. Unfortunately, Leo Mustonen had no living blood relations from his mother's side of the family. However, none of the samples provided by any of the other families proved a match to the sample collected from the Frozen Airman. Along with all the circumstantial evidence, JPAC therefore determined the Frozen Airman was Leo A. Mustonen.

JPAC concluded that Leo Mustonen's fatal injuries were consistent with either "a high energy perimortem event such as an aircraft crash or a fall from a height." In the face of what I considered to be evidence to the contrary (especially the unopened, undeployed parachute lying attached to the remains), JPAC still entertained the theory that "the absence of metallic objects [aircraft wreckage] and extensive skin lacerations are not consistent with this individual being in the aircraft when it crashed."

• • •

As summer of 2006 approached, I made plans to cross Lamarck Col and visit Darwin Canyon. For the past year I had immersed myself in the lives of William Gamber, John Mortenson, Ernest Munn, and Leo Mustonen. I read books, watched World War II movies and films about aviation and aviators, and listened to the Top 10 songs of 1942. I thought that by studying the four aviators' world, I would learn more about how they had lived. I felt confident that through my research I could fathom what happened the day they died.

I was strongly motivated to visit the crash site for one reason. After everything I had studied about Leo Mustonen's final flight, I wanted to stand on the spot where the Frozen Airman had been found. I had to see for myself where Cadet Mustonen had spent sixty-three solitary years. I tried twice in 2006 and failed both times.

Spring of 2006 came late to the high country and when it did arrive was unseasonably cool. Snow lingered long. When my longtime hiking partner Michele Hinatsu and I hiked to Lamarck Col from North Lake, we were unprepared for what we found. The col itself was completely covered in snow and ice, blocking access to Darwin Canyon and beyond to Mendel Glacier. We sat below the col and decided we were ill-equipped to make the ascent.

Michele and I did a different trip instead, hiking over Piute Pass into gentle Humphreys Basin. There we found the best wildflower displays I've seen in decades, furious blooms on the edges of snowbanks. A week later we hiked out and drove to the bristlecone pine forest in the White Mountains, which was an education in relief. Standing on a high point in the Whites and looking across the Owens Valley to the Sierra, we were not confronted with a continual vista of equally high peaks and ridges. The Sierra crest actually dips in some places, runs for miles like saw teeth at a constant lower elevation in others, and in still others, sends massive mounds of rock into the sky. You can see all of that from the other side of the Owens Valley.

Mounts Darwin and Mendel lie a short way west of the crest and are the highest things around. From our perch we could see a considerable distance, north and south, where the peaks and ridges looked significantly lower. A topographic map shows no high mountains to the west of Darwin and Mendel. To be in their vicinity and to ram an airplane into the side of Mount Mendel required some pretty fantastically bad luck. Less than a quarter of a mile's difference, north or south, and Lieutenant Gamber and his crew of cadets navigating their course home could have arrived safe and sound from their harrowing ride.

• • •

In October of the same year I planned a return to a completely snow-free Lamarck Col with another hiking companion, Gregg Fauth. I expected Mendel Cirque to be as bare as a baby's bottom by then. But this time something besides the weather brought me up short: my father died the day I was to leave and this ultimately affected my view of what I had studied for the last year.

The AT-7 crew were of my father's generation. With his death I realized how little I knew about him, or about my mother who had died two years before. Every day that passed reminded me of questions I'd thought to ask but had never gotten around to. The Frozen Airman's story, Leo Mustonen's story, had become personal, a way to resolve and bring closure into my own life while providing the same sentiment to families of the missing crew. None of them knew, truly, how these four boys had died.

The Gamber, Mortenson, Munn, and Mustonen families didn't know me and I didn't know them. But I felt a connection to them. There were unanswered questions in my life that would remain so, but maybe, I could provide answers for somebody else. In a way, this felt like passing a baton in a relay race—passing the truth from one person to another so they could carry on. I couldn't shake the feeling there was more to the crash of the AT-7 than it simply being off-course. I wanted to dig deeper into the airmen's lives and find significance for both their lives and deaths. And whether I believed that Lieutenant Gamber was lost or not, I lacked the power to prove otherwise. I resolved to return to Lamarck Col in 2007 and to let nothing keep me from reaching Mendel Glacier.

CHAPTER 9

The Frozen Airman Is Not Alone: August 2007

For a trail with the reputation of being a hard row to hoe, the way up to Lamarck Col is busy today. The lower stretch, after leaving North Lake, was busy with day hikers wearing anything from flip-flops to combat boots. There are over a dozen people in this upper section, huffing and puffing above lakes and forest at close to 12,000 feet. Sometimes a way is popular; sometimes it isn't. If Michele and I wanted the trail to ourselves, we should have crossed the col last year in the snow.

A sign at Lamarck Col announces the boundary between Inyo National Forest and Sequoia and Kings Canyon National Parks. It's the only thing marking the presence of the Park Service in this wilderness area until McClure Meadow, assuming hikers go that far down Darwin Canyon and into Evolution Valley and the John Muir Trail. At McClure is a log cabin, built for snow surveyors in 1940, staffed by a backcountry ranger from around May to October.

Mendel and Darwin glaciers are embarrassingly exposed from Lamarck Col. You can see everything: their ice, their bergschrunds, every dimple and flaw, every rock and boulder. Mount Mendel (13,710 feet) and Mount Darwin (13,831 feet) are in bare relief too, as is all of Darwin Canyon, its dollar-coin upper lake and four linear lakes down-canyon. Not a tree, not a bush, and not a blade of grass is visible. Tucked within the rocks around my feet are a few scattered sedges, an occasional mountain sorrel fitting snugly into deep shade, and an incongruously large-flowered, fuzzy yellow sunflower. The rocks have splotches of color—lichens—as if Jackson Pollock has been up here with a few small cans of paint.

On a clear day like today it's difficult to imagine Lieutenant Gamber being lost in Darwin Canyon, and it's hard to believe that an airplane could smack into the granite walls of the Mendel Cirque. Darwin Canyon is a canyon, not a valley, but it's a big and wide canyon, maybe a mile across, several thousand feet deep and three miles long with two sharp turns. In comparison, airplanes are small. Even big airplanes.

To collide with an offshoot of Darwin Canyon, a cavity in the canyon really, Gamber and his navigation cadets must have been terribly misplaced on their charts. Maybe flying southeast in zero visibility up the San Joaquin River drainage from the Central Valley, they ventured into wide and gentle Evolution Valley and then, following the lowest, easiest path, turned up Darwin Canyon. As the canyon narrowed and the ground began to rise, the lieutenant realized his mistake. He couldn't follow the terrain much farther. Darwin Canyon is a "box" canyon. Just past the Darwin and Mendel cirques, the canyon ends at nearly 13,000 feet with a vertical wall. Quick! Turn to the right! This could, maybe, be a way out. But no. And, moving at 150 miles per hour, the AT-7 plows into Mendel Glacier. They would have had just enough time to see the mountain.

Or, maybe the AT-7 was flying east to west. Crossing over Lamarck Col and the Sierra crest, a downdraft plunged the airplane toward the ground. Gamber didn't have the time or maneuvering room to avoid the inevitable. He would have crossed the mile or so from Lamarck Col to the glacier in a few seconds.

• • •

Once Michele and I are below the col and at Darwin Canyon's upper lake, the geographic enormity of the scene is overwhelming. Canyon walls extend to sharp ridges and peaks. There is the definite feeling of having been dropped into a trench. Boulders of granite, all fitting together like the dolosse in a harbor, are the foot of Mendel Glacier directly before us. In a quarter mile the slope gains 400 feet of elevation. Imagine the tallest pile of earth ever created by bulldozers. Then close your eyes and imagine that pile as tall as a forty-story building.

High above the trench wall is Mount Mendel and portions of its left and right couloirs. From this vantage within Darwin Canyon, the peak is a nearly straight-up mass of granite cut and scored by grooves, fissures, and ledges. It's a cliché to say this, but I'll say it anyway: the peak looms over us. The only sounds in Darwin Canyon are wind, falling water, and cascades of rock raining down from the cliffs. This is primordial landscape. Glaciers occupied this canyon as little as a few hundred years ago. Plants and animals have only recently begun to claim it. They have a long and uphill battle before they'll succeed. Michele and I spend a cold and windy night at Darwin Canyon Lake Number 5. I'm excited. She's excited. Tomorrow we walk into history.

• • •

My first trip to Mendel Glacier is almost my last. Leaping across talus, suddenly I'm falling through space. Unfocused blue sky and hard, white, granite flashes before my eyes. I land harshly within in a rock-walled cavity, my day pack a soft cushion. Seven feet above, the boulder that turned under my foot continues wobbling, teetering on edge, a vulture deciding to fall or fly. It turns, turns, covering and uncovering the lid of my box, and finally settles quietly on the rim.

Getting up, I cautiously climb out of the hole and look around. Had the rock that threw me in here followed behind I don't think I ever would have been found. Who would know where to search in this terrain, where so much looks the same? I hurry to catch up with Michele, though *hurry* is hardly the descriptive term for what I do in the thin air, and soon we're standing on a slippery amalgam of ice, sand, gravel, scree, talus, and running water. This is a glacier?

Around us a sports arena consisting of rock rises to a dome of deep blue sky. The ground is ice with rocks poking out of it. The uneven surface where we walk is a slippery rough-and-tumble world of inclines, declines, melt pools, running water, and other hindrances to movement. It's necessary for us to pick our way up- and downslope, wending around ice-embedded boulders and rock debris that have fallen from the vertical cliffs. The hard, sharp granite already provides enough barriers, but a long summer of sun has melted deep divots in the ice. Walking on sun cups is as much fun as running a three-legged race across bomb craters.

From the middle of Mendel Glacier, gazing up the cirque toward the bergschrund, I'm reminded of standing at second base in a sunken baseball stadium. The bowl I'm now in was created by ice melting more rapidly in the middle of the glacier than behind me in the outfield bleachers. Fewer rocks in the infield equates to less insulation under my feet, so there is more melting. Ice behind home plate at the bergschrund is saved because the ice is deeper, shaded and sheltered from sun. It also accumulates more snow in winter. Behind home plate the cirque walls climb skyward into the stands, the rows of stadium lights represented by horns, arêtes, and the jagged sawtooth ridge of gendarmes.

A gash across the north-facing cirque walls marks a split couloir, unimaginatively known as Mendel Left and Mendel Right. They are narrow and steep gullies leading up to the ridge so often blocked from the ameliorating influence of the sun's warmth that, once they fill with snow and ice, they may remain icy long into summer. The couloirs are difficult and technical climbing routes. Mendel Left is considered the most challenging ice climb in the Sierra Nevada—a sixty-degree pitch for most of its 800-foot length, with a seventy-degree pitch at the top for good measure. It's also a claustrophobic one-arm's width toward the summit.

• • •

Michele and I traverse the loose rocky slope above Mendel Glacier, keeping our eyes open to anything unusual or out of place. I wish I had binoculars, "eyeball extenders" as my friend Hal

Genger used to say. All I can see is rock and ice. I kick at a rock but it doesn't move. It's still embedded in ice. Last year the glacier was here. Now, it's hidden below the rocks.

We don't talk. It's hard enough to breathe. Michele points down the glacier. Something silvery and shiny is mixed within the speckled white and black of granite, definitely out of place, shape and colorwise. We drop straight down to the object, stepping on rock stairs poking out of the glacier.

Closer and closer, the object develops size and shape. Round, reflective. A mechanical smell. Not until we're nearly on top of the object do I see what it is. "It's part of an engine!" There are gears and tubing and flashing. The smell is engine oil dripping into the ice. It looks exactly like engine debris from one of Roy Sulzbacher's photos. I have a copy of the image with me. As far as I can tell, the engine hasn't moved very far in fifty-nine years.

Excited, we pore over the machine. A small, fast-moving stream of cold water flows directly under it. There are identification plates on various pieces of the engine. Mindful of the 1947 trip when engine tags were used to identify the wreckage, I clear grease off the plates and copy the numbers into my journal. I take photographs. What an incredible find! I had hoped to find pieces of wreckage but nothing as quickly as this and certainly nothing this big. I thought we would be lucky to find anything bigger than a house key.

Pulling out my GPS unit I mark the waypoint. Michele and I speculate on where the rest of the airplane could be. As far as I am aware, ours is the first confirmed sighting of this wreckage since 1948. If the AT-7 flew into the cirque in the area above us, debris easily could have fallen onto the glacier and slid down the ice to where we are. I remind myself that the glacier was much deeper and larger in 1942 than it is today. Kirby West's photo of Mendel Glacier from 1947 shows an expanse of ice. So do Roy Sulzbacher's 1948 photos. Below us is very little exposed ice. In 1942, none of this rock was visible. For wreckage to still be this high up, snow must have fallen soon after the crash and embedded wreckage into the ice. It's only now melting out.

Michele decides to continue downslope, fanning out to what she surmises to be a reasonable debris field. I choose to climb and look.

I pick my way, trying to stay on the surface rocks where I'll have traction. I get don't get far before running out of firm surface to step on. I turn around.

• • •

Before Mendel Glacier, I thought of glaciers as rivers of ice, massive ice cubes hundreds of feet thick and miles long. You can't know the High Sierra without seeing the effects of glaciers. Their signs are ubiquitous. Lake basins were excavated and scoured by glaciers. Canyons were carved from V-shaped to U-shaped by glaciers. Rock surfaces were polished smooth by grinding glaciers.

Most glaciers are in fact composed of vast stretches of ice. Ice age glaciers that advanced across North America were. Glaciers in Alaska's Glacier Bay are. The big glaciers on Mount Rainier are made of ice and so are the large Sierra Nevada glaciers found in Lyle Canyon in Yosemite or the Palisade Group in Sequoia and Kings Canyon National Parks. Darwin Glacier is like that too. But not the Mendel. Mendel Glacier, with its mix of rock and ice, is an oddity. It is not one of these so-called clean glaciers.

For glaciologists, clean glaciers are the archetype. Rockfall from the surrounding cliffs may contribute surface debris, but the glacier is predominately ice. Clean glaciers pluck rock from beneath themselves, carry it downslope, and produce moraines at their margins as they melt and recede.

Clean glaciers are still slowly at work in the Sierra, carving the distinctive shape of the mountains as they do in Alps, Himalayas, Iceland, and the mountains of Patagonia, and I expected the Mendel Glacier to be one of them. That's why I experienced such strong cognitive dissonance when Michele and I reached it and found it to be a rock or "debris covered" glacier instead. I'd heard of rock glaciers in the 1970s but always envisioned piles of rock debris flowing downslope like ice. What they really are is ice embedded with rock.

The difference in movement and melting behavior between clean glaciers and rock glaciers explains why it took over sixty years for aircraft wreckage and the body of Leo Mustonen to appear in Mendel Glacier. If the AT-7 had crashed into Darwin Glacier, a clean glacier, there would have never been a mystery of the Frozen Airman.

• • •

At his office in Bellingham at Western Washington University, associate professor of geology Douglas Clark explained how rubble on Mendel Glacier, ranging in size from grains of sand to railroad boxcars, is a significantly greater portion of the rock-ice mix than in clean glaciers. Where the amount of rubble is enough to continuously cover the glacier's surface, it acts as a very effective insulator, preventing or retarding the ice underneath from melting. And if you think clean glaciers in the mountains move fast, rock glaciers barely crawl. Maybe a few inches in a year.

Not only do they move slower than clean glaciers, rock glaciers in the Sierra are smaller. They're downright minuscule when compared to the giant continental and tidewater glaciers of Antarctica, Greenland, and Alaska. Rock and clean glaciers in the mountains are found in steep-walled bowl-shaped valleys called cirques. At this late stage in their career, Sierra glaciers have retreated most of the way up into their cirques from a time when they may have extended miles downstream. As they get smaller and smaller, lots of stuff is being uncovered and it isn't just rock. Several years ago the skull of a Bighorn sheep, buried in ice for hundreds or thousands of years, appeared at the foot of Lyle Glacier in Yosemite National Park.

In his outstanding book about Sierra Nevada geology, *Exploring the Highest Sierra*, James Moore writes that during the Tahoe and Tioga glaciations in the Sierra Nevada (20,000 to 75,000 years BP, equivalent to the Wisconsin stage of the continental ice age) "an ice cap covered much of the higher parts of the range except for narrow ridges and isolated peaks that protruded above it. This ice cap fed large trunk glaciers that flowed west down the major river valleys as much as ten miles from the margin of the ice cap." Moore figures that some of the lobes of ice were 1,000 feet deep and were instrumental in carving "the Yosemite-like canyons of the North,

Middle, and South Forks of the Kings River, the Marble and East Forks of the Kaweah River, and the Kern River."

Despite differences in types of glaciers they all have a common development. As Moore explains, "Individual glaciers are formed during cool periods, when the volume of snow that falls each year exceeds that which melts, causing snowbanks to linger through the summer, and perhaps many following summers." Accumulated snow is compressed and recrystalizes to form ice. When the mass of ice reaches a certain point, usually about 100 feet thick, it begins to flow downstream, like a slowly moving frozen lake or river of ice. The flow is laminar—without turbulence, eddies, or currents. Where the ice separates from the cirque wall, a crack is formed. This crack, or bergschrund, marks the head of the glacier.

As a clean glacier moves downhill, it cuts into the underlying rock. Water, freezing within the cracks, creates fractures. These fractures and naturally occurring joints in the rock expand and allow the glacier to pluck that rock away and carry it downslope. Clean glaciers act like a stupendous plow digging and pushing and grinding rock debris.

Any rock that falls into the bergschrund at the head of the glacier is carried downslope, beneath the ice, to the toe of the glacier. Rocks that litter the glacier's surface continue downslope on top of the ice. If the crew of the AT-7 had crashed into Darwin Glacier, rather than Mendel Glacier, bodies and aircraft debris would have been treated the same way. Given the short length of the Darwin, wreckage would have appeared a lot sooner than October 2005.

But Mendel Glacier is not a clean glacier. All of its rock has not been plucked from the bottom. Most has fallen onto the top from above. Snowfall fills in the gaps and freezes the whole thing together like rocky road ice-cream. And like the rock debris within and without, debris from the crash has remained pretty much where it fell in 1942. A distant photograph from 1948 by Captain Roy Sulzbacher shows some soldiers sitting high up the glacier around what is obviously an airplane engine. To me, it looks to be in the same place where Michele and I discovered engine wreckage in 2007.

Unlike clean glaciers, which appear to move upstream as they melt, rock glaciers like the Mendel appear to melt in place. It's almost as if they subside. "Rock glaciers like the Mendel don't retreat as the climate warms, they thin out, particularly in their upper portions where the rubble is not very thick," Douglas Clark told me. Something that fell on the surface of Mendel Glacier in 1942 was covered by snow and rock debris and became part of the glacier. Over time, that debris moved a few feet downstream and was probably uncovered and recovered several times over the years during light or heavy, long or short, winters and summers.

Mendel Glacier may have "thickened up" a bit between the 1940s through the 1960s during a general slight cooling trend in much of the world. Several heavy snow years following the crash covered the site with snow, which turned to ice. Low snowfall during the winters of 1947 and 1948 exposed engine wreckage, and continued accumulation after that covered it all up again. Since the mid-1970s, lower than average snowfall coupled with hot, dry summers has caused the glacier to thin out again to its pre-1940s level, exposing the remains. "This slow response to climate has allowed such rock glaciers to persist through warm periods, like recently, when normal glaciers have retreated or disappeared altogether," according to Clark. Right next door to the Mendel, the same conditions have lead Darwin Glacier to shrink rapidly and separate from its moraine. A warming climate affects Mendel Glacier too, but due to its blanket of rock debris it just won't melt as fast as the clean glaciers.

The Sierra, for all the dramatic effects of glaciers, has been ice-free longer than not. In *Exploring the Highest Sierra*, Moore writes that "even during the Pleistocene Ice Age, from about 1.5 million years ago to 10,000 years ago, the ice cover in the highest parts of the range formed intermittently." In the last 3,200 years, glaciers in the Sierra expanded and retreated three or four times, and the last 700 years of glaciation, termed the Little Ice Age, represents only the most recent period of glacier expansion in the Sierra. The latest Little Ice Age culmination came about 150 to 200 years ago. Sierra glaciers have been thinning and retreating since then, allowing us to find debris from the 1942 airplane crash.

Glacial change, suggesting as it does change over a long period of time, is actually fast enough to be measured. In some places, such as the High Sierra, it is possible to not only measure but see the expansion or retraction of glaciers within one person's lifetime. Comparing G. K. Gilbert's 1908 photographs of Mendel and Darwin glaciers with today shows little change in the amount of surface area of the Mendel but demonstrates extreme recession of the Darwin. Indeed, between my 2007 and 2008 trips to Mendel Glacier it appeared to have sunk, in places five or six feet (determined by the height of boulders on ice pedestals). Where my photographs show ice the first year was all rock the next. Yet beneath all the rock and rubble was still the ice core of the glacier.

The ice pedestals eventually melt and the boulders settle onto the glacier. Further reduction in the amount of ice exposes more rock, which also consolidates into the surface rock exposed in previous years. Eventually a continuous layer of rubble insulates the ice, retarding melting. Any airplane debris acts the same way, becoming buried under successive layers of rock.

Mendel Glacier's fate is intimately tied to climate change. Research demonstrates that Pleistocene and Little Ice Age glaciers responded to global warming, expanding or shrinking as the climate cooled or warmed. Whether anthropomorphic changes in climate occurring over the last fifty years are affecting Sierra glaciers is still undetermined.

A large problem for the lay public and certain political decision makers is that some climate-change projections predict that global warming will paradoxically lead to cooling in a few areas. This apparent contradiction is confusing. Climate change is not a simple matter. But the clear consensus among those actively studying the subject (paleoclimatologists, climate scientists, and meteorologists) is that it's happening. They are consistent in saying that the majority of the warming we've been seeing for the last fifty years is due to anthropogenic causes. That means us.

If California's low-snowfall winters and long, hot and dry summers continue, Mendel Glacier should continue to melt. Due to its blanket of rock debris, it just won't melt as fast as all the clean glaciers. Mendel Glacier will probably keep getting smaller but will not melt completely away. This is because the steep headwalls behind the glacier protect it from incoming solar radiation during the summer, which reduces melt. And they enhance the accumulation of snow from wind loading and avalanching. Snow gets blown off one side of the mountain and gets deposited down the other. Snow that avalanches down the steep cirque walls and couloirs ends up on the glacier where it consolidates into ice.

As the glaciers are retreating, they retreat up into these more and more protected areas. Basically, the smaller the glacier gets, the bigger the effects of the shading and enhanced accumulation are. And, if climate stabilizes, so will the glaciers. "They will still be reactive to climate but less dramatically," says Hassan Basagic, a geologist at Portland State University in Oregon. Without any climate stabilization, he told me, "as temperature continues to increase dramatically, the glaciers will become smaller and smaller and may become things like permanent snowfields," snuggled in shade under cirque walls. Permanent snowfields resemble glaciers but are much smaller and lack a bergschrund, meaning they no longer thick enough to flow downslope. "My prediction range of how long a glacier is going to be around here is really wide. Some will disappear over the next 50 years and others will persist for 150 years."

Glaciers have not only length and width, they have depth. Judging from the change shown in historical photos, Basagic guesses the deepest part of Mendel Glacier, which is most likely at the bergschrund, is 160 to 260 feet. This is an estimate based on comparing how high up the glacier climbs the cirque wall in the historical photos to measurements he has made in the field. But it's only an estimate because there have been no actual measurements. Basagic also estimates that the glacier could have been 65 to 100 feet deeper in the 1920s and 1930s when the Mendel was probably at its thickest.

Knowing all of this before my trip to Mendel Glacier in 2007 had me thinking that it would be highly unlikely to find anything in the way of airplane debris, so I was delighted when Michele and I encountered the engine. And it helped me to realize how fortuitous finding Leo Mustonen had been. Michael Nozel and Mark Postle had truly been on the glacier at the right time and right place. An earlier trip would have meant that Mustonen's remains were covered by ice, and a later trip most likely covered by rock.

• • •

In my GPS unit I have the coordinates of where Cadet Mustonen was found in 2005. Holding the unit in front of me, I angle downward on the glacier, to the left of the engine and toward a rib of talus. I stop to catch my breath and check on Michele's whereabouts. Gingerly, she is picking her way downslope. She stops now and then to peer at something at her feet and moves on. So do I.

Following the line on the screen, I don't pay close attention to anything except where I put my feet. When I look up briefly I see a small tree, maybe four feet tall, about a hundred feet in front of me. It's leaning over to one side against a small chunk of talus. Somebody has found a gold ring and threaded it onto a twig of the tree. It shines in the sun, especially since the little tree is so blackened.

At first, I'm not surprised by what I see. Dead trees are not unusual in the High Sierra. There is a fungus that grows in subalpine elevations called brown felt fungus (*Herpotrichia juniperi*). Buried under winter snows, prolific *Herpotrichia juniperi* growth can engulf human-sized trees with feltlike masses that cover twigs and branches. It can kill smaller trees, which over time hunch and lean to the side.

That is, I'm not surprised until I stop to think. Something is wrong with what I think I see. Something about what I know isn't here sinks slowly into my mind. It can't be a tree. There are no trees up here. Only people.

And there he is, hunched over, his left arm curled under his body. On the third finger of his left hand, a gold intaglio signet ring of a Roman soldier shines in the sun. "Michele! Michele!" She doesn't hear me. I can't shout any louder. My mouth and throat are dry. I feel suffocated with emotion, my heart pounding in my chest. Oh, I want to cry.

It is Wednesday, August 15, 2007, and another young man will finally be coming home.

CHAPTER 10

My Report

Michele and I descend the glacier, dropping like cannonballs into Darwin Canyon and then onto Darwin Bench, losing 800 vertical feet in less than a mile. Further elevation loss to the floor of Evolution Valley equals another 1,000 feet. You can cut the oxygenated air at the lower elevation with a knife.

We arrive at the McClure Meadow Ranger Station and are greeted by Paige Meier. Her husband, George Durkee, is the duty ranger but he's out of the backcountry, tending to Park Service business in Bishop. George is due back by helicopter express as soon as the Park Service can find a reason to justify the expense of a flight. The three of us go back a long way, having worked for the same outdoor-education company—Naturalists at Large—in the mid-1980s, and Paige and I knew each other before that at Humboldt State University.

Paige and I say hello. She's surprised to see Michele and me, but visitors are always welcome. After a little bit of chit-chat I say to Paige, "Ask me where we've been."

"Where were you?"

"Darwin Canyon. On Mendel Glacier."

A flicker of interest crosses her face—she knows I've been studying the Frozen Airman. Last winter I spoke with George several times, picking his brain about Sequoia and Kings Canyon backcountry history. "So? What did you find?"

"Another body," I say as simply as possible.

Shock, then surprise, and disbelief and, "No!"

In a few sentences I give Paige a broad outline of the story, Michele filling in the parts I leave out. Paige listens, still not able to believe it. And who can blame her? Serendipity alone is all that can explain finding Leo Mustonen two years ago. And serendipity, like lightning, rarely strikes twice in the same place.

After some maddening delays, Paige is able to make radio contact with park headquarters and transmit the barest of details: location, confirmation that the body is military, and our names. Park medic and district ranger Debbie Brenchley radios back at 6:00 P.M. She plans to fly out the next day to meet Michele and me and listen to our story. She will also stop by in Bishop to pick up George. That night, Paige cooks dinner for us and we stay up late talking about our favorite subject: Sequoia and Kings Canyon National Parks.

• • •

In the dark early morning, I feel fine to be here in the forest. Given the sweetness of midsummer I can appreciate the misery of Captains Lewis and Goulding, Ranger Perkins, and horse packer Sauter in late September 1947 when Bill Bond guided them up here. It was cold. The days were short, the sky grey. Snow had fallen and would fall again. They had spent all day riding twenty-seven miles on horseback to McClure Meadow. Next they would have more horse riding to lower Darwin Canyon and then walking over talus past the upper lakes and then worse talus to the glacier. Then, over the glacier's ice.

This morning's cool air is alive with a slight essence of breeze. It feels, smells, tastes refreshing, like a cool drink on a hot day. I want to keep this feeling but the rising sun will kill it. If I can only hold on to it a second longer. No rush. No place to be. Nothing to do. It's delicious to lie in bed. There is time for everything.

I lie in my tent and think about what to say, concentrating on what I truly remember and not what is speculation. District Ranger Brenchley will be making an official report—open to the public. This is not the place or time for excess talk or guesswork. Sergeant

Joe Friday of *Dragnet* fame whispers in my ear from a long time ago, "Just the facts, Ma'am. Just the facts."

- We descended from high above. Michele saw something below us. The color and shape didn't fit with the landscape, so we investigated.

- We found part of an aircraft engine and spent about an hour examining, taking photos, and recording data from the ID plate.

- I used my GPS unit to mark the location.

- Michele looked for more debris. I tried to locate the spot where Leo Mustonen was discovered.

- About a hundred feet from the engine, I saw something dark, leaning over a boulder like a dead tree. As soon as I knew it wasn't a tree, I called for Michele.

- The first thing I noticed was a gold ring on his finger. His fingers were curled.

- He wore a shredded sweater, hanging from his body. Blackened skin. Blond hair, tight waves. Crushed skull. I looked up into his face. Good teeth. My immediate thought: this is a real person.

- Beside the remains was a parachute, the cords and silk exposed. It was undeployed.

- His shirt collar, was it white? He was hunched over, left arm crossed beneath him. I saw teeth from a broken comb on his hip.

• • •

I have a lot to think of, watching dawn come slowly. A quiet morning is anything but quiet. Greyness spreads across the sky and slowly, birds awake to sing their songs—chickadees and peewees, sparrows, and juncos flit about. Out of my tent and walking about, I rouse a deer from the meadow's edge, in shadows. Trees reflect in a quiet pool. Small trout race through the shallows, raising a surge wave, leaving ripples behind them. The slight breeze shifts and the river sound shifts with it, growing louder by degrees and then fading. I have the feeling that I have always known this place. More than anywhere else I've lived, the Sierra Nevada is home. I belong here.

On mornings like these I get the feeling that time has stood still in the mountains, but of course that's not true. William Tweed touches on this in *An Uncertain Path*, when he writes about the future of national parks. "Everything in this landscape screams change. Less than 15,000 years ago, a microsecond in the geological time scale, glacial ice thousands of feet deep covered everything in sight but the summits of the highest peaks. In quick succession, over succeeding recent millennia, the ice melted, plants and animals colonized the landscape and human beings arrived seeking sustenance and perhaps beauty as well. The climate warmed and cooled; human culture ebbed, flowered, and changed. New people arrived, first to map and seek wealth but soon purely for the pleasure the country offered."

My reverie is shattered by the *pocka-pocka, pocka-pocka, pocka-pocka* of a helicopter arriving with Debbie Brenchley and George Durkee. I hurry to the ranger station and intercept George halfway up from the landing zone in McClure Meadow, and we shake hands. Michele, Paige, and Debbie join us. We sit on logs outside the station and talk.

Just the facts. Just the facts. The park people sit and listen and ask no questions. I talk and Michele adds details. The helicopter pilot, Larry Bartell, joins us and listens intently. Pilots love stories about other pilots and aircraft.

When I'm done, George says in his rough, gravely voice, "That's a pretty complete description."

"I sat there a long time."

"How are you dealing with all this?" Debbie asks me. "It can be pretty rough."

Michele says it wasn't a shock to find the body, since we both realized the possibility. "Had we not known somebody could be there and just stumbled on him, it would have been different."

George fiddles with his GPS unit, plugging in the coordinates of Mendel Glacier's latest revelation. "He's about a hundred feet away from the first guy," he says. George has a way of stroking his bearded chin when he's being reflective and he's doing it now. I see his point immediately. Chance doesn't work like that.

"That's pretty close together."

"Hmm," is all George can say, stroking his chin.

Another question from Debbie Brenchley. "With all the research you've been doing for this story, do you have any idea which of the remaining three men this could be?"

I do, actually, but I don't feel like saying unless Brenchley agrees to not take my speculation any further, not to include my guesswork in her report. I don't want word leaking out and then to find I'm wrong. That would be cruel. She understands and agrees. "It can't be Leo Mustonen," I tell her, "he was found two years ago. It can't be William Gamber; he had dark hair. That leaves John Mortenson and Ernest Munn, both fair-haired. I'm betting on Munn. A name tag for Mortenson was found in 1947, which suggests to me that his body was not in any recognizable shape."

We wind down and George, Paige, and Debbie discuss setting up a recovery operation to bring this new airman home. I end up talking with Larry Bartell, the helicopter pilot. Bartell has flown all over this part of the Sierra. He remembers the Beech 18 from his military days forty years before, when he flew in one from Korea to Japan. What he remembers best is that "it was an underpowered aircraft and not maneuverable at high altitudes." That's a scary thought. Lieutenant Gamber could have seen where he was and been unable to change course. What would that have been like?

CHAPTER 11

On the Trail of the Second Airman

The recovery of the second airman from Mendel Glacier went more smoothly because he wasn't frozen into the glacier. He was flown to the Fresno County Coroner and then to Hickam Field in Hawaii, where JPAC assumed control over the remains.

Forensic anthropologists Dr. Matthew P. Rhode and Dr. Elias J. Kontanis examined the remains to ascertain if they represented more than one person. They found "no duplication of elements." Age was established at between eighteen and twenty-five years old, and the anthropologists noted the "lack of any arthritic changes to the skeleton." They found "extensive perimortem trauma" through-out the body, with bones fractured multiple times. They noted that "the perimortem trauma and probable perimortem trauma present on the skeletal remains are consistent with, but not exclusive to, a rapid deceleration event," which caused "greater damage to the right side of his body than his left."

Associated with the remains was a U.S. Army Air Corps cadet identification badge, a wallet with driver's license and dance tickets from Wheeling, West Virginia, a U.S. collar insignia, spare change, a Ronson lighter and Lucky Strike cigarettes, a pocket comb, and chamois leather flying gloves. There was also an unopened and un-deployed S-1 seat-type parachute, serial number 41-1990 (only six numbers from Cadet Mustonen's parachute, number 41-1984), and the gold ring that initially caught my eye on Mendel Glacier. Like

Leo Mustonen, this airman was not dressed for cold weather or high-altitude flight. He wore a wool long-sleeve shirt, necktie, wool trousers, undergarments, and a wool sweater.

The investigation wasn't as extensive this time around. JPAC's historical record was on file as were all the DNA tests from family members. Still, JPAC needed six months to make the identification, and their determination verified my suspicion. The man was Ernest Glenn Munn, known as Glenn to his family. On May 17, 2008, under a grey and weepy sky, he was buried with full military honors in his hometown of Colerain, Ohio. At the invitation of the Munn family, I attended. They welcomed me like a son, a brother, a favorite uncle.

There must have been over 200 people at Munn's funeral, and most of them were twenty or thirty years older than me. His three sisters, Jeanne Pyle, Sara Zeyer, and Lois Shriver, were there along with their children and grandchildren. A local congressman made a speech. Bill Ralston and one of his sisters, Nancy Calvert, attended too, nephew and niece of William Gamber. Members of the local VFW post were pallbearers. An honor guard from Fort Knox accompanied the casket to Holly Memorial Gardens following a service at St. Frances Cabrini Catholic Church. Cadet Munn got a fourteen-gun salute and a soldier played taps. He was buried beside his parents.

Members of the Patriot Guard Riders were on hand to protect the ceremony and motorcade from disturbances. They are a group of motorcyclists, mostly veterans, who attend funerals of military personnel at the invitation of a service member's family. At funeral ceremonies they escort mourners to the cemetery and then stand guard on the periphery. They do not speak. They do not interact with mourners or the military. They pay all their own expenses.

Ohio State Patrol officers, parked on the highway above the cemetery, kept an eye on things. Several television film crews stayed a respectful distance away and made a point of being quiet, polite, and unobtrusive.

I didn't expect to be part of any of this. I expected that Michele and I would find airplane wreckage on the glacier, but never did I think another person would be found. I've already mentioned the serendipity of Leo Mustonen's discovery by Nozel and Postle. That find was fortuitous enough and all anyone could have hoped to occur. Had Michele and I succeeded in getting to Mendel Glacier in 2006, the same snow that turned us away at Lamarck Col would have completely covered Glenn Munn's remains. When I mentioned this to people in Ohio, most of them saw the hand of God at work.

What I felt immediately was the hand of the media. I told my story and told it again, in person and over the phone, echoing decisions made by Nozel and Postle, though I hadn't met either of them yet. This was a story bigger than myself. The only portion that related to me was my discovery and how my interest began with Leo Mustonen's discovery in 2005 and all the confusion about which glacier and why the AT-7 had been so far off course. All the rest had to do with the four boys on the airplane, where the plane might be, and who—or how many people—were buried in Golden Gate National Cemetery in San Bruno. And there was the biggest question of all: how and why they crashed.

The big pull for me, why I felt this story was an important one, was something personal. The four boys who died when the AT-7 crashed were nothing like the generals or movers and shakers usually featured in World War II books. They didn't die in a major battle. Their "moment of truth" did not turn the tide of war. I pictured the excitement they felt in joining up, leaving their small towns to see the world and learn to fly, and then coming home from the war with a good job skill. For me, the story of Gamber, Mortenson, Munn, and Mustonen was real history. This was the story of people I could relate to.

It turned out that others related to these lost airmen too. "This is a story that covers all the bases," Craig Miller, an independent PBS producer, told me. "Science, forensics, a very human component, adventure." Other people saw the newspaper stories and television reports and contacted me. They hoped I could help them locate information about their family members who disappeared or never came home from the war. I wanted to help them, putting them in touch with the agencies I'd used in my research, but the four missing airmen from 1942 remained my mystery.

• • •

Back home in Seattle, with the second airman still an unknown soldier, came an e-mail from Debbie Hessler: "I am so excited to hear that you found another body and that you are writing a book about the missing airmen. Ernest Munn was my great uncle. No one in the family called him Ernest, though. It was always Glenn. Jeanne Pyle [Glenn's sister] is my grandmother. I just wanted to say that I can't wait to read your book and I do hope that, eventually, the other two men will be found. This has all been very interesting for us, especially for my 10 year old son who has become sort of a celebrity in school during Social Studies!"

Hessler and I began corresponding and I sent her my photograph of the gold ring from the new airman's finger. I hoped her grandmother or aunts would recognize the ring, but they didn't. My first thought after that was, maybe this isn't Munn. Maybe it's Mortenson or Gamber.

Meanwhile, my friend Marge Carpenter was trolling the Web for ring information. She found a bunch of old newspaper advertisements for men's rings that were very close in character to what I had found on my aviator's finger. Based on descriptions in the ads, we were certain the ring was gold and the carving was in the intaglio style, a technique where an image is incised into, or below, the stone's surface.

Most of the rings ranged in price from $12.95 to $33.75. I was grateful for the data, but it also suggested that the ring would turn out to be nothing special—not a family heirloom or something handed down from father to son.

Through my bicycle-riding friend Mikki Lippe, I met with Karen Lorene, owner of Facèrè Jewelry and Art Gallery. Located in downtown Seattle, Lorene's gallery shows the work of some fifty jewelry artists as well as antique and vintage jewelry. After outlining the story's basics, I showed her my ring photos.

She confirmed that the ring was a popular style in the era between 1930 and 1940 and that the stone was most likely hematite or black onyx. She leaned toward the former because that was more the standard at the time for intaglio. She also dismissed it as nothing special except to the owner. When I asked her about the special jewelry men wore in the 1940s, she replied that a man's "watch and his ring were probably his jewelry. That's what men got from their fathers. One at high-school graduation and the other at college, if he went to college."

As for the design, "There's no particular symbolism," she said, pointing out that it was either a Greek or Roman soldier. "It's a man's ring. A warrior." What a perfect fit for a young man going off to war. And she added that intaglio rings were the most common man's ring of the period. Lorene thought that, though the ring wasn't likely to be passed to him from his father, it still could have been a present. From a girlfriend maybe?

She turned her eye to the craftsmanship and ring quality and told me it hadn't much value. As for the gold, it was probably ten caret like the cheaper versions Marge found in the newspaper advertisements and now only worth "$300—mostly to collectors." Not jewelry collectors but to collectors of memorabilia. "The ring would have more value to them if a photo appeared in a book," she added. As for other options, "A 14 caret gold ring would have a $600 value today and an 18 caret gold ring, rare, would be worth around $800."

Even without having it in hand, Lorene was confident that the ring was die-struck. That is, the ring was punched out of a flat sheet of gold, bent back on itself, and soldered together. The hematite carving wasn't done by a master but wasn't done by machine either. "Probably a medium quality carver who went, zip-zip," her fingers danced back and forth in a limited number of graceful movements to demonstrate what she meant. Then, removing several pieces from a display case, she showed me the work of a master carver and, for comparison, something less than master. Even my unpracticed eye could see the difference in quality, workmanship, design, and detail.

I thanked her gratefully for her time and she was happy to have helped. She said, "It's not much and it's generic knowledge."

"Not to someone like me."

"Every little bit of information helps, doesn't it?"

It was soon after that when Debbie Hessler asked what my plans were for the funeral. Initially I hadn't intended on being there. Funerals should be for friends and family and I felt my presence would not be necessary or needed. Debbie replied, "I've been talking with a few members of the family and just thought that I should let you know that we would all be very honored if you would be able to attend Glenn's funeral. If it weren't for you, we wouldn't even be having a funeral. Our family will always be indebted to you for finding Glenn. You will always be welcome in any of our homes. We can't even begin to convey just how thankful we are for all that you have done for our family." With that kind of invitation, I couldn't refuse.

CHAPTER 12

Understanding the
Beech 18 AT-7 Navigator

The airplane piloted by Lieutenant William Gamber, carrying John Mortenson, Glenn Munn, and Leo Mustonen, was formally known as the Beech 18 AT-7 Navigator. *AT* meant that the aircraft was an Advanced Trainer in this case, designed for navigation instruction. Configured for all sorts of other uses in World War II, including bombardier training and hauling freight and passengers, the pre-war Beech 18 became the first successful corporate airplane. Other airplanes built in the 1930s (the Beech debuted in 1937) could have assumed the mantle, including Lockheed's 10 Electra, the aircraft carrying Amelia Earhart and Fred Noonan when they disappeared July 2, 1937, during an around-the-world flight. But the Beech had the competition beat in the limited prewar market. A big reason for this must have been the plane's reputation for lacking any "nasty habits" and its relative ease and comfort of flight.

The Beech 18—a.k.a. Twin Beech, Beechcraft Model 18, or permutations and variations of all three names—had an impressive history. This included a thirty-two-year production run with 8,000 aircraft built in thirty-two basic design variations, all possible due to the innovation of using tubular steel for the Beech's truss-type center section. This design served like a bird's hollow bones to confer strength and light weight. Only the DC-3 had a comparable run for a twin-engine, piston-powered airplane.

Designed and constructed well, and infinitely changeable into a multitude of functions and purposes, the Beech served in peace and war. It continues to fly all over the world today, though it has been mostly relegated to collectors, as the cost of maintaining such a classic airplane is high. The Beech 18 also served in movies and is where most people continue to see it. Some of the movies prominently featuring the plane include the 1963 Spencer Tracy comedy *It's a Mad, Mad, Mad, Mad World,* a silly James Bond movie with Roger Moore, and the 2001 *Insomnia,* with Al Pacino, where an Alaska-based Beech 18 is outfitted with floats.

Cutting-edge design features of the Beech 18 included a semi-monocoque fuselage and low cantilevered wings. The planes were among the most progressive designs of their time.

Successful early airplanes, like Orville and Wilbur Wright's 1903 Flyer I and aircraft used during World War I, had a simple fabric-stretched skin over a wood skeleton. They were also biplanes, having two wings, top and bottom. Some were even triplanes. Their construction is similar to truss bridges. The wings were braced with crossed wires so they would stay parallel to each other and also resist flexing and twisting. The cables generated considerable drag, slowing the aircraft and reducing maneuverability, so the impetus to experiment with modifications was implicit in the design.

Next came the monocoque (French for "single shell") design. It relied upon the aircraft's skin to provide structural rigidity over an internal frame of hoops. This worked well until the skin was dented or torn. Consider this: Place a large weight on an aluminum beer can and nothing happens. Being a monocoque design, the can takes stress quite well. But put a dent in the can while that weight is on top and the can collapses.

Reinforcing the hoops with longitudinal members in semi-monocoque designs, along with riveting the skin onto the aircraft's frame, created a much stronger structure resistant to collapse. Once aluminum became affordable, it was possible to inexpensively manufacture steel-and-aluminum heavier-than-air machines.

The Beech 18's low cantilevered wings capitalized on advances in monoplane design pioneered by Hugo Junkers. His successful experiments with cantilevered wings placed the German Luftwaffe ahead of other countries at the outbreak of World War II. Cantilevers are beams supported on only one end, like a diving board, allowing for overhanging structures without external bracing. Cantilevered wings are heavy, but the absence of wing struts reduces drag and the design itself resists twisting and wing flexing. As with semi-monocoque fuselage designs, inexpensive aluminum made this a possibility too.

Its most distinctive design feature, for those of us seeing the Beech 18 today, was the aircraft's twin tails. At the time it was thought by aeronautical engineers that twin-engine airplanes needed a rudder behind each engine to optimize control. This tail design continued on through World War II with a number of other aircraft, including the Consolidated B-24 Liberator heavy bomber and the North American B-25 Mitchell medium bomber.

Adapting a Beech 18 into an AT-7 Navigator involved removing all eleven cabin seats and replacing them with student desks and chairs. Robert K. Parmerter writes in *Beech 18: A Civil and Military History* that "standard navigation training equipment occupied each of the three student stations along the right-hand side of the cabin, and included a drift meter mounted on the floor, a chart table, a student seat, and an aperiodic compass," which "minimized oscillation and overswing, even as the plane bounced and turned."

Sighting objects along the ground, drift meters helped calculate ground speed and whether an aircraft was wandering off-course to the left or right. Bill Davis, who trained with Leonard Spivey, William Bechter, and the crew of the missing Beech 18, told me that drift meters were designed mostly for over-the-water flight. They were hard to use and difficult "to get an accurate reading" with. What's more, they didn't work when flying in the clouds and were therefore no use in helping lost pilots and navigators find their way in overcast.

For high-altitude flights in 1942, Parmerter says the AT-7 had high-pressure oxygen systems with five oxygen cylinders and regulators, providing a constant stream of oxygen to the wearer's masks. Assuming there were no leaks or mask malfunctions, with fully charged tanks the regulators delivered almost four and a half hours of oxygen at 20,000 feet, with another hour when flying at 10,000 feet. That was more than plenty for any AT-7 mission that required high-altitude flying.

As navigators, cadets were equipped with everything necessary to help them find their way over the earth and through the atmosphere. This included radio command sets, a radio compass, marker beacon receivers, and interphone sets.

Unless invited in by the pilot, there was no need for any of the students to be in the cockpit. Parmerter writes, "An instrument panel was mounted in the cabin's forward left corner so it was visible to all three students." Instruments included an "altimeter, airspeed indicator, clock, directional gyro, and outside air temperature gauge." The forward student position had an azimuth indicator, remote controls for the radio compass, automatic pilot, and directional gyro. Each navigator station included a command set transmitter and receiver allowing students to communicate to base via voice or Morse code. Voice transmission was effective for approximately twenty-five miles. If lost or in trouble, pilot and cadets had plenty of ways to ask for help.

The final modification converting the Beech 18 into an AT-7, writes Parmerter, was "a metal navigation turret on the top of the forward cabin" that was "rotated by hand 360 degrees and locked into position every 30 degrees, with an eight-inch, square piece of flat optical glass mounted in it." Advanced students would stand below the turret with an octant on night flights and make celestial observations. Aft of the turret was a large, football-shaped object, called a fairing, which housed an automatic direction finder (ADF), a part of the airplane's electronic instruments. The ADF, using signals broadcast from nondirectional beacons (NDBs), helped navigators determine aircraft position and point the way to go.

The AT-7 Navigators built between 1941 and 1943 were painted a natural aluminum color. The wing surfaces were each marked with a five-pointed star; under the starboard wing was a large "U.S." and under the port wing a large "ARMY." Thirteen red and white, alternating horizontal stripes were painted on the twin tail rudders, with a vertical blue stripe on the leading edge of the horizontal stripes. The plane's serial number was painted on both sides of the rear fuselage, preceded by a single digit for the year the plane was built. So, Lieutenant Gamber's AT-7 number 41-21079 was marked 121079.

• • •

As I mentioned before, the Beech 18 had a reputation in its day for lacking any "nasty habits." As I learned about the airplane, I found that defining "nasty" was a moving target. The issue revolved around how the aircraft handled in the air, what it felt like to fly, how high it could fly, and how much power the engines delivered at high altitude.

Taigh Ramey helped me get a feel for the Beech 18 and how the airplane's characteristics may have contributed to the crash. Ramey is the go-to guy for information about the Beech 18, especially if you're thinking about laying down at least $150,000 to buy your own. He knows everything about the plane's history, design, form, and function. I found him at the Stockton airport in California, where he operates his plane restoration business, Vintage Aircraft. Three guys were at work in the hangar, a shop really—with welders, hoses, parts, tools, benches, and a whole lot more strewn about. Ramey himself is a big guy—maybe six-foot-three—blondish and in his midthirties, with a boyish face. He lives, eats, and breathes airplanes. He was as happy to see me as I was to see him.

I broke out my laptop and showed him my photographs, starting with the Mendel Glacier and cirque so he could get an idea of the lay of the land. Then we moved on to the wreckage and Ramey was able to identify everything he saw in my photos. The only thing he wondered about was whether we were looking at something from the port or the starboard side of the plane.

The back of a Pratt & Whitney R-985 engine, along with the main crankcase with pistons and connecting rod cylinders from both engines, were the largest and more interesting pieces of debris. In my photos, Ramey identified a magneto, generator, ignition harness, and lots of little things like wiring, nuts and bolts, bits of riveted aluminum sheeting, clamps, and rubber hoses. He was both amazed at the level of destruction and that many items looked as good as new. Only half in jest, I think, did he say, "I could make some of these parts fly again."

Ramey agreed with everything I'd ever read about the Beech 18 except for one thing. It was not the kind of airplane to train pilots itching to move up from single-engine to twin-engine aircraft. Unlike what I'd heard from others, Ramey told me, "it was pretty tricky to fly and could get out of hand pretty quick. Especially for a student." He added, "They're one of the most challenging, most difficult airplanes I've ever flown. Most of my experience and research indicates that the people who flew the Twin Beech were guys who had a fair amount of experience elsewhere." If the Beech 18 lacked "nasty habits," as I'd been told, Ramey said it definitely had a few quirks.

Ramey said that if he hadn't flown the Beech in as little as a week, he'd be rusty. "It requires me to get back in the groove of the airplane. It has certain rules that it follows. You have to listen to the airplane and pay attention to what it's doing. When it gets up to the edge of its safety zone, it goes over that edge real fast and things can get out of hand real quick."

For example, he told me, "it's hard to handle on the ground and very demanding of your attention at takeoff and landing." On landing, he said, "when the plane starts to settle, it wants to go off to the left. Sometimes it really wants to go and sometimes it's not as bad." Once it's in the air, though, "it's like most any other aircraft. It's a great flying plane. One of the things people said about the Twin Beech was that if you could taxi it to the runway you could probably fly it OK."

Ramey agreed with what I'd read in Robert Parmerter's book about the AT-7 having good instrumentation for the day as well as a good autopilot. "It's a good, stable instrumentation platform," Ramey said. Add that to Lieutenant Gamber's mission being navigation training, and Ramey had a hard time believing the airmen were lost. But, he added, "pilots have been getting lost ever since Orville and Wilbur." In fact, he continued, "it's easy to get lost, even if you have several people onboard trying to figure it out." One of many good things about the Beech, according to Ramey, is that if a pilot finds himself out of his element, flying above the weather trying to get home, and it's cold outside, "the Twin Beech can carry a load of ice." Given the belief in 1948 that weather was a mitigating factor in the crash, I pressed Ramey to explain.

Under the proper atmospheric conditions, ice can form on an aircraft's wings and create drag, increasing fuel consumption as well as slowing the aircraft. More importantly, icing deforms the wing surface, retarding lift so an airplane must work harder to remain aloft. Gamber's AT-7 most likely lacked deicing equipment, called boots. But if the lieutenant knew his aircraft was able to carry more ice on the wings than other kinds of airplanes, he may have been tempted to chance high-altitude flying or to cross the Sierra Nevada if it meant he could get around bad weather.

There are a lot of things that could go wrong in flight, as Ramey told me from his personal experience with the Beech. The plane has four fuel tanks: a 78-gallon left and 78-gallon right main fuel tank and two 25-gallon auxiliary, rear fuel tanks. "In the World War II planes," Ramey told me, "both engines would run off one fuel tank at a time. The 25-gallon auxiliary fuel tanks run out in about half an hour. So, when I switch to those tanks, I set my watch and I know in twenty-five minutes I have to start watching those tanks pretty closely." The issue is that both engines will quit if you run a tank dry because they're running off the same tank. "That can make things really busy in the cockpit, trying to get the engines going again," he said dryly. This is a problem that caused accidents and killed pilots all during World War II. "Guys ran their aux tanks dry and crashed because they weren't able to get the engines running again."

In Ramey's case, he'd been climbing through clouds and concentrating on instruments, navigation, and where he was when he ran his auxiliary tank dry. "I was in the middle of reading back an instrument clearance to Air Traffic Control when both engines quit!" Dealing with the problem required some quick thinking. "I continued reading my clearance back," he told me, "pulled the throttles back, switched an aux tank over, got on a wobble pump [a hand pump, inconveniently located on the floor under the copilot's seat, to build up fuel pressure], and got the engines running again." It was a close call. "Reading back my clearance I know that my voice changed a couple of octaves when my engines quit." This scenario didn't necessarily happen to Gamber, but it shows how quickly things could come to grief if there was a problem, mechanical or otherwise, in the Beech 18 cockpit.

Then, there's the question of airplane performance at different altitudes. Ramey says the Beech does "pretty good" at 5,000 feet, and he hasn't ever flown one higher than 14,000 feet. "Some of the books say [you can take them to] 20,000 feet, but I have a hard time imagining it could actually do that without burning all your gas." The Beech will run out of power beginning around 8,000 or 9,000 feet, which means the pilot doesn't have much margin of safety when things start going wrong. "In clouds, drift meters wouldn't work," said Ramey, because they relied on sighting ground objects to fly a straight course. "Clouds mean you couldn't use pilotage," navigating to a destination by observing landmarks. All of a sudden, navigators would start running out of ways to navigate, stay found, and stay on course. Another problem: "The higher you go, the plane is a little bit sloppier. It still does fine, but if something starts going wrong it could become a handful really fast."

If you were flying and saw an obstruction in front of you—say you're at 10,000 feet and saw a wall of cumulo-granite (what pilots like to call a mountain directly in front of their aircraft)—and you pull back on the stick, how does a Beech 18 respond? "It depends on your airspeed." Ramey told me. "If you're up at altitude even at fairly good power setting on your engines, you're not going to climb very fast. The higher you go, the more your performance drops off." The Beech 18 Pratt & Whitney R-985 engines had superchargers, but "the critical altitude in the Twin Beech is typically around seven or eight thousand feet. That means you don't have any more throttle. You don't have a whole lot of power the higher you go."

What's more, Ramey added, "You can't climb real steeply. You're not going to see a mountain and then pull up like in an aerobatic maneuver and go above it. You can climb very slow and gradual the higher you go, and at a certain point you're not going to be able to climb much at all. Maybe twenty-five to fifty feet per minute."

Taigh Ramey has flown the Beech over the Sierra and he told me you don't get a lot of performance at those altitudes. *"You do your initial climbing early on and then you level off and you cruise.* You see something coming, you know it's going to take you time to climb over it. If you can."* Pilots therefore plan ahead when taking a Beech 18 over mountains.

William Gamber was a knowledgeable pilot; he had 709 hours of flying experience. He must have known all this about his airplane. Ramey's comments lead me to think that Gamber was flying high for a reason, especially since he would have known how poorly his airplane would perform at altitude. The only reason I could think of for Gamber to be flying so high was that he knew he was in mountains, and that suggests to me he wasn't lost in the clouds of bad weather as the 1947 army accident report suggests.

•   •   •

Leo Mustonen and Glenn Munn were both found with their S-1 seat-type parachutes still attached. Did this mean the cadets were aware they were in trouble and might need to "hit the silk?" Not necessarily, Ramey told me. "All people in the airplane were required to wear a parachute at all times." Things happen fast, and waiting to put on a parachute until you needed one could mean not getting it on in time. Nevertheless, the S-1 chute constantly banged against the thighs and back of the knees. That made it uncomfortable, especially when having to walk and particularly when moving about inside an airplane. At least it was better than wearing the backpack-style parachute, which at about thirty pounds was heavy, poorly balanced, on top of being uncomfortable.

•   •   •

Ramey helped me understand the relationship between a World War II pilot's experience and the aircraft he flew. "They were cranking pilots out like crazy back then." He told me the story of a World

War II pilot he met who trained at Stockton Field. "As soon as he graduated from his class, he became an instructor. He had just learned to fly and because he was good in his class, he became an instructor and started teaching other people to fly." As for Lieutenant Gamber, with 709 flight hours in just nine months, "He was a pretty darn competent pilot, that would be my guess."

In 1942, the United States was fighting a holding action throughout Europe and the South Pacific. China had fallen. "You had a real pilot shortage back then," Ramey said, "and I think that a lot of these guys were going into these roles real fast with not a lot of experience. My initial impression is, Wow! 700 hours! That was a lot back then. Especially, if a lot of his time was in the Beech 18, he was probably getting into the groove of the airplane, flying it every day."

National Transportation Safety Board accident investigators today look at a pilot's time in the cockpit and their recent experience. "Obviously, this guy was right up there," Ramsey concluded. "He knew the airplane real well." When it comes to weather factors, though, Ramey wasn't as sanguine about the lieutenant's ability. "If he had very little instrument time, that could have been a factor." Referring to the 1942 accident report, I noted that Gamber had been instrument rated but had no instrument time.

Experience with instrument meteorological conditions and instrument flight rules flying would have been crucial in a big storm. "I've had several experiences in the Sierra that give you a healthy respect for these mountains," said Ramey. "It can get really nasty up there." Updrafts and downdrafts are prevalent, especially later on in the day. "There's stuff that builds up over there that you simply don't want to mess with. Whenever I plan my trips across the Sierra, I like to do it as early as possible because the weather builds up later on in the day."

Ramey related a story from his own experience about how quickly weather could affect a flight. He was crossing the Sierra, flying a Cessna 172 with a couple of students and got caught in some updrafts. "They took me up to 14,500 feet in a Cessna 172 that's only supposed to go up to 12,000 feet. I had the power back and the nose pointed down and it was still blowing me up." He fully expected to get hit by a downdraft and, sure enough, the downdraft came right after that. "I could see a spot in the rocks down there, exactly where the plane was going to impact!

"The guy in the back seat felt, 'We're completely in God's hands here and He can just rub you out with a wipe of a finger,' because we were like a piece of paper in this wind. And it didn't care if we were there. It's scary. That's why I say that mountain flying in the Sierra can be really ugly." He laughed at this point, but it was plain to me it wasn't all that funny. "It can really get you going pretty good!"

Bush pilots in Alaska will fly below a low ceiling, through river canyons and valleys. A pilot flying in the mountains and unfamiliar with what to do could be inspired to do the same thing—especially if the alternative is to climb through clouds with an indefinite ceiling, surrounded by cumulo-granite. "There are a lot of stories about people who crash on the side of a hill," Ramey mused, "and you constantly hear, if they just had another fifty feet they would have been fine; if they just had another quarter mile this way, they would have been fine. There are a lot of stories about people who survived because they *were* a quarter mile one way or the other and didn't know it."

In his 1939 memoir, *Wind, Sand and Stars*, Antoine de Saint-Exupéry wrote of the dangers facing pilots flying in bad weather from France to North Africa over the Pyrenees. "An airplane, of course, can be replaced. Still, the important thing was to avoid collision with the range." Saint-Exupéry's description of what aviators today call cumulo-granite is much more poetic. "A pilot in trouble who buried himself in the white cotton-wool of the clouds might all unseeing run straight into a peak." His understated point was, "Blind flying through a sea of clouds in the mountain zones was subject to the severest penalties."

Many conditions—airplane and engine performance at altitude, bad weather, unfamiliar terrain, uncertainly of location, student navigators, a pilot with limited instrument flying experience, and no experience with mountain flying—made flying over the Sierra a dangerous occupation for Lieutenant Gamber. To be successful in flying under clouds or up river valleys and mountain canyons,

Ramey says, "depends on the turning radius on the type of maneuvers you can do. But when you're up at altitude, you don't have a lot of margin for doing steep turns. The higher you are, the thinner the air is and the easier it is for your plane to stall. You can't be doing real steep turns to be getting out of canyons." This is true with any airplane. "A lot of guys have gotten killed going up into canyons and finding the terrain rises faster than their airplane can and they smack the hill." Ramey told me, "I've done it coming back over the Sierra when you're between peaks and, because we didn't have oxygen, we couldn't go over them. Flying between peaks—that's dangerous. Especially when you have weather going too. You can find yourself in a situation where the terrain has got you stuck and you just can't get back out of it."

CHAPTER 13

The Boys

Though in their twenties, young men were still called boys during World War II, and that is how their parents referred to them. On March 6, 1944, Leo Mustonen's mother, Anna, dictated her last missive to Glenn Munn's mother, Mamee. "For us, war has inflicted deep wounds in our hearts, we can only remember and think of our good boys, how they used to bring joy and sunshine into our hearts and homes." After the AT-7 disappeared, Anna Mustonen initiated a correspondence with parents of the other boys too, but Mamee Munn was the only one to save the letters. These letters between two grieving parents, the letters written home by Glenn, and a scrapbook built by Mrs. Gamber following the loss of her son led me further into the actual lives of the lost airmen than any other part of my research.

• • •

When I first called Ernest Glenn Munn's sister, now a great-grandmother, Jeanne Pyle mistook me for the neighborhood bee-keeper with a similar name. "Why is the honey man calling me so late in the evening?" she wondered. I had been corresponding with her granddaughter, Debbie Hessler, since I'd found a second body on Mendel Glacier—the body that turned out to be Jeanne's big brother and Debbie's great uncle.

Once Jeanne knew who I was, she was happy to finally talk to the person who had found Glenn. She admitted to me that the past nearly two years, since Leo Mustonen's discovery, had been emotional ones for her and her two younger sisters. "It's been an up and down thing with us. First it's one person who calls and then it's another person. After you reach a certain age, you just give out. Knowing about this, it's a closure. It's something you dream would never happen." I asked her what the family's plans were for Glenn and she said, "We have a cemetery right across the road from me. It's a public cemetery. My parents are buried there. Our husbands are buried there. We're going to have a service for Glenn and bury him next to our parents."

• • •

Ernest Glenn Munn was born January 18, 1919, upstate in Farmington, Ohio. As a youth, his father, Joseph, played a season of professional baseball before marrying Sadie Barton (known to the family as Mamee). Joe was employed in the coal mines of eastern Ohio, a job he kept until the mid-1940s when the after effects of a broken leg made that kind of work impossible.

By 1920 the young family had relocated south to Colerain. Three sisters for Glenn arrived over the next five years. First Frances (called Jeanne by the family) in 1921, then Sara (also known as Sally) in 1922, and finally Lois (also known as Lou) in 1925. They farmed twenty acres, the kids helping out, and Joe made trips to nearby Wheeling, West Virginia, to sell vegetables, milk, butter, and whatever else they raised.

I met with the three Munn sisters in May 2007, after their brother's funeral. Jeanne remembered their childhood family farm. "We had lambs that would come in our back door and go clear across the kitchen, out of the pantry, down the steps and go outside again."

With money saved up from coal mining, in 1935 Joe and Mamee Munn gave up country living and moved up the road, buying the only service station on State Route 250 between Cadiz and Wheeling. Though Colerain was little more than a wide spot in the road at that time, the sisters remember the event as marking the transition from country living to being city folks.

While Joe Munn worked away from Colerain, Mamee raised the kids and operated the service station. The girls worked in the convenience store associated with the station, and Glenn pumped gas and performed minor auto repairs. Everybody agreed it was something Glenn didn't like. "He didn't work there if he didn't have to," said Lois. "I don't think there was much he liked about the service station."

Jeanne remembers there was some tension between son and father as Glenn got older and demonstrated his disinterest in the service station. "Dad tried to make him do things he didn't want to do. And you know how it is when a kid gets around sixteen and eighteen. They know what they want to do and they don't want to go out and serve gas or change oil for somebody. He just didn't like that. He was more bookish. He liked books and liked to go to school."

None of the girls felt resentment toward their big brother for not wanting to share in the work at the station. In fact, they were madly in love with him. Especially Lois. "He was my hero." She was the baby of the family. "He took care of me a lot," she told me. "I was a mama's girl too, and he was always around my mother. I liked to be with them."

Glenn loved to dance. "He used to come home and turn the radio on and dance," said Lois. "I can remember my dad used to get mad at him because he thought Glenn was making too much noise and Dad wanted to go to bed! We would jig around with him," Lois laughed. "I think he was using us for partners when he was learning."

Glenn was popular with the girls at school and in town. If a movie about his life had been made in 1942, Glenn would have surely been portrayed by Van Johnson. They shared the same wavy pompadoured blond hair, the same startling handsomeness, and the same bright eyes and incredible smile. Wherever he went, six-foot-three Glenn Munn turned heads.

"When I was in high school," Lois said, "I had a job during Christmas vacation at a Sears Department Store [in Wheeling]. Glenn would come in and pick me up when the store closed at nine o'clock. He was going to night school then and he would pick me up and take me home. One night he came in and all the girls are, *Gasp*! Oh my goodness, here comes the Blond Bomber! And I laughed and told them that's my brother. Just after that, all the girls called him the Blond Bomber." He knew about it too, "And I think it tickled him."

By this time in 1936, Glenn had graduated from Martins Ferry High School and was taking night classes in business while working at Fidelity Investment Association during the day. He continued working at Fidelity, going full time in 1938, until his January 27, 1942 enlistment. Photographs taken of him at the time show a young man comfortable and at ease with himself, with an attractive girlfriend and with a stylish taste in good clothes.

Like many young men in 1942, Glenn knew he would eventually be drafted. Enlistees at least had a choice of what branch of the service they could join. If they tested high enough, they would also have a choice of which position to fill. His sisters recall that Glenn came to see military service as a way to position himself for a good job once the war was over. As I imagine many rural and small-town people felt during the 1930s, there was little chance of rising out from under the Great Depression without some sort of major change in education or work experience. Learning to fly held out that promise to Glenn.

Lois remembers how hard life was. "We didn't have a whole lot of money. We'd butcher, like, four hogs and that's what we lived on." Sara recalled that the family "raised chickens for their eggs and the meat, too. Mother made bread." And Jeanne contributed, "Mother canned, made cottage cheese, and things like that. And grew all kinds of vegetables."

The entire family was shattered when Glenn's plane went missing in November 1942. Something in the world shifted and nothing would ever be the same again. Sara was married and with a baby. "I was home, right where I live today," when she got the news. "I just don't recall what I did when I heard. It was such a shock."

Jeanne learned the news from her father. "Dad drove all the way to Martins Ferry, where I was working at a service station." She was surprised to see him since she normally rode the seven miles from Colerain by bus. Joe Munn told his eldest daughter, "Glenn's missing. He said that to me. It just struck me." She stopped speaking for a moment before adding softly, "He said Glenn's plane went down someplace and crashed."

Lois was still unmarried, living at home, but was over sixty miles away in Zanesville, Ohio, when she got the news. "I was in training to work at a service station and some man from the Standard Oil Company came in and said to me, 'That Munn boy lost on that airplane any relation to you?' I looked at him and I said, 'Who?' And he said, 'Glenn.' And I said, 'My gosh, that's my brother.'" She left the training station and hurried to her room at the YWCA. "I ran all the way so I could call home, to see if that was him." After sixty-three years Lois remains stilled by the memory. "And it was. I never got over it."

Mamee Munn told her daughters not to worry, that Glenn would be found. And for the longest time they held out hope. At first they didn't even know how Glenn had gone missing, only that he hadn't come back from a mission, which they assumed to be part of his training. Each thought that somebody from the army in California was looking for their son and brother. Somebody would find him. Nobody had a doubt that Glenn would be found. "Well," said Jeanne, "it just didn't happen."

• • •

For a month after the AT-7 disappeared, the army sent daily telegrams to the families. The sameness of the messages must have been maddening. Infuriating. Angering. Impersonal. "AIRPLANE AT 7 41 DASH 21079 MISSING SINCE 1911Z NOV 18 NOT YET FOUND SEARCH BEING CONTINUED." Then came the message on December 15 that no one wanted to see. "SEARCH DISCONTINUED." It didn't help to read, "FURTHER REPORTS WILL BE INVESTIGATED."

• • •

William Gamber is remembered in his home town of Fayette, Ohio, as an exceptional young man. His cousin Dick Christian, younger by five years, thinks Bill would have been a great teacher, influencing the lives of young people for generations. His other cousin, Barbara Christian Adams, remembers that Bill was smart. "He must have been a fantastic student because he advanced quickly through pilot training. And the mechanical engineering he studied in college? It must have been difficult in the era without calculators." Gamber graduated from Tri-State College in Angola, Indiana, in three, not four years.

Bill Gamber possessed the clean-cut and collegiate good looks people never forgot. He was tall—six-foot-four—and slender. Even photographs of him as a child show his piercing dark eyes. A teasing and playful smile frequently crossed his lips as if he was privy to some amusing secret. He was the kind of fellow everybody in a small town like Fayette knew and liked—the older boy all the younger boys looked up to and all the girls swooned over. He was a talented musician and athlete. Everybody in Fayette expected Bill Gamber to go far and do well in the world.

The second of four children, William Richard Gamber was born on Friday, June 13, 1919, in Fayette, Ohio. His parents were John Howard and Nelle McGowan Gamber. The Gamber family was well-established in Fayette, having arrived three generations before. Straightlaced Howard Gamber, a tall man with a narrow face and deeply cleft chin, was town barber. Nelle Gamber was the town's telephone operator. They lived in a large two-story brick house with a wraparound sunporch that faced North Fayette Street. Behind the house were nearly thirty acres of farmland, with a cherry orchard and fields of corn and strawberries. Here they raised three children: Millicent (born in 1913), Bill, and Elvira (born in 1922). A fourth child born in 1925, Raymond, died in infancy.

Gamber's cousin Barbara was eight years younger than Bill and a frequent summer vacation visitor to Fayette through the 1930s. "I loved visiting and being with them," she remembers, "because they seemed so connected to their friends and to everybody in the town. They all seemed to be pretty secure, pretty together." She especially loved visiting her Uncle Howard and Aunt Nelle's for dinner because the meal was always followed by a family concert with Millie on piano, Bill on trombone, and Elvira playing violin.

As for Bill, "He didn't spend a lot of time with his younger sister, Elvira, and me. But he was always around. He did all these athletic things. And he could do anything around the house and the barn and that kind of thing. Bill was very good looking and I'm sure he was popular with the girls." There was something magical about Bill Gamber that transcended being handsome and popular. "He was always somebody you hoped would hang around with you."

Trips to Fayette were as special to Dick Christian as they were to his younger sister, Barbara. "Bill was very nice to me. I was just a little kid yet he treated me like I was his own age." Not only that, "He got along well with his sisters. Unlike some families, they never seemed to argue or disagree." Losing Bill was a shock to Christian. "Bill was so likeable and so good with everybody that nobody ever had anything bad or nasty to say about him. Everybody loved him—his family and his friends. We all admired him."

Bill Gamber graduated from Fayette High School, class of 1937. With John Henry Alleman, Gamber served as cocaptain of the basketball team, leading them to a 13-6 season. The senior yearbook, *The Tattler*, has a who's who section, and Gamber registers his weakness as "Buying large pictures," his favorite song as "It's Got to Be Love," and his favorite saying as "Oh Boy!" When it comes to outlining his ambition, Bill wrote, "Doctor's Chauffeur." That seemed like an odd ambition to me, especially in light of the realistic choices given by his thirty-one classmates: "Policeman." "Surveyor." "Math Professor." "Aviator." Sure, there were some silly ambitions too, like, "To Own a Ford V-8," "Dictator," "Romeo," and "Living in Iowa." From what I had already learned about Bill Gamber, he didn't strike me as frivolous.

It turned out not to be a silly ambition at all. The Fayette town doctor, Ralph Reynolds, and his wife, Florence, had a son, James, and a daughter, Phyllis. The doctor's chauffeur would therefore have close contact with the doctor's daughter. That Bill Gamber would advertise this ambition in the class yearbook suggested to me that Gamber had a girlfriend and everyone in town knew who she was.

Gamber family scrapbooks revealed letters from Phyllis Reynolds to Elvira Gamber about Bill. The script is large and voluptuous, and the text swings from deeply personal and revealing to chatty—the typical teenager. One moment Phyllis is excited that Bill might be coming to visit at her parent's weekend cabin and that she could ride back to Fayette with him. "But tell him not to come just on that account." Two paragraphs later she describes a trip to Toledo to buy "the cutiest [sic] mules" (slippers) for only nine cents. She ends one missive with, "Tell Bill I'm still waiting for a letter."

There is one photo of Phyllis in the Gamber family scrapbook, adjacent to what I'm sure was Bill's high-school graduation picture. He's in a tuxedo with a firmly level bow tie and a high, white starched collar. His hair is long, in the style of the day, parted slightly off-center, and immaculately combed. His father, remember, was the town barber. On Bill Gamber's face, those piercing eyes and mischievous smile. The image of Phyllis is that of a smiling, happy teenager. Her good cheer radiates off the page. She's wearing a doubled string of pearls over a dark sweater, and her curly red hair is swept back from her face. Written below the photo in white ink on the black scrapbook page is "Phyl."

After high school, Bill Gamber took a year off before starting college and worked at a local grocery store, keeping him closer to Phyllis. A scholarship allowed him to enroll the next year at Tri-State College in Angola, Indiana, to study mechanical engineering.

College was less than an hour west of Fayette, which made it possible for Gamber to get home to visit his parents and, I suppose, Phyllis. In 1939 he joined the Alpha Beta chapter of the Alpha Kappa Pi fraternity. Bill played trombone in the school orchestra, served on the staff of The Modulus—Tri-State's yearbook—and played varsity basketball, where he was voted "Most Valuable Man" during his senior year in 1941. He was singled out for his sportsmanship, scholarship, and attitude while on the court.

A summer job in 1940 found Bill Gamber at the National Cash Register Company in Dayton, Ohio, working in their Engineering Designing Department and living with his cousins, Barbara and her older brother, Dick Christian. Barbara said it was great having her big cousin around the house. She was thirteen years old then. "My memories were of lots of fun because there I was with two older brothers. My own brother ignored me most of the time and Bill didn't. I thought that was pretty nifty. And I wasn't his sister either!"

The Beech 18, configured as an AT-7 Navigator. Note the turret aft of the cockpit where student navigators would take star sightings. The football-shaped object housed an automatic direction finder (ADF), a part of the airplane's electronic instruments used by navigators to determine their position. *Copyright The Museum of Flight, used by permission*

William Gamber (top right) and fellow pilot cadets beside a Stearman PT-13B during primary flight school, late 1941.
Courtesy Bill Ralston and the Gamber family

O'er the ramparts we watch. US Army Air Forces poster from 1945. Artist, Jes Wilhelm Schlaikjer.
Courtesy Northwestern University Library

Second Lieutenant William R. Gamber, summer, 1942.
Courtesy Bill Ralston and the Gamber family

William Gamber beside his Ryan PT-22 at the Ryan School of Aeronautics in Hemet, California, late 1941.
Courtesy Bill Ralston and the Gamber family

William Gamber. *Courtesy Bill Ralston and the Gamber family*

Cadet John Melvin Mortenson at Mesa del Rey primary flight school, King City, California. *Courtesy Carol Benson*

Leo Mustonen with his parents, Anna and Arvid, before his enlistment on October 20, 1941. *Courtesy Leane Ross*

Cadet Leo Mustonen at home on leave, spring 1942. *Courtesy Leane Ross*

Glenn Munn during primary flight training at Mesa del Rey in Kings City, California, with a Ryan PT-22. *Courtesy Munn family*

Ernest Glenn Munn, final portrait: "I am sending you a picture. I don't know whether you will like it or not, because it wasn't focused exactly right and it is a little blurred. The photographer here at the field told me I should have another sitting, but I told him I would have it done later. It takes about twenty to twenty-five days to get a picture here anyhow. However you can tell it is me and the farther you get away from it the better it looks (about ½ mile) ha! ha!" *Courtesy Munn family*

Glenn Munn, the "Blond Bomber," at Balboa Beach, California, summer 1942. *Courtesy Munn family*

Glenn Munn's US insignia collar pin from the right side of his uniform shirt recovered with his remains.
JPAC photo by Paul Emanovsky

Second Lieutenant William Bechter, who was one class ahead of the navigation students who went missing on the AT-7. Bechter was killed in action over France on July 14, 1943. Over his breast pocket is Bechter's navigator insignia. His US insignia collar pin and air service branch collar pin are identical to those found with Leo Mustonen and Glenn Munn's remains. *Courtesy the Bechter family*

Glenn Munn's air service branch insignia collar pin, found with his remains.
JPAC photo by Paul Emanovsky

Mendel Glacier from Lamarck Col area, August 1947. *Courtesy Kirby West*

Air Rescue Service recovery party in Evolution Valley en route to Mendel Glacier, guided by William Bond (farthest left, hands on hips), September 27, 1947. *Courtesy Julianne Lewis and Laurie Lewis Woods*

UC students William Bond and Thomas Hodges on Mendel Glacier, August 1947. *Courtesy Kirby West*

Engine wreckage from the Beech 18 AT-7 Navigator photographed by Captain Robert Lewis during the September 1947 recovery mission guided by William Bond. *Courtesy Julianne Lewis and Laurie Lewis Woods*

From left, Captain Robert Lewis, William Bond, and Captain Andrew J. Walton at Hamilton Field on their return from Mendel Glacier, September 29, 1947. *Courtesy Julianne Lewis and Laurie Lewis Woods*

Piece of wreckage from AT-7 number 41-21079, on file at the Sequoia and Kings Canyon National Parks archives.
Courtesy Sequoia and Kings Canyon National Parks; photo by Peter Stekel

Engine wreckage from the Beech 18 AT-7 Navigator, photographed by Captain Roy Sulzbacher, September 1948.
Courtesy Julia Sulzbacher

"Crack Army troops" and one of their horse packers pose with climbing gear used during their recovery expedition to Darwin Canyon and Mendel Glacier, September 1948.
Courtesy Julia Sulzbacher

Searchers Recover Bodies of Airmen

Brought down from their icy crypt on Mt. Darwin by trained army mountain troops, the bodies of four airmen lost when their plane struck the Fresno county peak in 1942 were shipped to sixth army headquarters recently for positive identification.

Also headed for the Presidio was the search party. Commanded by Capt. Roy F. Sulzbacher, the party recovered the bodies after four days of perilous climbing.

"Brought down from their ice crypt …"—the Inyo Register dated September 16, 1948, reporting on Captain Roy Sulzbacher's mission to Mendel Glacier. *Courtesy Laws Railroad Museum; photo by Peter Stekel*

Group burial October 15, 1948, at Golden Gate National Cemetery. Joseph Munn, Glenn's father, is standing behind the casket.
Courtesy Munn family

Aerial view from about 15,000 feet of Mount Darwin (rear left) and Mount Mendel (middle), from the northeast. *Photo by Peter Stekel*

Mendel Glacier, August 2007 (the seated figure at center gives a sense of scale). *Photo by Peter Stekel*

Ranger Edward "Ned" Kelleher (on left) and park archeologist Keith Hamm survey Leo Mustonen's burial site in the Mendel Glacier.
Courtesy Sequoia and Kings Canyon National Parks

Park rangers excavated Leo Mustonen from Mendel Glacier, digging around the remains until they were isolated on a pedestal, ensuring no personal effects were left behind. *Courtesy Sequoia and Kings Canyon National Parks*

Engine wreckage from the Beech 18 AT-7 , August 2007.
Photo by Peter Stekel

Front wheel of the Beech 18 AT-7 found on Mendel Glacier, August 2007.
Photo by Peter Stekel

A fragment from Glenn Munn's sweater, August 2007.
Photo by Peter Stekel

Glenn Munn's parachute lay beside his body. The canvas pack had rotted away but the parachute inside was still tightly wrapped and undeployed.
Photo by Peter Stekel

Magneto plate from Lieutenant Gamber's Beech 18 AT-7. The magneto provides an electric charge [the spark] to the spark plugs in each cylinder. Each Pratt & Whitney R-985 engine on the aircraft had nine cylinders. There were two magnetos per engine. *Photo by Peter Stekel*

The section of Mendel Glacier where Glenn Munn was discovered. *Photo by Peter Stekel*

Jim Shriver, Glenn Munn's nephew, examines engine wreckage from his uncle's airplane, September 2008. *Photo by Peter Stekel*

Glenn Munn's ring. *Photo by Peter Stekel*

Michele Hinatsu holds a piece of wing wreckage from the Beech 18 AT-7. *Photo by Peter Stekel*

A portion of the Mendel Glacier bergschrund, August 2008.
Photo by Peter Stekel

Mendel Glacier bergschrund, with Mendel Left and Mendel Right couloirs above, photographed by Captain Roy Sulzbacher, September 1948.
Courtesy Julia Sulzbacher

A greatly thinned and shrunken Mendel Glacier in 2007 from approximately the same location as photographed by Captain Sulzbacher in 1948. No longer a continuous surface of ice, islands of rocks and boulders embedded within the glacier when it first formed are emerging.
Photo by Peter Stekel

The original 1948 headstone marking the gravesite for 2D Lieutenant William R. Gamber, and aviation cadets Ernest G. Munn, John M. Mortenson, and Leo M. Mustonen. Note that Mustonen's middle initial is incorrect; his middle name was actually Arvid. *Photo in author's collection*

Headstone for William Gamber and John M. Mortenson at Golden Gate National Cemetery, January 2010. *Photo by Peter Stekel*

Barbara and Dick's father was a mechanical engineer and that's what Gamber was studying at Tri-State. "I'm sure Bill's parents were glad that he could come stay with us and have a working experience in the city."

There were five years' difference in age between Bill Gamber and Dick Christian, enough to make the younger boy idolize the older. Bill was great in sports, taught Dick to play basketball, and the two of them became close. "I thought of my cousin as the older brother I didn't have." When Dick made the varsity basketball team at Denison University in Granville, Ohio, he told his mother, secure in the knowledge that Bill Gamber would find out about it and be proud of him. It didn't matter to Dick that he'd made the team because "all the seniors had already gone into the service and I wasn't that good." He knew Bill would understand and be proud of him anyway.

The Gamber family wasn't especially devout, though Howard and Nelle Gamber insisted their children attend Sunday school. "When we would visit on a weekend, we would all go to Sunday school together," said Dick Christian. With Bill as instigator, "Occasionally, we left the house and we didn't go to Sunday school at all and went somewhere else."

In March 1941, British forces arrived in Greece and President Roosevelt signed the Lend-Lease Act, allowing the United States to "lend" military equipment to the British in exchange for deferred payment and promises of military bases in that country's overseas colonies. It was the best Roosevelt could do with a noninterventionist Congress unwilling to become involved in another European war. The U.S. military was more bellicose and was preparing for inevitable conflict. That month, like thousands of other young men, Bill Gamber received his draft notice. He graduated on June 13, 1941, from Tri-State and spent the summer at home. Like Glenn Munn, Gamber enlisted as an aviation cadet in order to get his choice of service branch.

Speaking to a reporter in 2006 before she died, Bill's older sister, Millicent Gamber Ewing, said, "He always wanted to be a pilot. He always wanted to do it in high school, and he talked about it all the time. That was what he wanted to do after graduation. He was very devoted to flying."

On July 11, 1942, in response to earlier plans to come home to Ohio for a visit, Bill sent a telegram to his parents. "Impossible to get home, not enough time." Four months of busy flying later, he was gone. At the time, his sister Millicent was living in Half Moon Bay, south of San Francisco, to be close to her husband who was in the navy. It was her duty to pick up Bill's car and personal belongings.

I was sad to learn that Phyllis Reynolds had died in July 2006, but some detective work turned up her son Jaime Stilson. He remembered quite well when news about the Frozen Airman flashed across his television screen back in 2005. "When it first came on the news, I brought it up to her because I thought it was an interesting story." And she replied matter-of-factly and completely to her son's surprise, "I almost married one of those guys."

"She spoke very highly of William Gamber and she was very picky about men!" said Jamie. Jamie thought that his mother and Bill Gamber had been awfully close. "They were pretty serious. I think she broke his heart. It was her choice to break it off, not his. I think it was a first love for both of them."

As part of her legacy to her grandchildren, Phyllis Reynolds Stilson penned her autobiography. Of her teen years in Fayette, Ohio, she wrote, "My first serious boyfriend was Bill Gamber. He was two grades ahead of me in high school. I had to go past his house to get to school. He always waited for me." As an example of how deeply she felt for him at the time, she wrote, "My folks were going ice boating one Sunday and wanted me to go along. I had never been and had always wanted to—but no—I was afraid to leave the telephone in case he might call." Of course, "Girls never called boys," in those days, and when Bill Gamber had to accompany his parents somewhere and didn't contact Phyllis, she felt, "How dumb I was." Her first big out-of-town date was to meet Bill at a dance at Tri-State College. "I was so thrilled!"

Away at college, Bill had no idea that Phyllis had another boyfriend—Jack Stilson, whom she eventually married. It all came to a head when "Jack invited me to the Jr-Sr Prom. Bill was in college in Angola, Indiana, and wasn't supposed to find out." Somehow he did. Phyllis was excited and flattered by the attention of two beaus but admitted in complete candor to her grandchildren that she was "very confused as to my feelings." Then, Gamber was called to the service and enlisted. "I never saw Bill again as he was killed in a plane crash in the mountains and never found. I was devastated."

I talked to Gamber family friend Pauline Jones, who remembered when Bill's plane was lost. "His parents stayed up, night after night, waiting for a call to tell them they had found Bill." That call never came. After that, "Mrs. Gamber didn't come out of the house for a long time—and she was an very active, lovely person. I know Nelle never got over losing Bill. It was a long time before they gave up on hearing what happened to him."

Following his disappearance, Jones said the Gambers didn't mention Bill too often. "It was a sad time for everyone, and the town too, because in those times everyone knew one another." She recalled the impact this young man had in his town of 800 souls. "I can still see him walking the streets of Fayette, with his head held high. Always dressed very nice. We looked on him as being a very fortunate young man. He was respected in the town and in the school. He excelled in whatever he did and was admired for it. He knew that but it didn't make him stuck up. He was a down to earth fellow." Giving him the ultimate compliment for someone of that era, Jones said, "I would class him as an admirable young man."

Barbara Adams remembered late 1942 as terrible times. "Not only was Bill missing and presumed dead, it wasn't too long after that my other cousin was killed when his plane crashed in England on takeoff. My remembrance of those years was of my mother crying a lot."

The family chose not to visit California in 1948 for the Golden Gate National Cemetery burial. Finally, in 1953, Howard and Nelle Gamber traveled west from Fayette to acknowledge the official military recognition that their son had given his life in defense of the United States of America. Because Barbara and Perry Adams lived close to San Bruno, Mr. and Mrs. Gamber stayed with them. "I don't remember a lot of emotion but I know there was," said Barbara. "They loved to play bridge, and Perry and I played bridge so we had a good time with them. It was good for them. We went to the cemetery. I don't remember either of them being overly emotional."

They did talk a bit, but not much, about Bill. At least Howard Gamber and Barbara and Perry Adams did. Nelle was quiet. "She had the personality of being very extroverted and talkative," and therefore her lack of involvement spoke loudly as to her feelings. On the other hand, "Howard was never very talkative," and there was nothing unusual about his lack of conversation concerning his son.

So, the four of them played bridge, one generation in grief communicating in the only way they knew how. "We played quite good bridge in those days. It was a fun time for them and it made it easy for them to come. That's why they didn't ever come to the cemetery before. I'm just guessing," said Barbara. "I think it was just too difficult."

• • •

On December 17, 1942, Anna Mustonen sat at the table of friend and neighbor, Hilma Hill, and dictated letters to the Gamber, Mortenson, and Munn families. "Friends that we have not met ... We understand perfectly your sorrow in this matter which is doubly hard, for the reason, that no trace of the plane or boys have been found yet ... Can you think of anything, that we parents, could do, so they would do more, to find our boys ... your sorrow is just as deep and heartbreaking as ours ... We have given up all hopes, of them, finding the boys alive anymore, nevertheless we would like to have them learn the details of the disaster."

Nelle Gamber responded five days later. "Dear Friends. For some time I have put off writing to you, hoping against hope that we might receive some information, but guess it isn't to be so." A California friend of the Gambers' had been in contact with Colonel Hewitt, base commander of Mather Field. "Col. Hewitt seems to be very nice and willing to talk, but there doesn't seem to be much to say ... It doesn't seem right that our boys should be taken from us in this way, and words can not express the sorrow that we know is yours and ours at this Christmas time."

Two days after the new year, Anna Mustonen wrote to Mamee Munn. "Oftentimes, we feel, that we would rather, be in California, and search, the woods thoroughly, by running, over every inch of ground, than sit here at home ... A mother's heart, is so full of impatient love, and concern, over her son. We were sorry to hear that Glenn is your only son also ... It just seems wrong, sometimes, that our boys had to meet with this disaster ... We received a letter, from our son, Leo, the same morning, that the tragedy happened. He urged us not to worry and said that they are careful." She closes the letter with the suggestion of writing to the commanding officer again. "Some day we will receive news that the boys are found."

• • •

Leo Mustonen was a shy and quiet boy with a love of music inherited from his father. Leo was a serious boy too, though he possessed an outgoing and happy spirit, always with a smile on his face. Anna Mustonen showered him with attention and affection, always cooking, always baking, taking care of her men: Leo, his half-brother Arvo, and their father.

The boy's father was stoic, very quiet. Born in 1890, Arvid Mustonen immigrated to America with his five brothers in 1912 from the area of Baltic Russia, bordering Sweden, that became Finland. Like Leo, he hardly said a word, but he would watch the world around him. Arvid had been married once before to a woman named Elli. They knew each other in the old country. Their son was Arvo, born in 1916. One day she was there, and the next was gone.

Arvid worked for the railroad, moving around the old northwest country. He met Anna Raiski, who left Finland in 1913 for the United States, when she was working in a boardinghouse frequented by the traveling workers—the way a lot of Swedes and Norwegians met in those days. In 1918 Arvid and Anna were married in Cloquet, Minnesota.

Leo Arvid Mustonen was born in Brainerd on March 1, 1920, right smack dab in the geographical middle of Minnesota. The family lived at 1220 East Maple Street and attended Messiah Lutheran Church, a Finnish Congregation that later merged in the mid-1960s with Brainerd's First Lutheran Church. Leo played in the brass section with the Brainerd High School band and graduated in 1938.

Marjorie Freeman is the only one left in town who remembers Leo and the Mustonen family. "They were a reserved family, a nice family. Quiet. Really kept to themselves. There is no getting around that." Freeman remembers Anna Mustonen as the ideal housewife of that era. "You could eat off of Mrs. Mustonen's floor—she was so clean. The curtains were always starched. Oh my! She had starched doilies on all the tables. The tablecloth was absolutely perfect."

Times were hard in the 1930s and 1940s for everyone, but the Mustonen family were fortunately better off than many others. "They had a very nice home, comfortable," remembers Freeman. "In that time it was considered a nice home." They also owned another house across the street that they rented out.

"They didn't have a lot of associations, as far as I know. My mother-in-law and Mrs. Mustonen were very close—probably best friends." In 1942, Freeman was a young war bride, staying with her in-laws while her husband served in the Pacific. "When it was Leo that was missing, it was my mother-in-law she turned to. Mrs. Mustonen would come over every day and visit." Over coffee Anna would talk, and cry, about her missing son. It was the same every day, carrying grief so heavy it weighed her down. "Oh my poor Leo—if only he could come home." Knowing he had disappeared, presuming he was dead, but never knowing how or why tore at her until her own death in 1969.

Younger than Leo by four years, Freeman knew him from the neighborhood, though they weren't friends. In the 1930s, Brainerd was a town of about a thousand people. It would have been difficult for any of the school kids not to know each other. "Before the war, he was an average young boy. He went to school and was liked."

Following high school, Leo attended Brainerd Junior College for two years. In 1940 he accompanied the college debate team to the state speech tournament in Eveleth, Minnesota. After that he enrolled in either the University of Minnesota or St. Clouds Teachers College—Freeman's memory and newspaper reports differ.

Leo enlisted in the Army Air Forces in Minneapolis, at Fort Snelling, on October 20, 1941, and did his basic training at Jefferson Barracks, Missouri. From there he was sent to Fort McDowell on Angel Island in San Francisco Bay. Following the Pearl Harbor attack,

Angel Island had become a processing center for prisoners of war and a major point of embarkation for troops headed to the Pacific war zone.

With his college experience and studious nature, Leo certainly couldn't have been stimulated as an ordinary garrison soldier, and perhaps that's why he volunteered for the aviation cadet corps. As Freeman remembered, "He always monkeyed around with planes. They were something to him—something that he had in his heart and mind all his life. It was not surprising when he enlisted in the air force." After three months leave back home in Brainerd, Leo showed up for the nine-week preflight training at the Army Air Forces Classification Center at Santa Ana, California, on June 15, 1942. The paper trail for Leo Mustonen ends at Santa Ana, and all we know for sure is that he eventually came to Mather Field, where he was assigned to a navigation training class with Mortenson and Munn.

The human story jumps to 1967 and a five-year-old boy named Wayne Renn delivering prescriptions for his mother who worked at the local Brainerd pharmacy. In those days it was OK for a little kid to run down a quiet street, hand off a prescription, collect the money, and take it back to the store. That's how Renn met Anna Mustonen. "She was so polite and so sweet. She wore dresses all the time and a button-up sweater with a handkerchief stuck in her sleeve," Renn told me. A heart attack had claimed Arvid in 1958, Arvo and his family had moved to Florida, and Anna lived alone. "I bet you think I don't know anything about little boys," she said to Renn when they met. "But I do." She bent over and hugged him. "You remind me of my little boy." And she began to sob. "I didn't know she had lost her son and had been grieving all these years," Renn remembered.

After Anna died in 1969, Renn's parents bought the Mustonen home for $7,500. It was completely furnished with all of Arvid and Anna's belongings. All their furniture. All their photographs on the walls. Anna's kitchen. "When we moved in there, at first I slept in Leo Mustonen's bed. There were his belongings up in the attic that had been shipped home from the service."

When Renn inherited the house from his parents and moved in with his first wife, "She insisted I take the dishes out because they weren't our dishes. And she insisted we take down the Mustonen pictures and put ours up and then demanded I get rid of the Mustonen pictures. She said it was so illogical to have those things around because they belonged to somebody else. So I went out and put those pictures in a garbage bag. When she went upstairs, I snuck a few pictures under my coat. Those are the ones I have now."

Leo's only remaining relatives are his sister-in-law Louella and nieces Leane Ross and Ruth Mustonen. When I spoke to Leane, she said, "Our family didn't talk much about personal issues. All I knew—there was an Uncle Leo." When Leo was identified as the Frozen Airman discovered on the Mendel Glacier in 2005, Leane and her family were overwhelmed with gratitude to all involved. "Each person showed us the gentleness, consideration, and sensitivity usually awarded to one's personal family members in times of grief."

Leane told me how having Leo brought home after all the years of not knowing him brought closure and, oddly, hope. "This story has worldwide appeal because it speaks for people. It gives hope that any missing relative—for whatever reason—can be found. And families can find closure. His discovery created an empathy and renewal of emotions that included hope during times of peace and war."

When Leo Mustonen was brought home to Brainerd in 2006, to have his ashes laid beside the graves of his parents, the hymn played was one Leane remembered singing when she combed her grandmother Anna's long hair:

Be still, my soul: when dearest friends depart,
And all is darkened in the vale of tears,
Then shalt thou better know His love, His heart,
Who comes to sooth thy sorrow and thy fears.
Be still, my soul: thy Jesus can repay
From His own fullness all He takes away.

• • •

Anna Mustonen wrote to Mamee Munn on April 13, 1943, after communicating with Colonel Hewitt. "They think that the plane has come down somewhere in the Sierra Nevada Mountains within the area of Yosemite Park and Placerville. He assured us that, they have done everything, humanly possible to do, to find the plane and boys." She writes of the snowstorm that occurred the day of the disaster and that snow continued for several days, "so it is probable, that they are covered with snow." She places her hopes that when spring arrives, the snow will melt, "which will enable someone to find them." And she doesn't give up on the idea of writing to "Mather Field, every once in awhile, so that they will not forget, our boys."

A week later, Anna wrote again to Mamee. The subject now is the subject all relatives face when the death of a serviceman finally sinks in. Will there be a body to grieve over? "If the boys have gone into a lake or ocean, we know that it will be impossible to find them. Let's hope, that nothing as tragic, as that, has happened ... It does seem so strange when they can't find them. I do have to admit, that oftentimes, I wait for Leo, to come home, it just seems that he is alive somewhere. Oh! If that were only true!"

In much the same vein, on September 30, 1943 Anna wrote once more to Mamee. "We had such high hopes last spring that when summer comes, at least the plane will be found ... but it looks as tho' we have to face another winter same as last." A separate letter to Colonel Hewitt asked "if they have given up all hopes for our boys to let us know the truth." She tells Mamee that Arvo has written he will use his vacation in October to visit Mather Field and personally "talk to the officers."

In this letter is her only indication of distrust in the army's process. "We cannot understand why they are so secretive to the boy's parents. For it does seem that we should have some rights to our own sons, whom we have tenderly cared for, and tried to teach beautiful and high ideals ... It would seem terrible if we have to accept the news that the government report them as dead before they are found or anything definite is learned. One thing bothers me also that they discontinued the organized search for them too soon."

• • •

We can only imagine John Melvin Mortenson. Of the boys who lost their lives November 18, 1942, on Mendel Glacier, his story is the most difficult to bring to life. But for one letter, a photograph, and faint memories of a young neighborhood boy, Mortenson never existed.

In 2007, Mortenson's older sister, Ruth, was still alive at ninety-seven but had lost most of her memory to dementia. She only remembered her brother as a good-looking man, very serious, and with mechanical abilities. His cousin Carol Benson, was four years old when John disappeared and had no recollection of him. Her family was tight-lipped about the past; no one spoke about the boy who had gone off to war and never come home. "Unless you lived during those times, it's hard to understand." She only remembered that back in 1947, when the crash site was first found, her mother talked about the importance of closure.

From census records I learned that John Mortenson was born as Melvin Mortenson in either 1917 or 1918, attended school in Moscow, Idaho, and lived at 824 East Seventh Street. In 1935 he graduated from Moscow High School. He attended the University of Idaho in Moscow, according to Carol Benson, and graduated in 1939 with a degree in business. From the family house on East Seventh Street he could walk to school every day.

They were a family of farmers. John A. Mortenson, Melvin's father, had emigrated as a young child from Sweden to the United States in 1868 and by 1884 had become a naturalized citizen. In the 1900 census, John A. Mortenson is listed as widowed and living in the Thorn Creek Precinct of Latah County, Idaho, with his older sister, Hannah, and Christ(opher?) Christoffers, whose relation is given as "partner" and occupation as "farmer." They are living on, and John owns, a farm. There are no children living at the house, but I know that John was father to Myrtle by then. She would go on to marry Melvin Hattan. Carol Benson is the daughter of Myrtle Mortenson and Melvin Hattan.

By 1910, forty-two-year-old John Mortenson had remarried to Ida Caroline Sampson, a thirty-one-year-old Swedish immigrant who had arrived in the United States in 1906. Their first daughter, Anna, was born in 1907, and in June 1910 a second daughter, Ruth Victoria, was born. They had left the farm and now lived in town with Manny Samuelson, a twenty-five-year-old Swedish laborer and odd-jobber. According to census documents, John Mortenson was also working as a farm laborer.

By the time of the 1920 census, Melvin had been born and the family were exclusively town dwellers, living in the Seventh Street house. Ida's younger brother, Swan, was also living with them. John Mortenson's occupation is listed as "none." As an adult, John was employed either as a farmer or farm laborer. He was unemployed during the 1920 census but by 1930 had a job working as a bank janitor. He died in 1930 at age sixty-six before Melvin entered junior high school.

Ida Caroline Mortenson died on February 17, 1940, at age sixty-five. Neither Anna nor Ruth ever married. Ruth moved to Seattle in 1941 to teach grade school, eventually becoming a respected employee of the Seattle Engineering Department. I'm betting that Melvin enlisted around this time. With their parents gone, the children were leaving small-town Moscow for the big wide wonderful world. I don't know when Anna left, but the sisters were eventually roommates in the Magnolia neighborhood of Seattle. Anna died there in 1989.

I haven't any idea of what Melvin Mortenson did for the approximately three years following college graduation, and there are no enrollment or alumni records at the University of Idaho for either a John or a Melvin Mortenson. I don't even know when Mortenson enlisted in the army. At the beginning of the war it was still possible for enlisted men to transfer into the cadet program, and maybe he had done that. At age twenty-five, he was older than Munn and Mustonen and one year shy of the upper enlistment age limit.

Among the limited possessions of her cousin's that Carol Benson owns is a letter dated April 27, 1942, to Anna Mortenson at the Seventh Street house in Moscow. The penmanship is excellent, the letters finely formed, and Mortenson's fine-tuned observations from cadet training in King City, California, indicate a person with a good eye for detail and beauty. The letter to Anna is signed "Melvin," so it's a mystery when he adopted the name "John."

According to this letter, Melvin has finished his preflight cadet training in Santa Ana and has just arrived for primary flight school at King City. He still hasn't flown an airplane yet. The beginning of his letter alludes to having been in the area before. It's impossible to know whether this is because he was stationed at nearby Camp Roberts before the war (assuming an earlier enlistment) or if he had spent time in the area, maybe farming, since college graduation.

I'm confident that Melvin arrived at King City with the same group of young men as Glenn Munn, because Munn wrote a letter home the same day appraising his family of his transfer from preflight in Santa Ana. What with the hundreds who were transferred that day and the others already at King City, there is no way of knowing whether Mortenson and Munn had met yet.

The training facility they left behind in Santa Ana was well-known for its unattractive two-story barracks set within a dull landscape lacking any sort of vegetation save that which could escape tens of thousands of marching feet. In contrast, the King City facility consisted of one-story barracks, sleeping six to a room (each room with its own shower), built around courtyards planted with shrubs and flowers. Melvin thought it a "swell place." With venetian blinds on the windows and air conditioners, he wrote that "all in all it resembles more a summer resort than an army camp."

Melvin's letter to Anna ends with evidence that the Mortenson farm is still in possession of the family but that it has been rented out. "No, Harry Egland is not much of a farmer and I would definitely not rent the place to him." The tone suggests this topic has been discussed before. Apparently somebody by the name of Levi has been renting the farm and is no longer interested in doing so. Melvin suggests asking their brother-in-law, Melvin Hattan, to "take a look at the place sometime and check things out." He leaves any decisions to his sister, though, writing, "Use your own judgement."

There's only one other small part of Melvin Mortenson's life I was able to learn about. Walt Griser grew up in the same neighborhood as Mortenson and was a year behind him in school. "I knew him by the name Mel," Griser told me. "We played football in the backyards and went to school together and went Halloweening together. He was congenial, a nice guy, one of the kids in the neighborhood." They lost track of each other during the war.

From these fragments, Melvin Mortenson remains an enigma—so little exists to mark his life and his passing. Even the few objects that belonged to him that were recovered from the glacier in 1947 (part of his watch and his name badge) have been lost. Yet, he was here.

• • •

Looking backward in time, I think Barbara Adams has the best perspective of the world in which these four boys lived. "These small towns in the Midwest were wonderful in the 1930s. There was a lot of camaraderie. There was a lot of wholesome activity. A freedom too. I don't feel like we're very free today. Our children—we're certainly afraid for them. We're either concerned about them riding their bikes and getting hit by a car or something worse.

"That wasn't the way it was in these small towns. There was freedom for those men, for those boys, to run around and pursue life to the fullest without handicaps. As I read about the other three men, I realized they all grew up in small towns in middle America. To think, all four of those men had similar backgrounds! I imagine they must have gotten along, all of them, pretty well. I think it was a very wholesome period of time. It was a great time to be young and be alive."

CHAPTER 14

Their Training

Few boys coming of age in the years preceding World War II had ever been up in an airplane. For them, joining the U.S. Army Air Forces (called the Army Air Corps until June 22, 1941) was partly patriotism, partly positioning themselves for job opportunities at the end of their service, and partly a romantic aspiration of soaring in the clouds. Perhaps they felt like Antoine de Saint-Exupéry when he wrote, "One of the miracles of the airplane is that it plunges a man directly in the heart of mystery."

When they enlisted, the boys were young enough to still retain some of the immortality of childhood. They realized they were caught up in something larger than themselves, with events completely out of their control. But they were also young enough to see it happening not *to* them but *around* them. With the patience always shown by children to their parents, the boys were willing to wait until this generation of adults had straightened out their mess. As Ivan Doig comments in his WWII-era novel, *The Eleventh Man*, they would serve as dutifully as they could for the duration of the war and reconstitute themselves when peace came in whatever measure.

I imagine the boys' impressions of flying came in large part from motion pictures and books. *The Dawn Patrol* was a popular movie for its depiction of World War I aerial combat. During aviation's first decades, a number of young-adult books focused on flying for the air corps and the U.S. Mail. One series from the 1930s, produced by the Stratemeyer Syndicate and penned by Edward Stratemeyer himself, was appropriately called *Airplane Boys*. As they grew older, kids with either a mechanical bent or interest in engineering, like William Gamber, were naturally attracted to aircraft. Barnstormers helped contribute to flying's fascination, as pilots performed aerial tricks and also offered rides for a fee.

When the four boys first took flight, they would have seen the earth in a new and different way. As they climbed higher and higher, they might have been amazed to see topographic relief fall away—mountains and canyons becoming inconspicuous and unimpressive and the natural wild landscape becoming a feature-less plain. All four were from farming communities and they were probably surprised to see that rural areas, from farm to farm, all looked alike from the air. Pilots experience this differently than passengers. This featurelessness is dangerous to the pilot not keeping an eye on the altimeter or paying attention to his height over land. As the land rises, altitude remains the same. A seemingly flat valley from high up metamorphoses rapidly into a narrow canyon when approached at 150 miles per hour. When trouble occurs, it comes even faster. Lieutenant Gamber would have learned this in flight school and the navigation students would have been aware of it too.

• • •

With GPS technology today, there is little need for an individual onboard an aircraft whose duty is to navigate. Leonard Spivey, who trained at Mather Field, told me that "during World War II, navigators were not only essential to guide an aircraft on transocean flights and on extended flights over foreign lands, but also to direct bombers on combat missions and to pinpoint aircraft position at any time. Even on long cross-country flights in North America it was prudent to have a navigator onboard a bomber or transport—especially where visibility was limited."

The B-17 Pilot Training Manual published by the U.S. Army Air Forces explains a navigator's primary responsibility. "Direct your flight from departure to destination and return." Determining geographical position, the navigator "must know the exact position of the airplane at all times." Among the techniques to know were pilotage, dead reckoning, radio operation and navigation, celestial navigation, and instrument calibration. Navigators were also expected to skillfully manipulate the .50-caliber machine gun at their station.

Before a mission, navigators took their map and plotted a course in much the same way as private pilots do today. Checkpoints were located and approximate time from point to point was calculated, taking such things as wind speed and direction into account to compute fuel consumption. Planning the trip was an essential duty for ensuring you knew how to get back after your mission.

Once in the air, navigators had plenty to do. Using pilotage they charted their position using visual ground references. This is very similar to driving a car with a map on your lap and checking off places as they are passed. Dead reckoning was the basic form of navigation beyond pilotage and added accuracy by plotting airspeed, windspeed and direction, and course headings on a map. A drift meter allowed navigators to determine deviation, or drift, of an aircraft from a straight-line course. This was very important, since drift increases distance and therefore time in the air. Radio navigation (i.e., following a radio beam) was still a new enough field in western North America during the early 1940s that it was used primarily to verify pilotage and dead reckoning.

There were two forms of radio navigation in use: nondirectional beacons (NDBs) and radio range. Navigation cadets would have no experience with either (though pilots were well-acquainted with both) until near the end of their training. In William Bechter's 1942–43 diary for his 100 days of navigation school at Mather Field, his first practical experience with radio navigation was on day 87.

On top of the AT-7 fuselage was a loop antenna called an automatic direction finder (ADF) located within a football-shaped housing. The ADF picked up nondirectional beacons broadcasting Morse code identifiers. Aeronautical charts marked the location of NDBs, their identifier, plus any other pertinent data such as height of the broadcasting tower. A gauge with a needle pointing to the compass point where the NDB signal originated was located on the aircraft's instrument panel. Pilots would turn their plane to the NDB magnetic heading and proceed in that direction until they saw the NDB source. As they flew over the source, their needle would flip 180 degrees and point to a heading behind them. One problem with NDBs as navigational aids is they say nothing about how far away you are from them. They simply point and say, "This way."

Pilots and navigators were trained to constantly seek any signal they could. For example, on a heading from Mather Field south to Los Banos a navigator would know where he was heading but not how close he was. For that, he might scan for an NDB broadcasting from San Jose, Merced, and Modesto. Then he could draw a line on his chart for each magnetic heading he recorded. Where all the lines intersected, that was his position.

There were several things to keep in mind with NDB navigation. It was always possible to turn off course by following a commercial radio station with a frequency close to the NDB frequency you were searching for. Also, ADF needles will point away from an NDB and toward lightning flashes during electrical storms. Static electricity builds up on aircraft flying in rain, snow, or clouds and causes ADF needles to wander. Mountains reflect radio waves like NDB signals and lead to incorrect readings. NDB signals could be refracted thirty to sixty miles or more from their stations by ionospheric disruptions. Keeping these shortcomings in mind, cadets got a lot of practice using this rudimentary radio navigation during the advanced part of their education as navigators. Yet, an indication of how effective the technology was, and remains, are the number of pilots worldwide who still navigate using NDBs.

An older technique still in use in 1942 while flying in the United States involved tuning to a radio range course. Radio range transmitting stations were established along a straight line and broadcast a Morse code identifier along with either the letter *A* (dot-dash) or *N* (dash-dot). If the pilot flew the middle of the course, he was "on the beam" and would hear the steady tone of the two melded signals. But if he strayed to one side of the course, he would hear an *A* and if he strayed to the other, an *N*. The farther the drift, the stronger the signal.

Radio range courses functioned like radio highways. There was one that ran down the valley from Mather Field to Fresno and another that went from Fresno southwest to northeast at 37 degrees (or 217 degrees coming northeast to southwest) over the Sierra Nevada to Bishop. Pilots flew to one side or the other of the beacon to avoid the possibility of midair collisions between aircraft being flown under Instrument Flight Rules. A major issue with radio range courses came from mountains interrupting or dispersing the beam.

In the last third of their training, navigation cadets used an octant to practice celestial navigation. Sequentially sighting at least two stars through a small telescope (or peep hole on older instruments), the navigator used his octant to measure his angle between the horizon and those celestial objects. The results were shown at the bottom of the instrument on a protractor's arc that represents an eighth of a circle, hence "octant" or "eighth." By knowing the time of day and determining the position of these celestial objects, navigators used triangulation to locate their place on the ground and in the air. Accuracy was crucial but challenging to achieve. Imagine yourself in a bouncing airplane, looking through a telescope at a star while trying to keep steady enough to take a reading on the octant's angle gauge.

Celestial navigation is the oldest form of finding an accurate position, yet World War II navigators relied on it more to confirm pilotage and dead reckoning than as the primary means of navigation. The AT-7 was equipped with a celestial dome located behind the cockpit. Barring clouds, standing below the dome on a stool, the navigator would have a confining but clear view of the night sky.

After gathering all his data from pilotage, dead reckoning, radio, and celestial navigation, the navigator returned to his desk to plot his actual location. This could take quite some time. Meanwhile, the airplane is still moving forward. This meant the navigator never knew where he was but only where he had been, which is why plotting a course was done continuously.

These were also the tools used by navigators for calculating fuel consumption during flight. The navigator balanced engine performance, weather and wind, payload, fuel reserves, passenger and crew weight, and maximum allowable weight for the aircraft to calculate fuel quantity.

Mortenson, Munn, and Mustonen would have learned these techniques in a classroom during preflight training. Theory would have been put to the test with day and, in time, night flying at Mather Field during advanced training. The cadets would also have learned more than calculating direction forward. Pilots needed to know their point of no return (especially during over-the-water flying) and their location relative to alternate landing fields in case the plane couldn't reach its target destination.

Accurate navigation demanded planning for contingencies upon contingencies. This preparation included filing a flight plan. Should a mistake occur, and mistakes happened all the time, aircraft were more easily located if rescuers knew where to look. And indeed, we have a flight plan for Lieutenant Gamber's final flight provided to us by base commander Colonel L. R. Hewitt: south from Mather Field to Los Banos, north and east of Mather to Roseville, farther north to Corning, and back to Mather Field.

• • •

Cadet aviation education began with preflight training, transitioned to primary, then basic, and ended with advanced training. Everyone took the same preflight training before winnowing separated pilots from navigators and bombardiers. Preflight for U.S. Army Air Forces aviation cadets included marching in drill, calisthenics, drill, sports, drill, classes in physics, mathematics, aircraft recognition, map reading, Morse code, drill, drill, and more drill. The day began at 5:15 A.M. and ended with taps at 10:00 P.M. Spare moments, when they occurred, were occupied with studying for weekly exams or sprucing up the barracks for inspections, both anticipated and not.

Every cadet suffered through a battery of tests. First were medical exams and the embarrassment of standing naked with a hundred other men while doctors did their tapping, poking, prodding, and probing. They took motor skills tests too. To be worthy of piloting an airplane, cadets had to prove their depth perception by lining up two vertical pencil-like sticks down a long narrow box by pulling on attached cords. Potential bombardiers were required to demonstrate their dexterity with a device that mimicked the Norden bombsight used on heavy bombers.

Hazing from upperclassmen, as senior cadets were termed, was common. This added to the general hazing from officers as well as from the noncoms who lead cadets in their physical training and drill. The harassment didn't begin letting up until cadets entered primary flying school. At the end of April, when Glenn Munn arrived for primary fight training, he was still complaining in letters to his mother about all the hazing from upperclassmen. Munn was realistic and understanding of the process. "This will continue of course until we solo and become upper classmen ourselves."

• • •

Following his January 27, 1942, enlistment in the Army Air Forces at Fort Hayes in Columbus, Ohio, Glenn Munn began regularly writing letters home to his mother. Sadly, none of the letters he received were preserved, but his mother did keep the twenty-six letters he wrote home from California between March 28 and November 6, 1942. Many of his letters end with an exhortation not to work so hard, to take more time off, and, "I am always thinking of you and home."

Munn arrived for his five weeks of pilot preflight training at Santa Ana Army Air Base (SAAAB) on March 28, 1942, with one of the first cadet classes to train at the newly renamed Army Air Forces Classification Center. SAAAB was part of a stepped-up program to train pilots, navigators, bombardiers, and other specialists for the army—after the December 1941 attack on Pearl Harbor, pilot training had been instantly accelerated at all U.S. training centers. As a basic training facility, the approximately 900- acre SAAAB (increased to 1,283 acres by 1945) also served as an airbase, though without airplanes, hangars, or runways. At the end of 1942, 23,470 soldiers had passed through SAAAB on their way to primary flight training.

The first set of buildings at SAAAB to accommodate the influx of recent recruits weren't completed until May 1942 so a fourteen-by-fourteen-foot canvas tent with eight cots served as Munn's first home in Santa Ana. In a letter full of hope and promise, he wrote home that "the plan of the whole camp is excellent. They are working night and day to rush it to completion. It will be a very nice place when they get it all finished."

Daytime temperatures in Santa Ana were triple digits and the nights dove down into the low forties, with stiff ocean breezes making it feel cooler. After several cold and sleepless nights, Munn managed to collect four blankets and sleep comfortably. He wrote to his mother that he liked the food, but it was "nothing to brag about."

● ● ●

In his book *The SAAAB Story*, local historian Edrick J. Miller makes the base sound like a cross between college and summer camp—hard-core academics alternated with intense physical conditioning. The mood at SAAAB was upbeat but serious, and Miller doesn't mince words about the country's unrealistic appraisal of the path before it after the surprise attack at Pearl Harbor. "The average American citizen felt that 'good ole Uncle Sam' would put a finish to these Japanese upstarts within 90 days or even less. What a mistake in judgement that turned out to be."

Leonard Spivey reminded me of the military situation in 1942. "We were faced with two foes who had been preparing for and engaging in war for years—Japan since about 1935 and Germany since 1939, with practice in the Spanish Civil War in 1937." After Pearl Harbor, "The United States was pitifully not prepared for modern ground warfare in strength and equipment. Thankfully we had a fairly good navy—with aircraft carriers—which the Japanese appreciated as the primary obstacle to their goals in Southeast Asia." For the defense of the continental United States, those carriers in the Pacific happened to be out of harm's way at sea on December 7, 1941.

People like Spivey, and his friends Bill Davis and William Bechter, joined thousands of others, including John Mortenson, Glenn Munn, and Leo Mustonen, to train as navigators on the big bombers of 1942: the B-17 Flying Fortress. These were potent, high-flying, and long-ranging aircraft that carried immense destructive force to the enemy. Massive bombing raids were a thing of the future, though, when these boys were in training. The first planned attack by the Army Air Forces in Europe was on August 17, 1942, when only a dozen B-17s bombed marshaling yards at Rouen, France.

• • •

Life at SAAAB meant long hours and hard work. Glenn Munn didn't like the physical training all that much. But he put a positive spin on it for his mother. "I think it will make a better man out of me after seeing some of these healthy specimens that have been here for awhile." Marching around base the first week was made rougher for all the cadets because they lacked proper clothing and shoes. The army wasn't nearly as organized as it expected its cadets to be. Everyone marched in their regular civilian clothes for several days until receiving two pair of coveralls called zoot suits. Proper footwear arrived two weeks later. "The only thing that bothers me is my feet," Munn wrote home, "they seem to be one solid blister."

Talking with a good friend of mine who has made the army his career, I began to understand what life was like for Munn as a new soldier. "I can still relate to what they experienced," Thomas "Sandy" Sandbakken told me. "Basic training for soldiers is pretty much the same. The shock of the initial transition from that of a free civilian to being ordered about and having every hour of your day dictated to you takes some getting used to. Our individual freedom was left at the door and put in storage for a while. We constantly wondered if we made a mistake in giving up our precious freedom."

Loss of personal freedom wasn't the only adjustment. Many enlistees in 1942 were overwhelmed with the quantity and value of military clothing issued to them. Most had gone through life with barely a change of clothes and now they possessed two sets of shoes ($10/pair), twelve pairs of dress socks, half a dozen pairs of white shorts, six undershirts, three pairs of wool olive drab (or "OD") khaki pants ($16/pair), three pairs of regular khaki pants ($4/pair), one OD coat ($45), an OD overcoat ($65), a raincoat, three wool dress shirts ($8 each), three khaki shirts ($4 each), four ties, six white linen handkerchiefs, three sets of gold wings and U.S. pins and other insignia, four garrison hats, an officer's style service hat ($12), and a pair of tan-colored leather dress gloves. Always the snappy dresser in civilian life, Munn was quite pleased with how sharp he and his cohort appeared in their new uniforms.

A footlocker was also issued, as well as tennis shoes, sweat pants, sweatshirts, and t-shirts for use in sports and calisthenics. There were also two barrack bags, a shaving kit (shaving brush, razor and blades, towels), mess kit, utensils, canteen (plus cover) and cup, wool cap, leggings, and belt. A big surprise came for the cadets when they learned that their gym clothing distribution was charged against their paychecks. There were also deductions for room and board, laundry, and required donations to base beautification and groups like the Red Cross.

Money was also withheld in an "accumulation fund," dispersed when the cadet left preflight for primary flight training. I guess the army brass were afraid of the cadets gambling their money away. They certainly had no opportunity to spend it at the post exchange or in wild sprees in nearby Santa Ana. Perpetual quarantine for communicable diseases (measles was a big worry) kept the cadets confined to base.

Part of preflight training included time spent in a pressure chamber where cadets could experience how it felt to be at high altitude without supplemental oxygen. The reactions of the boys ranged from no effect, to acting drunk, to passing out. Munn thought it great fun. "I suffered no ill effects at all though, in fact I enjoyed it, watching it affect the other boys when I hardly felt it at all." There was also poison gas training. Wearing a gas mask, cadets were taken to an open field and exposed to phosgene, mustard, and other killers. As each one was released, cadets opened their masks and took a quick whiff in order to smell and identify the agent.

Classes involved lectures and demonstrations followed by exams on Saturday, with the results posted the next Monday. Competition was fierce, but cadets were encouraged not to compete against each other but against themselves, to do the best they could. In fact, cadets with special skills, advanced knowledge and ability, or who were quicker to pick up concepts were pushed to help out the others by tutoring those most in need of assistance.

Determinations of who would be a pilot, navigator, or bombardier were not made until the boys finished preflight training. All three flying specialties led to second lieutenant commissions in the Army Air Forces, though it took more time for pilots because they were in training much longer than the other two groups. The roles of navigator and bombardier were filled by cadets who "washed out" of pilot training, and the weeding-out process was intense. Accruing too many demerits and lackluster academics were two big ways to wash out. There was no shame in not making it to pilot training. Every man was needed. Munn wrote that only half of his preflight class at Santa Ana expected to make it as far as primary flight training. He felt proud to be one of them.

•   •   •

Passing through a bucolic and greening golden California, at about 8:30 P.M. on April 24, 1942, Glenn Munn arrived by rail in King City and was transported to the Army Air Forces airfield at Mesa del Rey. Construction of the airfield had taken place during the winter of 1940–1941 and the first cadets were welcomed in March 1941. According to the California State Military Department Web site, when Munn arrived, Mesa del Rey had five barracks, a hospital, administration building, mess hall, and two hangars. Munn knew from rumors that his group of pilot trainees would soon leave Southern California but, in keeping with wartime restrictions and secrecy, he didn't know until ten minutes before departure where he was heading. "Our train was loaded with G-men and guards to prevent sabotage in the big troop movement," he wrote to his family.

Mesa del Rey, on the east side of King City in California's Salinas Valley, was one of many primary flight schools for the Army Air Forces. For a boy raised in the green and rolling hills of eastern Ohio, spring in Salinas Valley was in beautiful contrast to dry, dusty, brown Santa Ana. The oaks were impressively large in the valley, and their spreading branches cast enough shade on hot summer days to protect a house. West of King City, beyond the lettuce fields, conifers cloaked the deep ravines of the Gabilan Range that overlooked the valley. East, the far slopes of the Diablo Range rose to 5,258-foot San Benito Mountain. "We see beautiful green grass and flowers again," Munn wrote to his mother. The accommodations were a step up as well. "The rooms are very nice here [and] only slightly crowded. We have Venetian blinds and perfectly white plastered walls for a change."

· · ·

In his only surviving letter home, Melvin Mortenson describes the King City camp on April 26, 1942, two days later than Munn. To his sister Anna, he wrote in glowing terms, "This is ... a swell place. The barracks are all long one story structures. There are courts in between them and the whole place is planted with shrubs and flowers. We sleep six to a room but the rooms are large and we have elaborate single beds. Each room has its own showers. The quarters are also air conditioned."

Mesa del Rey may have been nicer looking than Santa Ana, but the work continued on pace. "Our days here are long and we are kept very busy," Mortenson wrote. "We get up at 5:20 and reveille is at 5:30. Breakfast is at 6:00 after which our day's work starts. It consists of flying, exercises, sports, ground school, etc. we have an hour off at noon and the evening dinner is at 7:00. After dinner we have two hours more of ground school. You can see it is pretty rugged!"

Munn also wrote home, discussing the schedule. "Flight line from 6:55 to 1:00 P.M. Athletics from 1:30 to 3:30 P.M. and ground school classes from 3:45 to 6:30." After dinner, "from 7:30 to 10:00 P.M. we have classes again." He didn't have any problem with the classes, but he still didn't like all the strenuous exercise. "It gets one in good condition, but you go through torture for a while with every muscle in your body sore."

Within a day of arriving at Mesa del Rey, Munn was excited to write his mother about receiving his "flying suit." It included "a fur lined helmet with ear phones and chin strap and large heavy duty goggles that are form fitted to the face, a big leather jacket with fur lining and straps that go around the neck to keep out the wind, a flying suit of overalls with zipper legs and pockets and a pair of fur lined leather boots with rubber soles." He sent home a photo in his regalia, posed in front of his trainer, a Ryan PT-22 airplane. Munn pronounced it a "honey."

Given the military proclivity for arranging everything alphabetically, I think it's reasonable that, among the 400 students in training at the 249-acre facility, Mortenson and Munn met here. From their letters home we know they were at Mesa del Rey at the same time and at the same level of training. Mortenson's letter says he picked up his pilot's garb on April 25, the same day as Munn. Unfortunately, neither mentions the other in their letters home, so we'll never know for sure if they first met each other here or at Mather Field five months later.

• • •

At primary flight school cadets got their first taste of piloting an airplane, going up every day for forty-five to fifty minutes. To pass they would need sixty-five hours of flying time. The Ryan PT-22 Munn described as such a honey turned out to be quite a handful. "It looks easy and one would think it would be fun, but the way the army wants you to fly it's all work and no play," Munn discovered. "They say that these are the hardest planes they have to learn to pilot because they are so fast and touchy on the controls." Munn found landing the PT-22 the toughest thing to do "because they land at 65 miles per hour," and the constant 30-mile-per-hour winds on the mesa increased the chance of ground looping or other mishaps. He also didn't like how crowded the sky could be when "about 200 airplanes get in the air."

Cadets continued attending ground school at Mesa del Rey. In his letter home, Melvin Mortenson describes studying "motors, navigation, theory of flight, meteorology, physics, etc. It is imperative that we learn this as we are given examinations regularly. We can be washed out for failing in ground school as well as inability to fly." Mortenson was philosophical about the odds he faced. "I hope I don't wash out but a large percentage do. I guess after all it's just life; you are either born without that inherent flying ability or with it, as the case may be." He signed off, promising to keep the family advised about his progress, "If I have any."

Nobody at Mesa del Rey enjoyed a social life. Munn found King City small and with little to do "except walk around on the streets or go to a show." One Saturday in early May a USO dance was organized in town. "I enjoyed myself, but the dancing and the music isn't like it is back home or I could have had a better time."

Flying was fun but, to his surprise, Munn discovered it wasn't for him. "Yesterday in some preliminary stages of air acrobatics we dove 3,000 ft straight down and it wasn't nearly as thrilling as I thought it would be." He did enjoy doing loops and flying upside down in the open-cockpit PT-22 with only a safety belt between him and Mother Earth. It wasn't frightening at all. "When one gets up there it is altogether different [and] it's just like I always have been there."

With no love of flying, Munn recognized he'd made a big mistake in pursing his ambition to pilot aircraft. "I think and know now that I am better qualified for dealing in airplane navigation exclusively." With the blessing and cooperation of his flight instructor and squadron commander, Munn applied for an "automatic washout" that would provide a transfer to navigation school rather than the normally required demotion to infantryman. He would retain his cadet rating, train in the big bombers, and ever mindful of advancement, he wrote, "I will get my commission 3½ months earlier with a higher pay than [an] ordinary pilot." Looking to his future, Munn realized, "This gives me a higher type education and I will be better fitted for a good job after the war." He predicted pilots would be "a dime a dozen" after the war, but good jobs would always be open for navigators.

It was at about this same time that Munn's letters take on a plaintive tone. "I guess this sounds like I am suffering from that well known disease called home-sickness, but darn it all any man who pledges his life to the current cause and to his country no matter how much he steels himself against the actual truth, the largest and softest spot in his heart is retained for his home and family."

· · ·

As Glenn Munn would do the following January, William Gamber enlisted in the U.S. Army Air Forces at Fort Hayes in Columbus, Ohio, on September 25, 1941. Gamber then started with sixty hours of training at the Ryan School of Aeronautics in Hemet, California. Gamber joined what would end up being 14,000 pilots graduated from the nine-week primary flight training programs taught by the Ryan schools in Hemet and Tucson, Arizona.

Unusual for a small-town boy of that era, this wasn't Gamber's first trip out west. Back in 1937, to celebrate his high-school graduation, Gamber rode the Greyhound Bus to Southern California with his older sister, Millicent. Several weeks were spent in Los Angeles at the home of transplanted Fayette friends before bussing up to San Francisco in July and returning home.

Gamber completed his own primary flight training in a Stearman PT-13B biplane at Ryan Field, a civil airport located 2.5 miles southwest of Hemet. He followed that with nine weeks of basic flight school at Lemoore Army Air Forces Field, due west of Sequoia and Kings Canyon National Parks. The 1,460-acre Lemoore Field must not have been much of a place. A 1944 U.S. Army/Navy directory of airfields describes the field as having a 6,500-foot unpaved hard-surface runway, "available only when dry." The current Lemoore Naval Air Station is a few miles north of the decommissioned Army Air Forces field.

Had Glenn Munn hung on at primary flight training, he would have found basic and advanced flight school more pleasing. Gone were the hazing and continuous threats of washing out. By this point in flight training, the army had a lot of time and money invested in cadet pilots and worked hard to keep them. Also, though the spit and polish routine remained, there was less of it because the men were expected to spend more time and effort on the practical application of flying.

In *Song of the Sky*, Guy Murchie describes flying during the 1940s as more a practical art than a theoretical science. "Although in those days the average training time before flying solo had been increased from a couple of hours to six or eight, it was still largely a practical preparation with a minimum of theoretical understanding of why and how." He goes on to recall a soloing flyer "who was unable to explain how the rudder worked." This student didn't know whether the rudder was moved by the hands or the feet but could fly well enough "without thinking, like a bird."

The focus at basic flight school was on accumulating seventy hours of flight time. Bill Gamber moved on from the Stearman to a twin-seater closed-cockpit Vultee BT-13, equipped with 484-horsepower single Pratt & Whitney R-985 radial engine, with a top speed of 156 miles per hour and a service ceiling of 16,500 feet.

Gamber would have found the Vultee a huge step up from the Stearman in maneuverability, power, and cockpit complexity. As a pilot's training progressed from primary to basic flight training and through advanced training, so did the cockpit. Guy Murchie, who came of age as a flyer in the 1930s, recognized the value of all that complexity but also resented it a bit. "There are lots of warning lights, bells, horns, and other devices in modern airplanes to tip off the pilots when gas is dangerously low, airspeed too slow, wheels not locked down for landing, a door not properly shut." Nevertheless, reliance remained on human alertness to avoid trouble. "Anyway," Murchie writes, "there is a limit to how many gadgets you can cram into a cockpit and leave peace of mind enough to fly."

Gamber likely made his first cross-country flights in the Vultee. His lessons would have included operating a two-way radio, night flying, flying blind on instruments, flying in formation, along with takeoffs and landings in formation. Safety would have been another big lesson for Gamber. "The causes of air accidents range all the way from playfulness to panic," writes Murchie, "with the biggest factor usually just human carelessness or poor judgement—often fatigue and boredom contributing."

Gamber moved on to advanced flight school at Mather Field and was assigned to seventy hours of training in the twin-engine Curtiss AT-9 "Jeep" Transition Trainer. The AT-9 was an aircraft used for teaching mastery of flying multiengine planes in formation and increasing a pilot's ability to fly on instruments at night. Larry Ball writes in *The Immortal Beech* that the AT-9 was "considered by some senior Army Air Force officers to have difficult handling characteristics similar to that of fully loaded bombers." It was additionally "unstable, tricky, and considered to be quirky in many respects," such as having "a high approach speed for such a small, relatively light twin-engine trainer." This made it ideal for teaching new pilots the coping mechanisms necessary for more demanding aircraft like P-38 fighters. The AT-9 was one hot little number, "A real pilot's airplane," according to Ball." In a letter to his parents written during advanced flight school, Gamber included a photo of the AT-9 with a caption identifying it as his favorite airplane.

On April 24, 1942, Gamber graduated in Class 42-D at the top of his class. He was then commissioned a second lieutenant and was asked to stay on at Mather Field as an instructor. The proud and happy pilot sent his wings home for his younger sister, Elvira, to wear. Congratulations poured in from family and friends, including a glowing "Salute to our Lieutenant Gamber" from Gamber's former babysitter, Mrs. Eva R. Crane. She wrote, "I am confident that while your duties will often keep you literally in the clouds, your feet will be, figuratively, on the ground. And to maintain this balance requires mental, moral and physical characteristics of superior order." Mrs. Crane also enclosed a check for "some small extravagance—perhaps a dashing necktie to go with similar dress when stepping out of official life," or, perhaps, "a good meal at some swanky place."

Lieutenant Gamber was soon flying Beech 18 AT-7s, ferrying navigation students from Mather Field, up and down the Central Valley and beyond to places like Salt Lake City, Tonopah, Arizona, and Lancaster-Palmdale in Southern California. Between April 24, when he received his twin-engine certification, and November 18, when he disappeared, Gamber racked up 505 hours in the Beech

18. In the three months leading up to the crash, Gamber spent an average of 21 hours a week flying the AT-7.

• • •

After leaving Mesa del Rey flight school on May 25, Glenn Munn was soon back in Santa Ana and entering a holding pattern as he transitioned from pilot to navigator training. He expected to be there no more than two or three months, and he loved all the free time associated with not being assigned to any particular unit or having specific assignments. His only duty was to drill freshly arrived cadets. He enjoyed this at first but the novelty wore off. With his ample free time, Munn made trips to the beach, started dating a local woman named Marilynn Dick, and spent a lot of money on having his uniforms made by a tailor in Hollywood. "The pants alone will cost about $20.00 which really knocks a hole in your pocket book," he wrote home.

Army inefficiency finally caught up to Munn in June. A cadet group he managed to join left for navigation school in Florida but, lacking papers, Munn couldn't leave with them. He was bitterly disappointed—he had seen the move to Florida as a way to visit family in Ohio along the way. Navigation classes in session at SAAAB and elsewhere were full. It appeared he wouldn't be able to leave SAAAB and continue with his lessons until September— or later. The scheduling hassles arose from a shortage of bombers to train in, "because they are sending them to the war fronts." He spent most of his time avoiding anyone who would detail him to "a lot of undesirable things."

Munn's morale suffered with the indignity of inactivity and increasing homesickness. He asked for but was refused a furlough to see his family. Due to being transferred from squadron to squadron, letters from home were lost or not delivered. "I hear about them [his letters] from different fellows but I just haven't been able to locate them myself. I spend about 2 hrs every evening checking all the squadrons for my mail. I hate to lose any mail from home."

With over a month of this, Munn's luck changed at the end of July. An opening occurred in a navigation class and he got in. "We go to school six hours a day and have two hours of drill and two hours of athletics every day." He found it difficult to "get back in the swing of going to school" after his enforced idleness. His letters are still full of discouragement at the tack his training has taken. "They certainly make life unhappy here at times."

Classes continued into August, and summer heat arrived in Santa Ana. Munn disliked the monotony of Southern California weather. "It seems funny having beautiful and endless sunshiny days." Leave days were spent at the beach with his girlfriend, his buddies, and their dates. Perhaps it was around this time that Munn had an opportunity to purchase the gold ring I saw shining in the August sun in 2007. Or, maybe it was a present from his girlfriend, Marilynn. He also took up cigarette smoking and purchased the Ronson lighter that JPAC found with his remains.

Munn studied arithmetic, algebra, geometry, solid geometry, both spherical and plane trigonometry, physics, map reading, naval identification, airplane identification, weather and meteorology, radio code, and blinker signals. All were considered preliminary training, laying groundwork for the actual subjects presented next at advanced navigation school. Perhaps reflecting the tedium of the weather, Munn began losing interest in his studies. "Navigation has its possibilities and adventures," he told his family, "but a person's enthusiasm sort of wanes with what you have to take and the way they teach it here."

Classrooms were stuffy and sleep-inducing in the summer heat. As classes began to wind down in preparation for the next phase, detail work ramped up. It was filled with, "shall we say, the more unpleasant chores." Munn was disillusioned, but philosophical: "I suppose it can't last forever. Some day, these things will probably seem quite laughable."

Expressions of homesickness were always reserved for the endings of Munn's letters. "It seems ages and ages since I have been home. I am so hungry to see dear old Ohio and home again that I hesitate to describe it." He sent his greetings to his father and three sisters and encouraged them to write as often as they could. "I enjoyed it [their letters] tremendously." He expressed remorse at not seeing his niece, Patty, who was born shortly before he left home. "I'd give almost anything just to be able to touch her once more."

Mostly Munn expresses concern for his mother. "Mother Dear, may God keep you well and happy and above all please don't work too hard and take care of yourself."

Each letter ends with, "Your loving son, Glenn."

• • •

After Glenn Munn left Mesa del Rey, Melvin Mortenson continued with primary flight school before washing out and being sent in early October to Mather Field for advanced navigator training. Munn arrived there October 9. Leo Mustonen, after first reporting to SAAAB on June 15, arrived at Mather at the same time. The alphabetically inclined army assigned the three men to be roommates and training partners. Three cadets who trained together were referred to as an "element."

Their first two weeks at Mather were as brutal as anything experienced at SAAAB, with eleven hours of school each day along with two hours of drill and athletics. "This really is a rugged life," Munn wrote. He estimated all the marching back and forth from one activity to another consumed five miles of shoe leather every day. They were up an hour before the sun to drill before going to class until noon. After lunch, more class until 5:00 P.M., followed by athletics. After that, showers and supper and nose to the grindstone for more instruction from 7:15 to 10:00 P.M.

Another cadet from the same time, William Bechter, spelled out the situation in even greater detail in his diary. "Our daily schedule is as follows: 6:20—first call; 6:30—reveille; 7:10—breakfast; 8:00 to 11:50—school; 12:00—dinner; 12:45–5:00—school; 5:10—athletics; 6:25—drill; 7:10—supper; 7:45–10:00—school; 11:00—taps!"

Though he found the physical training arduous most times, Munn understood the urgency of training for combat as well as anyone. "Please don't worry about me," he wrote his mother. "I am getting along OK. It's tough I know but I think I will be able to stand it."

As difficult as the course of study was, the boys had plenty to look forward to. Finally, after nearly a year of military life, they were all embarked on an exciting journey. At advanced navigation school they were doing what they had enlisted to do. They were flying. They were navigating. They were serving their country. Everyone knew the value of what they did and this balanced some of the trepidation they felt about what would happen once training concluded.

Eugene Fletcher unflinchingly tackles the perspective of a young man and his country committed to all-out war in his memoir, *Mister*. I asked him about being so young, living in such danger. What did they tell their parents? "We had no desire to worry the home folks. They were already apprehensive of the danger of just being in the service." Fletcher said that cadets weren't too worried about anything happening to them during training except qualifying as pilots.

Eighteen days into training, on October 26, 1942, Munn wrote, "I must tell you about my first big flight with me navigating the ship. It certainly was funny." Standard procedure was for navigators to be given their assignment, allowing ample time to plot their course. Munn had a problem though. The route that day was to fly south to San Bernardino, but fog along the entire route necessitated a change of plans. "I had to plot a new one [i.e., course] in the air, along with navigating the plane at the same time." With a million things to do, keeping on course and figuring out where to send the pilot, Munn also learned how different the high-altitude chamber test he'd taken months earlier in Santa Ana was from being in an airplane. "You would be surprised how much one's thinking power decreases at 10,000 ft. and above." The Beech 18 AT-7 he flew in that day presumably lacked supplemental oxygen.

He could, at least, still retain bragging rights about one thing. Evidently everybody had a bumpy ride that day. "About 30 Cadets in our squadron got terribly sick, we had a big laugh on them when we landed."

Despite complications involving the new course after takeoff, Munn thought he did well. Writing to his mother the following day while in class, his prose is clipped. "We flew over the snow capped

Rockies at 15000 ft. into Reno, Nevada about 600 Mile hop. I just missed my course about 5 miles, I was very lucky ... we circled the city, called the radio station there and headed home." He thought it was a good trip. "We were up for about 6 hrs, we have a twin engined trainer ship about 1500 horse power, it flies like a dream." This "dream" was the Beech 18 AT-7 Navigator.

There are some intriguing passages in Munn's letter. He says their route went over the Rockies and not the Sierra, flying for 600 miles in six hours and without stopping to refuel. Michael Kopp, a Seattle-area pilot owns a Beech 18 and has taken me flying several times and was dubious of Glenn Munn's calculations. He reminded me that the AT-7 had a fuel capacity of 206 gallons and then laid out the figures for fuel consumption during flight: 60–65 gallons per hour for takeoff and en route climbing, with 45 gallons per hour for cruising. "Thus," he told me, "typical flight duration is in the three to three and a half hour range, leaving another thirty to sixty minutes for reserve." In reading the pilot's manual for the AT-7, Kopp found that under certain situations the aircraft could be coaxed into a six-hour flight—but only if it (the aircraft) started in the air and not on the ground and, of course, that's impossible. "Fuel burn for taxi, engine run-up, takeoff, and climb would typically be 20 to 30 gallons," leaving no reserves during a six-hour flight. "I have a difficult time believing that the military would not require an adequate reserve of at least 15 to 30 gallons."

Then there is the issue of Munn's accuracy. Being off by five miles doesn't strike me as being a cause for celebrating good luck. Five miles is actually pretty sloppy, especially if you're trying to hit an island in the South Pacific. Or avoid a storm in California.

There are two other items of interest in this letter. The first is Munn's comment that "I think we will go to Salt Lake City this week, I hope we land this time, it is a pretty long jaunt and I think we will have to refuel." The shortest distance between Mather Field and Salt Lake City is still slightly more than 500 miles. If Munn suspected the Salt Lake City trip required stopping to refuel (which it does), how did he fly 600 miles in six hours without refueling in the trip he describes in the letter?

The last intriguing thing Munn wrote in this letter was that he thought the San Joaquin Valley "stretches from Northern Calif all the way down to Death Valley." But as the crow flies, Death Valley is over 150 miles east of the San Joaquin Valley. Not to mention on the other side of two tall mountains ranges, including the Sierra Nevada.

• • •

Glenn Munn's last letter home was written thirteen days before his death and is postmarked November 6, 1942. In it Munn finally articulates the dangers of what he's doing. He tells his mother about a training flight, probably his third, where he was to navigate from Mather Field to Salt Lake City. They ran into a storm over the Sierra Nevada and were turned back. "They don't like to fly over those high mountains when it is stormy, because they are afraid of downdrafts forcing the plane into a side of a mountain ... it gives one a funny feeling to be flying in a cloud with hailstones beating against the wings and windshield when you can't see ten feet ahead of you." He jokes, "Not that I was scared, but I was glad when they decided that we had better go back." He was certainly caught in a storm that hit California on November 3. In Placerville, a small town in the Sierra foothills west of Lake Tahoe, a whopping 2.33 inches of rain fell that day. Placerville would have been along their route to Salt Lake City.

Four weeks into his advanced training, and with another approximately eight more to go, Munn was again contemplating his future. Assignments after graduation were a function of "how good we are and the different demands for navigators in different branches of work." Assessing himself against the huge cohort of college educated cadets, Munn wrote, "I don't think I am smart enough to become an instructor."

Munn liked the Ferry Command, shuttling aircraft, because it would take him to further training in St. Joseph, Missouri, which was closer to home than California. That or cargo and transport, which would send him to training in South Carolina—also closer to home. Both would only be for a little while, but a few weeks or a month was better than not at all. A reluctant warrior, Munn still missed his birthplace. "Gee, I'd like to see some Ohio winters again."

Munn realized that his fate was ultimately out of his hands. "I guess I will have to go where they tell [me], this army you know, they have their own way to do everything." He suspected his actual future lay with "tactical duty," which meant Las Vegas for "six weeks gunnery training before being sent to one of the fighting fronts."

Following completion of their training, most navigators found themselves assigned to bomber crews where they were required to complete twenty-five (later in the war increased to thirty-five) missions before coming home. By war's end, the average life expectancy of a bomber and its crew was fifteen missions. Bill Davis, a classmate of Mortenson, Munn, and Mustonen, was shot down on his third mission. Leonard Spivey was shot down on his thirteenth. William Bechter, good friend to Davis and Spivey, was killed in action on his ninth mission. Survival statistics for bomber crews were grim. Spivey told me he went to England with 372 others in the 381st Bomber Group H. Of the original group, 86 completed the tour of twenty-five missions, 72 were killed in action, 185 became prisoners of war, 5 were shot down and evaded capture, and the remainder suffered wounds that prevented them from flying again. Spivey's group was part of the 350,000-strong Eighth Air Force which suffered a total of 26,000 airmen killed in action between 1942-1945.

• • •

When Marilynn Dick learned that Glenn Munn did not come home on November 18, 1942, from a training mission, she was inconsolable. She tried writing to Munn's mother several times but could never finish. Finally her own mother did the writing, two weeks after Munn's airplane went missing, full of admiration for the young man. "I can tell you this Mrs. Munn, Glenn had very fine principles."

Anna Mustonen couldn't let go of her son and wrote passionate-ly to the army to continue their search. In 1943, her husband Arvid traveled to California and met his eldest son in San Pedro where Arvo was working in the shipyards. Together they journeyed to Sacramento, rendezvousing with Joe and Mamee Munn. Their mission was to make personal inquires and convince the army to not give up. They had no success.

Only Joe Munn and Glenn's brother-in-law, Ralph Zeyer, attend-ed the 1948 army burial service for the four aviators. Anna Mustonen was still too grief-stricken to attend and Arvid stayed home with her. Ever after, Anna would always talk about her younger son and say, "He's in those mountains somewhere." When she died at age seventy-eight, grief at losing her only natural son had only deepened with time.

And so, training for World War II ended for William Gamber, John Melvin Mortenson, Glenn Munn, and Leo Mustonen on a gla-cier deep within the High Sierra. "I hope you do not feel so heart broken as I'm afraid you do," wrote Mrs. Dick to Mrs. Munn. She tried her best to offer consolation. "I wish I could say something to ease the pain that I know will be there a long time." In the end, all she could offer was a story told about a soldier in the Solomon Islands who wrote to his mother, "Pray for me constantly, not that I may return, but that I have the courage to do my duty."

CHAPTER 15

They Weren't the Only Ones

Between 1932 and 2002, forty-eight military and civilian aircraft crashed within the boundaries of Sequoia and Kings Canyon National Parks. Most involved fatalities. Not all were located quickly or easily. One airplane wasn't found for sixteen years. Two have never been found. With a range of mountains pushing nearly three miles into the sky, the High Sierra has always presented a significant challenge for air travel.

Total crash numbers for the remainder of the Sierra Nevada are sketchy, but the Air Force Rescue Coordination Center does list 177 wreckage sites between Walker Pass and Lassen Peak where debris is still present on the ground. Anthony J. Mireles, author of *Fatal Army Air Forces Aviation Accidents in the United States, 1941–1945*, counts more than 900 fatalities throughout California. Training accidents were common during World War II and could be considered a third battle front. Mireles writes that 15,530 pilots, crewmembers, and ground personnel were killed in the United States in aircraft accidents. Lieutenant Gamber and his crew were only four of them. More aircraft were lost to accidents (7,100) than were lost fighting the Japanese (4,500).

George Bibel points out in *Beyond the Black Box* that "modern airplane crashes usually result from a series of improbable, almost random events and pilot-system interactions that are difficult to predict" and that "mechanical failures are usually a series of events that never happened before." Bibel also contends that aviation accidents occur from "pilot error," though I'm reminded of a comment made to me by Lieutenant Colonel Tom Betts, a retired Air Force command pilot and crash investigator: "No pilot intends to make an error. These unintentional actions result from fatigue, a mistake, oversight, lapse in judgment, or failure to exercise due diligence— that is, failure to do everything possible to prevent a mishap."

Aviation archeologist Pat Macha says the causes of accidents include tailwinds, crosswinds, bad weather, flying at night, and maintaining radio silence. Weather is the top factor in 98 percent of the accidents he's examined. Macha attributes most World War II accidents to the times. "This was because of a massive training program, highly accelerated—taking eighteen-, nineteen-, and twenty-year-olds and rushing them through primary, basic, and advanced training." The training was rigorous. "They were not being careless about it. You still had to take so many hours of flight training, take so many tests, and you kept advancing." As pilots advanced, "the learning curve would set in and guys would stall, spin. There were midair collisions. Accidents happened with a pilot's first instrument training or during cross-country flights."

Each of the following stories of airplane crashes in and around Sequoia and Kings Canyon National Parks illustrates what could have happened to the AT-7 piloted by Lieutenant William Gamber. The individual and compounding accident factors in these cases show many similarities with the missing AT-7: a lost and off-course pilot; equipment malfunction and poor night-time navigation; an inaccurate weather report, bad weather, and faulty navigation gear; pilot inexperience and equipment failure; a pilot's inexperience coupled with unfamiliarity with geography; and, worst of all, all these factors in combination.

● ● ●

Shards of aluminum and melted beads of metal strewn across the southern slope of Panther Peak a few miles east of Moro Rock in southern Sequoia and Kings Canyon National Parks are all that's left of a Slick Airways (some sources say California Air Freight)

Curtiss-Wright C-46F-1-CU Commando that crashed at 1:30 A.M. on January 13, 1959. The plane was registered to Axxico Airlines and was en route to Seattle from the Hollywood-Burbank Airport. The pilot and copilot were killed when the C-46 flew into Panther Peak at an altitude of 8,600 feet. They were forty-five miles off course.

Designed to carry fifty passengers and a crew of four, the C-46 was initially meant for commercial, high-altitude aviation but found its greatest use during World War II as a military transport flying cargo "over the Hump" between India and China. A "tail dragger" with conventional landing gear like the Beech 18, the C-46 was ideal for its mission, flying to high-mountain, poorly developed, and frequently flooded airfields. Following the war, many C-46 aircraft, like the one that impacted with Panther Peak, were sold by the federal government to commercial operators.

The Panther Peak C-46 was the first airplane crash site I ever visited. In 1970, I'd heard about the wreck and hiked up there. To put it mildly, I was disappointed by what I didn't find—there was nothing to see. It wasn't until conducting research for *Final Flight* that I learned from aviation archeologist Pat Macha that major salvage of the wreck had occurred in the mid 1960s by someone using a portable smelter. No wonder the site was littered with aluminum marbles.

• • •

Even pilots with years of experience are not immune from accidents, as illustrated by the crash of a Douglas B-18 piloted by General Herbert Arthur "Bert" Dargue. The general's accident is a classic case of cascading incidents, where one error or mistake leads to another, culminating in disaster.

Following the Japanese attack on December 7, 1941, General Dargue was in transit to Hawaii from Mitchel Field in New York to relieve General Walter Short and assume command at Pearl Harbor. Flying up Owens Valley, Dargue crashed his B-18 above Birch Lake in the eastern Sierra, near the town of Big Pine. All eight people onboard were killed in the fiery crash. A pilot with twenty-eight years and 5,800 flying hours of experience, Dargue had begun his flight training in a 1910 Wright Model B.

Dargue's B-18 was last reported over Palmdale in the desert northeast of Los Angeles, en route to Hamilton Field, across the bay from San Francisco. How then did Dargue find himself flying northward through an overcast Owens Valley with the Sierra on his left when he should have been in the Central Valley with mountains on his right? J. J. Snyder tackles this question in the article "Dargue's Destiny," his attempt to answer the question of what went wrong the evening of December 12, 1941, when the general's plane went down.

Night air navigation in those preradar days was heavily dependent on tracking nondirectional beacons. Aerial celestial navigation was a possibility in some aircraft, but Dargue's B-18 was not equipped with a celestial dome like that found on the AT-7. Snyder hypothesizes that a communication failure involving the aircraft's radio transmitter and receiver forced the B-18 captain and navigator to rely on dead reckoning to continue the flight.

Using dead reckoning, the plane's navigator would have marked his chart with his last known position and then calculated true airspeed, course, time, and wind speed and direction. This would provide a fairly accurate, but still estimated, idea of distance traveled over time. Unfortunately, in this case their dead reckoning plot was wrong, maybe due to headwinds, and the pilot turned north too soon instead of traveling farther west. Thinking he was in the Central Valley and that the mountains were *east* of him, when Dargue encountered the Sierra Nevada he turned the wrong way, actually turning into the mountains when he thought he was turning away. As the ground rose, the general realized his mistake too late, and the B-18 flew straight into the Sierra.

Dargue was a competent and confident pilot, accustomed to flying cross-country and off established routes. Yet his accident demonstrates the dangers inherent in night flying over unfamiliar geography, of getting lost and encountering rising terrain. General Dargue's B-18 wreck was discovered the following May by the copilot's father, guided by legendary Sierra hiker, climber, and explorer, Norman Clyde.

• • •

Bad weather, an inaccurate weather report, and faulty equipment were a dangerous combination made fatal in a B-24E Liberator training mission piloted by Second Lieutenant Charles Turvey. His airplane disappeared on December 5, 1943, during a night navigation training mission that was supposed to go from Fresno's Hammer Field to Bakersfield to Tucson and back. Onboard as copilot was Second Lieutenant Robert Hester, along with a crew of four others.

With 613 flight hours, including 260 hours in the B-24, Turvey was well-versed in piloting the Liberator. He had 38 hours of night flying experience too, 7 of which were in the previous thirty days. For 1943, Turvey could be considered a highly experienced B-24 pilot.

Though the weather forecast given to Turvey mentioned a cold front moving into Northern California, no bad weather was expected along his planned route. Two weeks after the plane disappeared, investigators questioned another pilot who had been coming back from Arizona to Hammer Field at 3:00 A.M. the night Turvey and his B-24 disappeared. "Returning from San Diego that same evening," Second Lieutenant John K. Specht said, "we encountered strong winds from the northwest at 12,000 feet and we were flown about forty miles off course to the southeast." When Specht arrived at Hammer Field, it was overcast with light rain at 3,000 feet and a cloud deck of about 2,000 to 3,000 feet thick.

At 2:10 A.M., Staff Sergeant Howard Wendtake, Turvey's radio operator, transmitted his last position report: fifty miles east of Muroc (now known as Edwards Air Force Base), flying at 18,500 feet. Their heading of 280 degrees would take them south of the Sierra Nevada before they altered course to head north up the Central Valley and home. Like Specht, Turvey's crew must have encountered strong winds that blew them east, off course.

Specht's final comment to the investigators sheds some light on why one crew could be aware of these strong winds and correct for them while the other did not. "The compass radio in 463 [Turvey's

B-24] was not in very good operating condition," Specht surmised. "For a celestial mission that could have been a very good reason for them to get quite a ways off the course without realizing it." Weather crossing the Sierra would have been marginal, according to the Hammer Field weather officer: "Broken cumulus clouds, bases on the mountains, tops twenty to twenty-five thousand, visibility zero-zero in the clouds and 10 miles outside of clouds, moderate icing in clouds, moderate turbulence."

The father of Turvey's copilot was devastated by the loss of his son, Lieutenant Robert Hester. A Los Angeles resident, Clinton Hester spent the following fourteen years searching the Sierra Nevada for signs of Robert's airplane. In 1959, Hester died from a heart attack. The following summer, two U.S. Geological Survey researchers were working in a remote section of the High Sierra, west of LeConte Canyon in Sequoia and Kings Canyon National Parks. They encountered airplane wreckage in an unnamed lake and along the slopes above the lake. Army investigations revealed that the wreck belonged to Lieutenants Turvey and Hester. The missing crew had been found. This lake is now known as Hester Lake.

Another B-24 Liberator was lost during the search for Turvey and his crew. Squadron commander Captain William Darden lifted off along with eight other B-24s early in the morning of December 6, 1943. Experiencing high wind turbulence, Darden lost hydraulic pressure. Seeing what looked like a snow-covered clearing, he gave his crew the choice of bailing out or crashlanding with him. The copilot and radio operator chose to jump and survived.

Captain Darden, his airplane, and remaining crew were not seen again until 1955, when Huntington Lake reservoir was drained for repairs to the dam. It seems the "clearing" spotted by Darden was the reservoir's nearly frozen surface. The B-24 was found resting 190 feet below the reservoir's high-water mark, the five other crew members still at their stations preserved by cold water and anaerobic conditions.

The loss of both B-24s demonstrates the role of faulty equipment in causing airplane accidents. When weather is added as a factor, the crews have even more to worry about. And like the loss of General Dargue in 1941, night flying adds further navigational challenges.

• • •

When Leo Mustonen was first found, many people were amazed that human remains and an entire airplane had been hidden in the mountains for so long. But the Sierra Nevada is a big place. It took twelve years for Captain Darden's and sixteen years for Lieutenant Turvey's B-24s to be found, and another military airplane is still missing.

On May 9, 1957, First Lieutenant David Steeves left Hamilton Air Force Base in Marin County, north of San Francisco, en route to Luke Air Force Base near Phoenix to ferry a Lockheed T-33A T-Bird to Craig Air Force Base in Alabama. The T-33 is a two-seat jet trainer first flown in 1948. It saw combat service in Korea but quickly evolving designs made the straight-winged T-33 inferior to swept-wing aircraft, so it assumed new functions like teaching propeller-trained pilots to fly jets.

Steeves received his pilot rating on June 15, 1955, and with 914:45 flight hours, over half in jets, the twenty-three-year-old lieutenant was considered experienced enough to fly the T-33 solo. In 1942, William Gamber had built up two-thirds the flying time as Steeves and in half the time.

At 11:20 A.M., within thirty-five minutes of takeoff and approximately sixty-seven miles from the base, flying at 33,500 feet over the Sierra Nevada on a course for Bakersfield, Steeves felt an explosion. He blacked out and the T-33 continued in flight, angling earthward. At about 5,000 feet, the pilot regained consciousness just in time to comprehend his predicament. He ejected, landing harshly in the rock- and snowbound High Sierra somewhere in or around Dusy Basin—a few miles east of Hester Lake. Both his ankles were severely injured and Steeves was unable to walk for several days.

Bundled in his parachute, the lieutenant spent four freezing days and nights awaiting rescue. When it didn't come, Steeves set out to save himself. He spent fifteen foodless days dropping 6,000 snowy feet into forested LeConte Canyon until, some twenty miles from Dusy Basin, he reached the Simpson Meadow Ranger Station alongside the Middle Fork Kings River. There he found tools and, more importantly, a small food cache and a map. He now knew where he was. After days of bad weather, the lieutenant continued hiking downriver in hopes of reaching Hume Lake. He failed, halted by a deep gorge, and returned to Simpson Meadow. With food from the cache dwindling, Steeves attempted to hike out over Granite Pass, succeeding on this second try. It was July 1 and he'd been gone for fifty-three days.

The survival story of Lieutenant David Steeves is a triumph of will, youth, and vigor. The twenty-three-year-old pilot lost forty pounds during his ordeal. Newspaper photographs show a thin face with hollowed eyes and a big bushy beard. In photographs taken a month later for *Life*, a debonair Steeves poses beside his Jaguar convertible. He's at the top of the world with television appearances, reporters clamoring for interviews, and a book contract. Not many people survive airplane crashes in the Sierra, and Steeves is probably the only pilot who has ever self-rescued. It's a happy story with a cruel ending.

Spurred on by a *Saturday Evening Post* article, the popular idea soon developed that Steeves had spent his time, not trying to survive a High Sierra mountain winter, but hiding in Mexico after first selling his airplane to the Soviets. For one thing there was that *Life Magazine* photo of Steeves with his Jaguar. It also didn't help that not a trace of the lieutenant's aircraft could be found.

In 1977, some Boy Scouts from Southern California were backpacking in Dusy Basin. There they chanced upon cockpit pieces from a T-33 and they reported their discovery to the rangers. Newspapers recorded their find. A few freelance magazine writers wrote a feature or two, exonerating Steeves. The gist was, well, well, well—he wasn't really a Soviet agent after all. By then it was too late to do anything for the reputation of David Steeves.

In late 1957, tired of the negative attention, Steeves left the air force. He hoped he would leave the scandal behind as well. Steeves continued to fly and eventually was killed, along with his passenger, in an October 16, 1965, crash in Boise, Idaho, when his Stinson V-77 collided with the ground. At the time, David A. Steeves was thirty-one years old.

. . .

Military pilots are not the only ones to leave their aircraft in pieces on the ground within the High Sierra. The Sequoia and Kings Canyon National Parks database of airplane wrecks includes at least twenty-three civilian airplanes. Ten of them are in a small region bounded by Center Basin, Forester Pass, and Vidette Meadow in the upper Bubbs Creek area. There is a very good reason why so many pilots end up here. They all made the same navigation mistake. Sequoia and Kings Canyon have also seen many private pilots defeated by high mountains, poor planning, inexperience, bad weather, treacherous winds, and just plain bad luck.

Crossing the eastern crest of the High Sierra is a dangerous proposition even for experienced pilots. As the sun heats the mountains, updrafts and downdrafts along with extreme turbulence are common. Winds along the crest can be fierce as well. In September 2008, I had an opportunity to fly out of Bishop to investigate Mendel Cirque from the air. Steve Ivey, a longtime pilot with several thousand hours of flight experience, has made the crossing from Owens Valley to central California scores of times. Nevertheless, he insisted we meet at dawn, when the atmosphere would be most settled. He had no plans to take any chances. As Ivey circled over Mount Mendel, I took photographs. An hour later, as we began our homeward approach and crossed the Sierra crest eastward above Piute Pass, the air was bumpy enough that we were bounced around like a couple of dice.

The dangers of mountain flying are acute for small aircraft, and pilots must perform special flying techniques to remain safe. As the next story demonstrates, it's easy for a pilot to become geographically challenged when flying *through* the mountains rather than *over* them. There is also the danger of the ground rising beneath an airplane even though the pilot is flying level.

. . .

Lauren Elder didn't know anything about the dangers of mountain flying on April 26, 1976, when she was invited to fly in a Cessna 182P from Oakland to Furnace Creek in Death Valley National Monument. The 182 is a four-seat, single-engine airplane with an ample baggage compartment. Besides the pilot, Jay Fuller, and Elder, coming along was the pilot's girlfriend, Jean Noller. Elder slipped into the back of the airplane for the flight and had plenty of room to slide back and forth from side to side, taking photos and admiring California from the air.

Acquainted with the forecast for strong northerly winds, and getting a late start, pilot-in-command Jay Fuller headed east at around 3,500 feet. After crossing above Fresno at 9,000 feet, Fuller probably angled east to meet the Middle Fork Kings River and fly up Bubbs Creek in Sequoia and Kings Canyon National Park. The pilot's target for crossing the Sierra was Kearsarge Pass (12,598 feet). The pass is high and wide. Many small-airplane pilots like flying over Kearsarge for that reason—there's room to move.

Following FAA directives for high-altitude flying, Fuller kept the Cessna below 12,500 feet. The rules state that pilots flying longer than thirty minutes above 12,500 feet must use supplemental oxygen. Above 14,000 feet, supplemental oxygen must be used at all times by pilot and passengers. The FAA recognizes the danger of flying too long without enough oxygen to breathe. In "Advisory Circular 61-107," the FAA estimates that if a person is sitting quietly, the time of useful consciousness for a person at 22,000 feet is ten minutes. This drops to five minutes during moderate activity. These numbers drop further to less than two minutes at an altitude of 30,000 feet.

During preflight training, Glenn Munn spent time in a barometric chamber that simulated high altitude. He wrote home that he suffered no ill effects. Real life was much different, and during his first flight above 10,000 feet Munn lacked supplemental oxygen and experienced difficulties in thinking. This problem is duplicated in airplanes like Jay Fuller's Cessna 182 because they are not pressurized and don't always carry supplemental oxygen. Pilots flying at high altitudes in such aircraft therefore risk succumbing to hypoxia.

George Bibel explains in *Beyond the Black Box* that "hypoxia can be defined as insufficient oxygen being supplied to tissues for their physiological needs, despite an adequate supply of blood." Hypoxia is not caused by a lack of oxygen; if it were, the body's ventilation system could compensate with an accelerated breathing rate. "Hypoxia is actually caused by an insufficient oxygen pressure to adequately drive the diffusion mechanisms of oxygen across the tissue in lungs."

Hikers at high elevations don't suffer hypoxia because they have taken a longer time to get that high—they have acclimatized. In order to cross the Sierra at Kearsarge Pass, Fuller had to sustain an altitude of 12,598 feet (the height of Kearsarge Pass), plus a cushion of air space to remain above the highest visible object. The FAA recommends that cushion be 2,000 feet above ground level. The aeronautical chart for that area shows the highest points around Kearsarge Pass as an unnamed peak (13,977 feet) and Mount Williamson (14,432 feet). Fuller should have been flying at over 16,000 feet.

By choosing the keep the Cessna below 12,500 feet, when Fuller entered the mountains he found himself flying below high peaks and within canyon walls. That can be dangerous because, in a canyon, there might not be enough room to turn around, and terrain can rise faster than an airplane can climb. Rising terrain is a serious issue when flying an airplane like the Cessna, whose climb performance degrades with increased altitudes. The aeronautical chart for this region clearly states in the area leading up to Kearsarge Pass: "CAUTION—RAPIDLY RISING TERRAIN."

Understanding rising terrain is easy. There you are, leaving your home airport at sea level, climbing to and flying at a constant altitude of 12,000 feet, heading into the mountains. But as you travel on your course, the mountains begin to rise beneath you. Soon, though you haven't changed your altitude, the ground below is no longer so far below. What was a 12,000-foot cushion at takeoff is now an uncomfortable and insignificant amount of space underneath and alongside your airplane.

The issue of flying among the peaks is compounded by the lack of atmosphere at 12,000 feet. Less oxygen for the pilot also means less oxygen for the engine. In turn this means less fuel is burned, producing less power. Less engine power equates to less engine performance. This equates to less power when you really need it—like when that wall of cumulo-granite makes its appearance.

An unseasoned mountain flyer could be easily confused as to the proper route through Bubbs Creek. From the ground, and with a topographic map, the way is plain. Moving up this major tributary of the South Fork Kings River, the way to Kearsarge Pass follows a little glacial bump to the east, which becomes the obvious path of least resistance. From the air, this isn't quite so obvious. The route is left, to the east, but it involves a sudden, steep climb. On the other hand, continuing up Bubbs Creek feels like the proper route. The creek goes on, bending to the southeast, in an inviting and wide, classic U-shaped glacial canyon. It sucks you in, it's so inviting. And at its head is a low spot that just might be Kearsarge Pass—if you didn't know any better and weren't paying attention to your altimeter. But the Bubbs Creek glacial canyon ends with a bang: a basin with rapidly rising terrain rimmed by a high ridge and three peaks that exceed 13,000 feet: Mount Bradley (13,289 feet), Mount Keith (13,977 feet), and Junction Peak (13,888 feet). It's a classic box canyon.

In Lauren Elder's book about her experience, *And I Alone Survived*, she clearly says that Jay Fuller knew what he was doing. Following good rules of navigation by pilotage, he flew with an aeronautical chart on his lap, checking off landmarks as he flew over them. He knew his target. He knew he had to fly high but was not worried by the altitude because it would be "no more than ten or fifteen minutes" before coming back down again. The thirty-six-year-old Fuller had 213 hours of flight time under his belt, including forty-six in the Cessna 182P. He performed confidently and Elder expresses freedom from doubt in his abilities.

Fuller was also aware of updrafts and downdrafts when crossing the Sierra. Had he been where he thought he was, Kearsarge Pass, Fuller would have squeaked over the crest with about 200 feet to spare at the altitude he was flying at when he crashed in Center Basin. But he wasn't where he thought he was and, approaching the crest, Fuller was flying too low. "Hang on," he told his passengers.

"You're going to feel a big jolt as we clear the crest. We'll drop with the air currents." That assurance was the last thing Lauren Elder heard before the accident. They were fifteen feet too short.

The rest of the story is tragic and grievous. The front section of the Cessna absorbed nearly all the airplane's forward momentum. Fuller's girlfriend was severally injured in the accident. She survived the crash but soon died of her injuries. After hanging on throughout a subfreezing night, Fuller died from internal bleeding. Elder was able to make her way down from the High Sierra to Owens Valley and Highway 395. More than thirty-four hours after leaving Oakland, her ordeal was over.

• • •

Each of these airplane accidents in the general vicinity of Darwin Canyon and Mendel Glacier has something to teach about what conditions may have contributed to Lieutenant Gamber's final flight. Being lost or off course, equipment malfunction, poor navigation, inaccurate weather reports, bad weather, and pilot inexperience with mountain flying demonstrate that what happened on November 18, 1942, was not an isolated case. Another crash is even more eerily parallel, because it happened in the area where the AT-7 was found. At about 4:30 P.M. on October 23, 1983, a twin-seat, dual-engine, turboprop, U.S. Navy OV-10 Bronco BU 155444 found its way into the Sierra Nevada. Traveling up the South Fork San Joaquin River, the two pilots entered Evolution Valley. For some reason they turned their craft from Evolution Valley to the narrower Darwin Canyon.

By chance, David Evans, Ken Hoffman, and Jim Angione were there to witness what happened next. They had climbed Mount Darwin that day and were camped a few hundred feet below Lamarck Col, cooking dinner, when they heard the sound of an airplane coming up-canyon. The weather was deteriorating, with snow flurries and a steady wind. "We all stood up to investigate and sure enough we spotted the plane very low in the canyon making the turn around Mendel," Evans told me. "The plane sounded like it was struggling. The engines just didn't quite sound right."

Suddenly the three mountaineers realized the Bronco was approaching the dead end of Darwin Canyon and there wasn't room for the airplane to turn around. "The bottom of the canyon was getting closer and closer and the plane was barely climbing." From their vantage point the plane was nearly at the climbers' same elevation. A Bronco has a climb rate of 2,600 feet per minute and can climb as high as 30,000 feet. Unfortunately, the pilots were apparently dealing with mechanical problems, which precluded their craft from performing correctly.

The issue of rising terrain, so instrumental in Jay Fuller's Cessna crash in Center Basin, is equally apropos here. But it isn't quite the same. Fuller had an aircraft performing at its optimum. As witnesses to the Bronco crash realized, the airplane was not functioning properly. Under normal circumstances, it would have been fine.

The Bronco barely cleared a cliff band below a tarn on Darwin Cirque's north side. Evans says it was still climbing when they "heard an explosion or two and the two guys ejected, shooting straight up quite a way into the air. One fellow's chute instantly tangled up in his seat and he dropped to the glacier like a rock from what looked like at least a hundred feet in the air." Wind caught the other man's parachute and carried him up the glacier a few hundred feet. He experienced a rough landing and was dragged along the ground for several hundred feet." The plane dropped straight down and completely disintegrated upon impact," Evans told me.

The three men hurried back to their camp and turned off their stove. They quickly changed into boots and grabbed what little emergency equipment they had, preparing to drop back down into Darwin Canyon and climb steep talus to Darwin Glacier. It would take them the better part of an hour to get there. Already it was late and the sun would be down awfully soon. They had to make time. And fast!

"Before we had gone more than a hundred yards or so we heard yelling from across the way." Two climbers who had summited Mount Mendel that day called across the canyon for Evans and his two friends to hike out and report the crash. They would stay with the injured pilot. "The other guy was clearly dead."

Evans and his two companions hurried out of the wilderness, arriving at the sheriff's office in Bishop around 10:30 P.M. "He made some calls and found that there was a plane reported missing from the base near Lemoore Naval Air Station," Evans remembers. At 5:30 A.M. the next day, Evans met a navy doctor, nurse, and two soldiers at Bishop Airport and guided a helicopter to the Darwin Glacier crash site. "The plane was so totaled that the biggest piece I saw was a section of the wiring harness."

More than any other aircraft accident in the High Sierra, the circumstances of the OV-10 Bronco crash parallel what could have happened in 1942 to Gamber and his crew. Evans described a doomed airplane with engine problems encountering rising terrain in Darwin Canyon. Just past Mendel Glacier, the pilot attempted a right-hand turn, saw he wouldn't make it, and ejected along with his copilot. The aircraft crashed near some tarns below Darwin Glacier.

The maneuver the Bronco pilot attempted is called a steep turn and is an accepted technique for making a canyon turnaround. The pilot banks the airplane at an angle exceeding twenty-five degrees. Lift and drag increase while turning. Speed decreases. It's essential for the pilot to pull back on the stick and increase his throttle to maintain proper attitude and speed.

Banking as steeply as forty-five degrees or more is known as a box canyon turn, according to Sparky Imeson, who writes about it in *The Shirt Pocket Mountain Flying Guide*. "Regardless of the distractions [beautiful scenery, engine problem, downdrafts, turbulence, or whatever] you must always adhere to the basic premises [of flying]. In doing so you will never be in a position where the box canyon turn is required." Any amount of skill or airplane design technology isn't going to help a pilot turn if there isn't enough space.

I was unable to locate the surviving pilot, and the navy's accident report was so heavily redacted it was useless for my purposes. All I knew for sure was that the Bronco's maneuvers were outside the ability of a Beech 18.

• • •

Each of the preceding stories contains an element of what might have brought Lieutenant Gamber's AT-7 down in the High Sierra. What we know about geology and glaciers explains why Leo Mustonen and Glenn Munn appeared in Mendel Glacier when they did. History tells us of the efforts made to bring these young men home when the crash site was first found in 1947. Personal tragedy explains the lack of follow-through. Wilderness explains how the remoteness of the area contributed to so few people exploring the crash site over the next sixty years. All that is left to understand, before speculating on a reconstruction of what happened on November 18, 1942, is the weather.

CHAPTER 16

It Rained Cats and Dogs All Day

In letters written to his mother, Glenn Munn decried Santa Ana's monotonous sunny summer days with the pain of a boy raised in Ohio's green spring and summer seasons. But hidden behind California's mythic hearty, healthy, wholesome, salubrious climate are orographic and geographic variability contributing to some of the most dynamic weather in western North America. One August in 1982 I left home in Arcata, on California's north coast, in a heavy fog with my thermometer pegged at 40 degrees. A few hours later I drove into the town of Williams, in the Central Valley foothills. The temperature was pushing 105 and it wasn't even the hottest time of day yet. Climate involves long-term records, trends, and averages. Weather is the day-to-day experience. Or, as Mark Twain supposedly said, "Climate is what you expect, weather is what you get."

Weather reports from the 1942 and 1947 army accident reports were in opposition. One predicted no severe weather, and the other pointed to extreme weather as a possible cause of the crash. In order to reconcile conflicts about the weather, I needed to understand some weather basics. That way I could determine what pilots faced in 1942 and what could lead to inaccurate forecasts.

• • •

Heated air expands and rises and has less pressure than cold air, which sinks and compresses. This pattern of circulation can be seen with boiling water in a pot. Hot water rises in bubbles, or cells, from the bottom of the pot to the top. There, it spreads across the surface, cools, and sinks along the sides of the pot to the bottom, where this process of convection begins over again.

Clouds consist of water droplets. A given volume of warm air is capable of containing more water vapor than in the same volume of cooler air. Dew point is reached when air cools enough that water vapor condenses. We see dew above the surface as clouds. Dew at the surface is formed when the ground is cooler than the surrounding air. There are many reasons for precipitation, but it's easiest to think of it as occurring when clouds can no longer hold water vapor against the pull of gravity.

Frost occurs when water vapor comes in contact with objects cooled below freezing. These objects can be the ground, trees, cars, whatever. When frost forms on an airplane wing, it's called icing, and while this can occur at higher altitudes, as long as there is moisture and temperatures are cold enough, icing can occur at low altitudes as well. The problem with icing is that it deforms wing shape and decreases that wing's ability to create lift. Enough wing deformation can lead to zero lift. Lift is what keeps the airplane in the air. Propellers are actually long, narrow, wings spinning around and around. If frost forms on the propeller, the blade cannot spin efficiently and the plane loses power.

As Glenn Munn observed in a letter to his mother on October 26, 1942, between early November and late March, California's Central Valley experiences long periods of a deep and widespread fog called Tule fog. Visibility often drops to as little as ten feet. When I attended UC Davis, west of Sacramento, I recall weeks of fog so thick it was too dangerous to ride my bike—from my fifth-floor dorm room I could not see the ground.

• • •

The Sierra is an effective moisture barrier, creating a rain shadow for the Owens Valley and White Mountains and causing deserts to the east. Winter storms stall at the crest; the east side can be experiencing clear skies while the west side is getting hammered.

In summer, as hot, moist, air rises and cools over the Sierra, the water in that air condenses and forms clouds. This accounts for late-afternoon cloud building in the Sierra and summer afternoon thunderstorms. Huge updrafts and downdrafts are associated with thunderstorms, along with windy conditions and lightning—sometimes, even rain. Thunderstorms are dangerous conditions for airplanes.

All this air moving around from side to side and up and down causes turbulence, especially where there are mountains. Picture an air mass as a river, flowing placidly along. When the flow encounters a rock, surface and subsurface waves are created, forming eddies and swirls of turbulence. All of a sudden, the river flows over a sharp edge, forming a waterfall and the water splinters into chaos and spray as it falls. Downstream, all the water coalesces and the river again flows placidly along. Air does pretty much the same thing as it flows over plains, valleys, and mountains.

• • •

Weather worries increase with mountain flying. Aviators must contend with variable wind speeds, crosswinds, updrafts and downdrafts, wind shear, turbulence, and electrical storms. All are pretty bad weather factors, one at a time, but in thunderstorms they appear all together—which is why thunderstorms are avoided. Any bad weather Lieutenant Gamber experienced on November 18, 1942, would have concerned him. But his biggest concerns that day just might have been phenomena that weren't described by science until after World War II—the laminar air flow that accounts for mountain waves and atmospheric rotors.

Mountain waves are incredibly dangerous weather events that regularly form on the lee side of mountains. In the Sierra, they're formed as air is pushed up the gentle windward west slope of the range and over the crest. Once on the other side, the air mass is pulled by gravity down the steep eastern face, generating waves, spatial and temporal changes of upper-level wind speed and direction, severe updrafts and downdrafts, turbulence, and horizontal tornado-like clouds called rotors—just like a waterfall flowing over a rock or a cliff.

Updrafts and downdrafts in a mountain wave can exceed 2,000 feet per minute, horizontal wind speeds can reach forty miles per hour or greater, and the wave train may extend 100 miles or more downwind. Condensation at the crest of these standing waves produces lens-shaped, lenticular, clouds. Lenticular clouds remain fixed in position relative to the obstruction responsible for their formation, unlike run-of-the-mill powder-puff clouds hurriedly scurrying across the sky. It's cold in lenticular clouds too, with wing icing at the top of the clouds and in rotors, creating serious hazards for pilots.

To visualize mountain waves it's helpful to return to the river analogy. With no obstructions, a laminar flow of water moves smoothly downstream. There are parallel layers of water moving at varying speeds (slow at the bottom and fast at the surface), but the whole mass essentially moves together. If an underwater barrier interrupts the flow, a series of standing waves appear on the surface. The larger that barrier, the larger the waves. The sharper the fall on the lee side of the barrier, the taller and more turbulent the wave. This same thing happens when a laminar flow of air encounters a tall barrier like the Sierra Nevada. Extending the analogy to the ocean, mountain waves range in size and severity from gentle swells to a storming colossus.

The laminar flow of a mountain wave breaks just like ocean waves crashing on the beach. When this occurs, atmospheric rotors, or roll clouds, are produced. These rotors are intense, low-level, horizontal tornados found parallel and downstream of mountain ridges. They range in height from 12,000 feet above the surface to the surface itself. Along the eastern crest of the Sierra, researchers at the Terrain-Induced Rotor Experiment (T-REX) report that these breaking waves are most prevalent in March and April, though they can occur any time of year when atmospheric conditions are right. Rotors are always associated with mountain waves, usually found in the trough of the first wave. They can generate so much turbulence that a pilot can easily lose control of his aircraft. Engines, wings, and other essential parts have been ripped off airplanes by these winds.

An Evergreen International Airlines Boeing 747 cargo jet near Anchorage, Alaska, in 1993 suffered in-flight separation of an engine due to wave turbulence. Citing other historical convergences between mountain waves and aircraft, T-REX researchers point to 1966, when 124 people on BOAC Flight 911 were killed after their Boeing 707 was ripped apart by a mountain wave as the craft flew near Mount Fuji in Japan. A Fairchild F-27B lost parts of its wings and empennage to a mountain wave in 1968, and a Douglas DC-8 lost an engine and wing tip in 1992 in a wave-related accident. Meteorological conditions surrounding the Paradise Airline N86504 crash of March 1, 1964, in the Lake Tahoe area suggest that a mountain wave was involved.

Glider pilots based in Bishop on the east side of the Sierra did the initial exploratory and research work on mountain waves in the late 1940s and early 1950s with the U.S. Air Force–sponsored Sierra Wave Project. An indication of how much lift exists in a mountain wave can be seen by the altitude records reached by Wave Project scientists. In 1948, Paul MacCready sailed his glider to 27,500 feet, climbing at the amazing rate of 2,000 feet a minute. John Robinson rode mountain wave updrafts to 33,500 feet on New Year's Day, 1949. In late 1951, pilots Dr. Joachim Kuettner and Larry Edgar sailed their Pratt-Read glider to 40,000 feet, climbing at an astounding 2,500 feet a minute. On March 19, 1952, Edgar joined Harold Klieforth to achieve a record of 44,255 feet.

Today, it's well understood among meteorologists, and among pilots who frequent the Owens Valley, that large-amplitude mountain waves and strong rotors are formed by the steep topography of the Sierra Nevada. This was not known in 1942, even though mountain waves were discovered in 1933 by two German glider pilots, Hans Deutschmann and Wolf Hirth, when they were flying above the Riesengebirge between the (now) Czech Republic and Poland. Deutschmann and Hirth and subsequent glider pilots experienced these atmospheric events, but science had yet to describe them.

What is it like to fly through a mountain wave and rotor? Simply horrible if you're prepared. And if you have no idea what's happening, as violent an epic as ever befell Odysseus. Without knowing he was experiencing a mountain wave, Antoine Saint-Exupéry described it in 1945 as "brutal and overwhelming." He was afraid of piling too many adjectives together and then being accused of "an embarrassing taste for exaggeration." In *Wind, Sand and Stars* he writes that "very soon came a slight tremor," and then all movement stopped except for a shivering in the aircraft. His engines screamed at maximum power, but Saint-Exupéry remained exactly in place in the sky, almost as if surfing an upstream wave. The danger was immediately apparent and "for the first time I understood the cause of certain accidents in the mountains when no fog was present to explain them." Stationary as he was, suddenly his plane lifted 1,500 feet straight up, as on an elevator. For the first time in his flying life, he says, "I began to worry about the strength of my wings." A moment later his ship was broadsided by a gust of wind and spit out to sea "by a monstrous cough, vomited ... as from the mouth of a howitzer."

• • •

On November 20, 1942, two days after the AT-7 disappeared, Mather Field base commander Colonel L. R. Hewitt sent a teletype to U.S. Army Air Forces headquarters in Washington DC. Beside reviewing who the missing crewmembers were, he gave a weather synopsis.

WEATHER OVER ROUTE AT 14:30Z [6:30 A.M.] CONTACT 2000 TP. 4000 FT CEILING MATHER TO STOCKTON. 5000 TO 7000 FT FROM STOCKTON SOUTH. VISIBILITY 3 TO 4 MILES AT STOCKTON; UNLIMITED REST OF ROUTE. 2000 TO 3000 FT. CLEARING IN VICINITY OF RED BLUFF WITH BROKEN CLOUDS AND OCCASIONAL LIGHT RAIN ALONG ROUTE BEFORE 1700Z [9:00 A.M.]. NO WORD RECEIVED. SENDING SEARCH MISSIONS.

It wasn't the best weather in the world for a scenic flight, but there is nothing in the telegram suggesting anything a pilot with Lieutenant Gamber's experience couldn't handle. On the other hand, I have the diary entries for that week by William Bechter, the cadet one class ahead of John Mortenson, Glenn Munn, and Leo

Mustonen. On November 16, Bechter wrote, "I'm afraid we will not fly tomorrow, for the wind & rain are howling outside tonight almost as bad as the weather used to shriek back in Nebraska." It must have been a serious storm because he wrote the following day, "It rained cats & dogs all day (you could see the 'poodles' on the streets). Our flight was of course canceled." The next day, the eighteenth, Bechter wrote, "We flew part of an interception mission this morning but had to turn back short of the goal because we ran into a bad storm and low ceilings."

The contradiction between Bechter's journal and what Colonel Hewitt telegraphed was very unsatisfying. Newspapers from that week convinced me that the colonel's weather report had, well, inconsistencies. There had been wet weather throughout the state several days before the eighteenth, and more importantly, an extreme weather event had hit not only California but the entire West Coast that day.

My friend Frank Glick, chief of the geology section of California's Department of Water Resources, looked at old weather records for me and verified Bechter's journal entry, telling me that Sacramento on the seventeenth had nearly an inch of rain. But Frank wasn't too impressed with the amount. "One inch of rain isn't all that much," he said, adding that "I think we get several one-inch events each year." The day Gamber and the AT-7 disappeared, Sacramento had 0.04 inch of rain—hardly anything at all.

The reason for this rainfall distribution has to do with geography. Sacramento and Mather Field are located smack-dab in the middle of the Central Valley. For simplicity, I've been referring to the Central Valley as one distinct geographical entity. But it's actually two separate valleys. North of Stockton is the Sacramento Valley and south is the San Joaquin Valley. Their rivers meet at Suisun Bay and flow as one into San Francisco Bay through Carquinez Strait. For as close as they are, the two valleys have different weather. This reflects the great geographical variability of California, also its size. The state spans 800 miles north to south, more than eleven degrees of latitude.

In Redding and Red Bluff, at its northern extreme, Sacramento Valley gets precipitation as much as a full day earlier than Fresno near the southern end of San Joaquin Valley. For instance, on November 17, Red Bluff received 1.8 inches of rain and Sacramento 0.92 inch, while to the south Modesto got 0.1 inch and Fresno got nothing. The following day, when Gamber was flying into the wild, Sacramento and Red Bluff had hardly a trace of rain. To the south, Modesto got 0.42 inch and Fresno got 0.29 inch.

To the east, the Sierra Nevada was being hammered with rain and snow on both days. The foothill town of Placerville, east of Sacramento, received 2.04 inches of rain on the seventeenth and 3.13 inches on the eighteenth. Other foothill towns got significant precipitation on the seventeenth and eighteenth. Nevada City received 2.85 inches and 3.21 inches respectively, with 0.94 inch and 2.6 inches falling in Grass Valley.

Reviewing the rainfall timing and amounts, Frank Glick saw a typical California precipitation pattern. "My interpretation of the data is that a storm moved across California on November seventeenth and eighteenth." Following that typical pattern, the highest amount of rain in the Central Valley occurred on the seventeenth in the north and on the eighteenth in the south. Frank also reminded me that "when there is rain in these valley towns, there is certainly bad weather in the High Sierra."

The *Reno Evening Gazette* bolstered Frank's interpretation. Farther up in the mountains on November 18, Rubicon Point at Lake Tahoe got 4 inches of snow. West of Lake Tahoe, Yuba Pass got buried in 16 inches of snow. Farther north, the Lassen Peak Highway was closed by "a severe storm which began" four days earlier, dumping three feet of snow.

In Reno, normally a dry place in the Sierra rain shadow, 0.43 inch of rain fell on the eighteenth. Carson City, less than an hour south of Reno, experienced a deluge and by the next day had accumulated 2.65 inches of rain. That same day, Winnemucca, 170 desert miles northeast of Reno, culminated five days of stormy weather with an almost unheard-of rainfall total of 1.13 inches.

Every record I found between November 18 and 19 was diametrically opposed to the weather report Colonel Hewitt and his staff submitted to their superiors in Washington DC two days after the accident. Not until I saw a copy of climatological data prepared by the U.S. Weather Bureau did I have an inkling of why. Between those dates, as the Sierra Nevada was receiving record rain and snow, the Central Valley and Sacramento were relatively dry. Whoever wrote the Army report at Mather Field in 1942 had not been a meteorologist. That person likely assumed that weather throughout California was consistent from place to place, not knowing how stormy the Sierra could be when out the window was clear blue sky.

The route described in the 1942 army accident report said that Gamber was flying south from Mather Field to Los Banos, and then turning around and heading north to Corning before turning back south to return to Mather. Plotting rainfall for November 18, 1942, onto a map of California, I could see that this route would not encounter any severe weather hazards. But flying anywhere around or over the Sierra would have. All of a sudden, the timing of the storm became very important to me because I felt confident that nobody at Mather Field would have let a training mission leave the area if they suspected bad weather anywhere along the route.

I turned to Eugene Fletcher to explain how Gamber would have been allowed to fly in bad weather when he lacked IFR, or instrument fight rules, experience. Fletcher flew thirty-five B-17 combat missions during the war and wrote about that experience as well as his pilot training in *Mister* and *Fletcher's Gang*. "It is true that he would not be overly proficient in instrument flying," Fletcher told me, "but he did know the basics and he should be able to keep his aircraft aloft and flying. However, his navigational skills may not have been all that great, and with the fledgling navigators on board it may have been the blind leading the blind."

Pilot certification for instrument flying worked like this. "When Lieutenant Gamber graduated from instrument training he was given a 'white card' saying he was cleared to fly under IFR conditions," Fletcher said. However, "He could not clear himself to take off under IFR conditions. Only those who possessed a 'green card' could act as their own clearing authority. To receive the green card required a certain number of hours of actual instrument flying plus some other requirements."

Somebody carrying a white card could not take off under IFR conditions unless they were cleared by someone else who had a green card. That meant somebody such as the director of flying, operations officer, or squadron commander had given the go ahead. "But since they have authorized the flight," Fletcher continued, "they are also very particular about how this authority is used and would not do this lightly." Of course this could have proved irrelevant too, because as Fletcher reminded me, "The weather could change after the flight took off." In that event, though, Fletcher is sure that a change from visual to instrument flight rules conditions would have prompted a radio call home for Gamber.

What I didn't understand was how Cadet Bechter's pilot could turn around in bad weather without Gamber doing the same thing. Two weeks after her son disappeared, Mamee Munn got a letter from Jessie Dick, the mother of Glenn's Santa Ana girlfriend, Marilynn. "I understand seven planes left on their assignment. They ran into a storm, two planes continued, while five turned back." Whatever happened to the other pilot and crew, they apparently got home in good shape, because no record exists of two planes being lost that day. Surely, if Gamber hit bad weather he would have turned around too. He might even have sent a radio message to Mather Field, though no such transmission is noted in the army's 1942 accident report. And if his radio malfunctioned, just as surely I thought the lieutenant would have landed at any number of Army Air Forces auxiliary fields to have it fixed. I now realized that not only was the timing of the November 18 storm important, so was Gamber's route. What had kept Gamber from turning around? Had he *not* encountered bad weather?

• • •

On the advice of Frank Glick, I spoke with Dr. Laura Edwards at the Desert Research Institute in Reno and her colleague Dr. John Lewis. Her research focus is on measuring regional climate change and variability, including trends and extremes, while Lewis is interested in combining the subjective and objective components of meteorology to produce synoptic weather analysis and predictions.

Edwards interpreted contemporary weather maps and gave me further evidence contradicting the weather forecast from Mather

Field. "It appears that a frontal passage occurred about the time the pilot took off from Mather. Assuming he went south first, it is possible that he was ahead of the front for a time. The surface winds are not exceptionally strong, only about 20 to 25 knots from the southeast ahead of the front and about 5 to 10 knots from the northwest behind it." She thought conditions were ripe, though for "strong upper-level winds."

Next, she turned to cloud cover, saying that poor visibility should be factored into any crash scenario. "On the November 18 map, precipitation is falling ahead of the front and it's mostly cloudy to overcast in Fresno and Reno, with partly cloudy skies in Tonopah." Not only that, it was cold. "Reno reported thirty-six degrees Fahrenheit the next day. Supercooled water in the clouds over the Sierra Nevada may have been another factor," raising the possibility of wing icing and loss of control of the aircraft.

The assumption by the army in 1947 was that Gamber was lost and somehow drifted east of his route, across the Sierra Nevada, in bad weather with zero visibility. Laura Edwards broached the idea that on such a west-to-east flight from the Central Valley over the Sierra to Owens Valley Gamber might have been flying below the cloud deck and in the clear. "I know that bush pilots in Alaska fly within sight of the ground, which leads to pretty low flying in river canyons during inclement weather." She pointed to the steepness of Evolution Valley and rising terrain as very real hazards to attempt for a pilot unfamiliar with the area. "There's a vertical gain of about 2,300 feet over about two or three miles horizontal distance from Evolution Lake coming up to the Mendel Glacier." Neither Edwards nor I could understand why a pilot would knowingly place himself in such peril, especially in bad weather.

Edwards explained how any forecast that Gamber received could be so incorrect. Back in 1942, weather maps were drawn by hand from data collected by observers across the country. There were no automated stations feeding data into a central computer that then spit out forecast maps on demand. Weather bureau maps were drawn for every twenty-four-hour period from data collected at 1:30 A.M. Eastern Standard Time, which means the November 18 map was actually drawn from observations made at 10:30 P.M.

Pacific Standard Time on the previous day. The maps were released one week later. A lot could go on within those twenty-four hours between observations.

The November 18 weather map shows a band of precipitation extending from Portland, Oregon, to San Francisco, reaching eastward to the California-Nevada border; the map for the November 19 (drawn from observations the evening of November 18) shows the remains of the storm all the way south to Los Angeles and a pocket of moisture in northern Nevada, around Winnemucca. That is, within twenty-four hours the front had moved 900 miles, meaning its average speed was thirty-eight miles an hour. The maps show maximum winds speeds of thirteen to eighteen miles per hour. Whatever hit Gamber and his crew and dumped snow all over the Sierra, creating gully washers in Placerville and Carson City and 1.13 inches of rain in Winnemucca, had come in fast. The state of weather observations in 1942 was not up to the task of predicting such a storm. So, off they flew that morning of the eighteenth.

Given how bad the weather became, and given where the AT-7 ended up, there are two possible scenarios for how the crash occurred. The first is what the 1947 army accident report concluded. Lost in a storm, or perhaps blown east over the Sierra, Lieutenant Gamber flew into cumulo-granite. Controlled flight into terrain: CFIT.

The other scenario is that, encountering stormy conditions, five pilots turned back. We know from Jessie Dick's letter that two pilots did not: Gamber and one other. The only reason I can see for Gamber and the other pilot not turning back with the other five planes is they had not flown anywhere near them. Where they flew the weather was different—some place like Owens Valley on the eastern side, the rain-shadow side, of the Sierra. Did they cross the Sierra early in the morning while the other planes practiced in the foothills?

Under either scenario, the weather bureau climatological data report showed me that to get bad weather and be forced to turn around, the pilots that day had to be flying over the Sierra Nevada or in the foothills. That's why storm timing is important. When did that bad weather arrive, since the weather was good when Gamber and the other six pilots left Mather Field? There is also no reason to assume that all seven aircraft flew to the same place or on the same schedule. After all, William Bechter doesn't say in his diary how long they flew on November 18 before bad weather forced them to turn around.

CHAPTER 17

Carried by Flight:
A Scenario for Disaster

Lieutenant William R. Gamber awoke the Wednesday morning of November 18, 1942, with the rest of Mather Field. At 6:00 A.M. the sun still had nearly one more hour of sleep before rising and an undefined several minutes more after that before cresting the Sierra Nevada. Gamber was eager to fly. The navigation cadets were anxious too because their instructors were anxious. Nobody liked being grounded due to bad weather when there was a war to win.

But nobody could be blamed for canceling flights, Gamber thought. An inch of rain is what he heard had fallen yesterday. These California storms were different than back home in western Ohio. One day it's sunny and warm and the next it's raining cats and dogs. Dangerous updrafts and downdrafts, especially near the hills, and big cumulonimbus rising halfway to the moon.

At the mess hall, Gamber ate his breakfast, washed down with lots of coffee. Afterward he picked up his assignment for the day—chauffeuring three cadets on a navigation training mission. He stopped in for the weather report. Not good, but not so bad given the previous days: Mather Field south to Stockton, 4,000-foot ceiling, and 5,000 to 7,000 feet south of Stockton. Visibility three to four miles at Stockton and unlimited beyond that. That meant the previous day's rain was gone, but marginal visual meteorological conditions over the Central Valley today meant he would have to keep one eye on the weather and the other eye on his students and their navigation. At least there would be none of that horrible fog from a couple of weeks ago. After over 700 hours in the air, Gamber found he desired only a few things: a smooth-running machine, favorable winds, and a sky clear above with visibility unlimited.

He strode out to the field to check on his airplane, number 41-21079. The morning felt warm, not like winter at all. A bit blustery was all. The stars were bright.

With the crook-necked military-issue flashlight he carried in the moonless dark morning, Gamber circled the AT-7 and ran through his preflight checklist. His two main and auxiliary fuel tanks were full, giving him approximately three and a half hours of flight time in stable conditions, with a thirty-minute reserve. His musician's hands ran over the smooth aluminum-painted skin of his airplane, searching for dents and dings and anything that might signal a loose rivet. Where he could reach, he felt the edge of the aircraft's propellers. With his tire pressure gauge he checked the two balloon Goodyear tires forward and the smaller aft tire. By hand he moved the ailerons on his wings then moved to the tail to check the aircraft's twin rudders and elevator, insuring the mechanisms and their cables moved freely without binding and without too much play.

Satisfied with the outside of his airplane, Gamber opened the rounded coffin-shaped portside door, pulled down the stairs, and climbed into the cabin. His inspection here was quick. The lavatory functioned, the student desks were secure, fire extinguisher filled and secure, nothing loose. He moved into the cockpit, bending his tall slender body through the small door frame and trying not to hit his head. Taking off his leather flying jacket and pilot's "crusher" cap, he hung them on a hook and out of the way. He settled into the left seat, the pilot's seat.

Gamber let his eyes dance across the instrument panel of the Beech 18. Flying! The young man in him loved the feeling of being up in the air, circling around like a hawk and knowing the control lay with him. The engineer in him loved aircraft and engine design and function. And the student in him loved the theory of flight, airfoils and lift, physics and math—how it all worked together to keep him up in the air.

With his feet on the rudder pedals and his hands on the yoke, once again Gamber moved ailerons, elevator, and twin tail rudders. He made sure his radio functioned correctly and switched on cabin, landing, and navigation lights. He checked his propeller anti-icing system, saw that it was working correctly and thought again of how nice it would be to have wing deicing boots as well. Wing ice can form at any time of year if the aircraft surface temperature drops below freezing, but especially now, as California moved into winter, the danger of icing was ever-present in every pilot's thoughts. It helped that the Beech could carry a load of ice if need be, because when conditions are bad enough it takes less than five minutes for a couple of inches of ice to cover the leading surface of a wing, creating drag, and decreasing lift.

From outside came voices, other pilots showing up—six more, according to the morning's assignments—as well as ground crews and marching navigation students. They marched everywhere. Splitting into their elements of three, the cadets singled out their aircraft and clambered aboard. There were quick introductions all around, the cadets giving sloppy salutes within the confined space and referring to him as "Lieutenant." Gamber noticed that one of his cadets had as much trouble moving himself around the cabin as he did. That would be Glenn Munn: tall enough to make the lieutenant feel of normal height.

Gamber asked who would serve as first navigator and John Mortenson raised his hand. As the three cadets took their seats at the student desks in the main cabin, Gamber was amused to notice that they sat in alphabetical order.

The pilot completed his cockpit check while his navigators readied charts, flight computers, protractors, rulers, and other equipment. With the sky gradually getting brighter, Gamber had the ground crew slowly pull the propellers four complete revolutions before switching the ignition on. He continued running through his preflight checklist, ending by priming the two Pratt & Whitney engines and firing them up. He ran the engines at 1,000 rpm, continuing his checklist, checking and rechecking his instruments. The engines rumbled and roared like happy beasts. All was ready for takeoff. Gamber motioned for the ground crew to remove the aircraft moorings. He released the parking brake and the AT-7 began to move.

At 7:11 A.M. they left for the sky, smoothly racing the rising sun into the firmament. A broad sheet of red spread across high and lacy clouds to the east. It put in mind a verse about spring he'd learned in Bible school. "For, lo, the winter is past, the rain is over and gone; the flowers appear on the earth; the time of the singing of birds is come, and the voice of the turtle is heard in our land; the fig tree puts forth her green figs, and the vines with the tender grape, give a good smell. Arise, my love, my fair one, and come away." Arise. Arise!

Gamber leveled off at 5,000 feet and watched the day grow brighter. He checked his trim, read his gauges. With the AT-7 up, up and away, Lieutenant William R. Gamber was ready for his first set of instructions from his first navigator, Cadet John Mortenson.

● ● ●

They flew south, toward Eagle Field, a bit beyond Los Banos, 120 miles down-valley as the crow flies. At top cruising speed, and flying straight, they would make it in under forty minutes, but navigation training flights never flew straight lines or at top cruising speed. Gamber knew his way to Eagle Field and back by heart from his own training days and from piloting months of navigation training flights. He had mastered the rudiments of navigation from his own flight training and was proficient at pilotage, dead reckoning, and radio navigation—following radio range courses and picking his way through the Central Valley using nondirectional beacons.

Sometimes the cadets made mistakes and got off course, so Gamber used his own knowledge and ability to check on the students. If the students made errors, he tried to let them figure it out on their own before letting on that he knew better. It was his duty to get the cadets where they needed to go and get them back, but they also needed to learn how to identify and rectify their mistakes.

As they flew, Gamber received instructions from his first navigator, as Mortenson computed air and ground speed and confirmed his checkpoints. And, as Gamber had promised himself that morning, he kept his eye on the sky and on the ground. Using dead reckoning and pilotage, they followed State Route 99 from town to town and turned due south at Turlock. The flat valley looked pretty much the same from place to place, farmers' fields and curlicue creeks and agricultural dirt roads, but the towns all had different shapes. If the navigators lost their way, Gamber would show them the old barnstormer trick of dropping low to the ground and reading town names on their water towers.

Radio navigation worked well to check dead reckoning, but the cadets were just forty days into their training and didn't have any practical experience with it. This was probably only their fourth flight. Therefore, Gamber also kept his eyes on the automatic direction finder needle, listening to valley NDBs and mentally tracking their position from the familiar stations. Down the center of the valley was also a radio range course to follow and he paid attention to that as well. It intersected with another course farther south in Fresno that led northeast over the Sierra Nevada to Bishop, should their assignment point in that direction. Gamber had done it many times.

He was a bit bothered by clouds developing over the Sierra Nevada and south of his position. According to his weather forecast, as they flew south the ceiling should be rising and visibility increasing. It didn't look that way to Gamber. Quite the opposite, actually.

He knew bad weather doesn't always come at you like a wall. It grows. And there are gaps. Pilots have to pay attention and be aware of the gaps, because bad weather can come at you like a suspicion of weather. And then a little more weather. A layer of cloud here and a layer there. Virga falling from the clouds. And you begin to maneuver. Gently. Gently, at first. Because the weather has sucked you in and you're still focused on going straight.

• • •

Everybody involved in this story, from the 1942 and 1947 army accident reports, through R. W. Koch's 1979 account, to twenty-first-century journalists, assumed that Gamber was lost in stormy weather. Looking at all the facts, I've tried to come up with a reasonable explanation for how this might occur, but conjecture is all I have for deciding what happened next.

Supposedly, no radio or visual confirmation was ever received that Gamber and the AT-7 had reached Eagle Field, Los Banos, or anyplace else along that route. As part of his preflight check, Gamber would confirm whether his radio functioned. If he didn't transmit his position, either he chose to practice radio silence or he experienced catastrophic radio failure involving not only his own set but the transmitters and receivers students used for communication via voice and Morse code. If all their radios conked out, Gamber might not stop along the way to have them fixed. How would he know if parts and a technician were available? How many days would he have to remain away from Mather Field for repairs? I can see him thinking, "No—I'll just carry on without it." After all, a radio isn't essential for safe flight, especially if you know the area. He would rely on remaining alert to avoid trouble.

I don't know how, or where, Gamber became swallowed by clouds, but he must have if we are to believe that he became lost. The cloud deck must have dropped awfully fast, forcing the pilot to attempt climbing out of it, since the AT-7 was never sighted nor heard at Los Banos, his first point of contact according to the 1942 army accident report. A cloud ceiling can rise while clouds form below, so pilots try mightily to stay on top of such clouds until they can climb no higher. If there are layers of clouds, they keep between the layers. And when the layers close off, they try to turn around. And if they can't turn around, if they suddenly realize they have been flanked, they're facing bad news.

The storm that turned away Cadet William Bechter and four other flights must have caught up to Gamber as well. To end up being east of his flight line there had to be a pretty stiff wind, blowing the AT-7 across the Sierra. The cadets' drift meters were useless in cloud conditions with the ground obscured. As I imagine occurred with General Dargue's fatal flight the previous December and Lieutenant Turvey's crash into Hester Lake the following year, Gamber's crew would be plotting their dead reckoning and pilotage courses based on weather and wind data secured the morning they took off. As soon as the pilot popped out of clouds, or flew under them, or found a hole to peek through, they would have realized they were no longer in the valley and would have begun to rectify their error. Surrounded by mountains as far as could be seen, would they know enough of where they were to plot a different course? An airplane can't drop crumbs on the ground, turn around when lost, and follow them back home.

Perhaps the radio compass in their AT-7 was faulty, as would happen to Lieutenant Turvey a year later, and they drifted east in the clouds without knowing it. But why not use their radio to inform Mather Field of their predicament? Had their radios conked out? Maybe breaking out of a lower strata of clouds over the Sierra Nevada foothills was Gamber's first inkling of how far off course he had drifted. Mountains peeked and poked from the clouds and resembled island archipelagoes. Frighteningly, some disappeared back into higher cloud strata.

The only possible way to get the AT-7 from the Central Valley to Darwin Canyon and crashing into Mendel Glacier at nearly 13,000 feet is to have Gamber flying up the South Fork San Joaquin drainage. He couldn't do that and *not* hit cumulo-granite unless he could see his route. I'm certain the pilot did not spend much time at altitude before crashing, because neither Leo Mustonen nor Glenn Munn was found with an oxygen mask, which they would need for extended high-altitude flying. Perhaps Gamber flew up-canyon, following the terrain as Jay Fuller did before he crashed his Cessna in 1976 with his girlfriend, Jean Noller, and Lauren Elder.

Whatever the series of events that got them there, the AT-7 turned, probably above Blayney Meadows, and headed up the wide and safe-looking Evolution Valley. Gamber, good pilot that he was, likely made his choice and flew up the left side of the valley, rather than up the middle, maximizing his turning radius in case a quick turnaround was needed. They would have run out of ground eventually, but everything sped up because the AT-7 flew straight ahead into Darwin Canyon when Evolution Valley turned obliquely right. Did clouds obscure the way?

To be blown so far off course in the Sierra Nevada, maybe in a storm—or a storm about to happen—Gamber would have been dealing with stiff winds, turbulence, and possibly rain and light snow, too. The mood in the cockpit would have been tense, with the students in back working hard to figure out where they were. Bound in a relationship as old as mankind, Lieutenant Gamber and Cadets Mortenson, Munn, and Mustonen were facing danger together and working toward a solution. In the heart of danger there would not have been much else to do except what they were already doing. They wouldn't have been thinking about survival so much as waiting. Thinking and waiting. Waiting for something to happen, and perhaps scared just a bit that it might.

• • •

I asked William Langewiesche about what happens in a cockpit in bad weather when the whole world has gone topsy-turvy. He's written about flying in *Fly By Wire* and *Inside the Sky* and he's flown through a lot of bad weather. He's flown the Beech 18. He's flown in California and knows the weather there—the hot stale-air summers and the autumn and winter storms.

"You can see the weather coming at you up ahead," Langewiesche told me. "It never takes you by surprise. The weather doesn't come up fast. You know what is happening. You see it. And if the weather is getting worse and worse, maybe clouds are blowing in, maybe you see some rain falling in the hills. Or the clouds are lowering and you're descending with it."

You can always turn around, because "climbing out of it is not at all assured. It's nothing, in California, at 20,000 feet, to be deep in the weather." And there comes a time when, if you don't turn around, you're going to die. The problem for pilots is, "That's not an obvious threshold. What's happening is that your choices are getting narrower and narrower. You're feeling a little bit ... you're not feeling good about it. You're feeling tense. But you keep going and you can allow yourself, if you're not being careful, to be carried by flight itself."

Being carried by flight is easy, Langewiesche said. "Flight is a forward progression. More than a car. You can't stop. You can't pull off to the side. You have to keep going. In *some* direction. It takes enormous and surprising mental energy to make the decision, especially for beginners, to deviate or turn around." That's how pilots get in distress. "Through basic inertia, or the mental momentum of flight, they allow themselves to be flown by the airplane into trouble."

There's one thing Langewiesche is certain of. "We're not talking about a scenario of panic," especially with how far off course Gamber appeared to be when his airplane was eventually found. "If they're that far off course it means they were deep in the weather for a long time. You can't sustain panic for very long. I would assume that the mood in the cockpit would be one of varying degrees of anxiety. Not panic. If they were flying, clearly, sustained in the clouds, they were in control." On the other hand, conditions in the cockpit would have aroused varying "levels of consternation," Langewiesche said, "especially with the people in the back"— Mortenson, Munn, and Mustonen.

Langewiesche shook his head and contemplated the fate of these four men. "World War II fatalities for aviation were high because they were cranking these guys out. The guys who flew fighters in combat, they had like, 300 hours!" He estimated his own flight time at somewhere between 15,000 and 17,000 hours. "A 300-hour pilot?" he asked in amazement. "They weren't people of the air, they were people of the ground!"

Langewiesche put his finger on the problem faced in the AT-7 cockpit: youth and inexperience. In World War II they called young men boys, and when I looked at the crew's portraits I was struck by how much like kids they appeared. But they were doing adult work. And they must have thought of themselves as highly experienced. The tone of our whole conversation had changed, from Langewiesche being interested and speculative to expressing complete wonder at the whole thing.

"I think you can imagine the inside of that airplane easily enough. There would have been nobody in the cockpit with that kind of experience in the clouds." There are a few possibilities for what happened inside the AT-7 or what they thought and felt. Langewiesche wagered the students didn't realize they should be concerned. "They invested huge faith, that they shouldn't have, in their pilot. A 700-hour pilot [like Gamber] was a high-time pilot in their world."

In thinking directly about the pilot's experience, Langewiesche told me, "I assume that if the guy had no instrument training himself, that being in the clouds was a *very* unusual situation for *all* of them. But what do you do? It's a noisy airplane. You're sitting there. You simply go along for the ride. You hope like hell it's going to work out all right." He chewed that over a few seconds before reiterating, "I doubt that anybody was panicking. A thing like that? It would just be, sitting there and enduring it."

● ● ●

I believe it's plausible that Gamber ended up flying southeast and then east into Darwin Canyon because he was carried by flight—blown off course, buried in clouds and buffeted by high winds and attacked by rain, fighting downdrafts and updrafts. But to crash into the northeast-facing Mendel Glacier, the AT-7 needed to be coming about, turning around, in narrow Darwin Canyon. Upper Darwin Canyon ends abruptly: a wall of rock rising a thousand vertical feet in as equal a horizontal distance. No way out. Just as happened to the navy OV-10 Bronco in 1983, reaching the end of Darwin Canyon the lieutenant would have attempted a right-hand box-canyon turn and would have been met with cumulo-granite.

For any of this to happen, the weather had to be really heinous. Was it? For that I really needed to know when the storm arrived on November 18. From newspaper accounts and the U.S. Weather Bureau precipitation records, all I knew was that several inches of rain and snow had fallen that day all over the Sierra. For a more precise answer I turned again to scientists at the Desert Research Institute in Reno.

Climatologist John Lewis had a good idea of what kind of weather the AT-7 crew faced after completing the first leg of their down-valley mission. It was pretty nice. Other than some blustery or variable winds in Sacramento that morning, there was little indication of a major storm event on the horizon. "They [weather forecasters] may have had an observation at Eureka, on the coast, and one at Redding," foretelling stormy weather, Lewis told me. "My suspicion is they took off before the front arrived. I don't think they would have sent them on a training mission if this strong a system had already passed through Mather."

Turning around from their southernmost leg at Los Banos, Lewis believes the crew wouldn't have met with any bad weather until after returning north, past Mather Field on the second leg of their assignment. That's because the storm was moving slower than the AT-7 and there was plenty of time to fly south and then north in good weather.

If they flew north of Mather Field, they would hit the same bad weather that forced Cadet Bechter's pilot to turn around. Lewis is emphatic that the storm could not move fast enough to catch up to a southward-heading aircraft traveling at 150 miles per hour. They would have to be flying toward it to experience its worst effects—strong headwinds and a wall of clouds developing in front of them. From a distance they might see deep cumulus blowing off cirrus clouds on top. Severe updrafts and downdrafts would bang the plane around and throw them every which way. As they closed in on the front, visual references would be lost in thick fog and rain. Bear in mind that this storm moved so rapidly that it overwhelmed the observation and recording stations along its path. "For a front to be traveling that fast in one day you have to have tremendously strong winds at 10,000 to 30,000 feet," said Lewis. How fast? "Maybe sixty-mile-an-hour winds." Lewis was amazed at what this storm suggested. "To have a frontal system move that fast is very unusual."

The pilot in command would be faced with few choices. Flying into the type of storm Lewis described wasn't one of them. "I've spoken to a lot of the pilots who went through meteorology instruction of that time. My guess is the pilot was quite knowledgeable about the weather," said Lewis. "They had good instruction, good books. They knew a lot about the weather associated with these advancing fronts and they knew what to expect." They also knew to stay away from them.

Avoiding a large-magnitude storm is a compelling reason for Gamber to have intentionally flown off course. Even if the timing, as Lewis suggested, was all wrong, consider what Gamber might have seen and thought to encourage such an action had the timing been correct.

Since May 2, when he got his rating, Gamber had not accumulated any instrument hours. He was a smart guy, not the kind to take chances with the weather. Returning north from Los Banos or Eagle Field he saw weather that he wasn't expecting blocking further progress to Sacramento and Mather Field. Tuning the AT-7 radio to KCU 344 for a local weather update, Gamber confirmed what he'd seen: a big storm up ahead. He knew enough about weather to recognize the need to stay ahead of it, to stay out of thick overcast or deep clouds. In his mind he might think, "Let's go east. Let's get around this thing." He would instruct his three navigators to plot their courses independently for Fresno with a plan to find clear weather and cross the Sierra Nevada and come home by way of Owens Valley, Reno, and Lake Tahoe.

On the other hand, if Gamber had never flown across the Sierra around Fresno before, he would need to be very careful and precise. He might not be able to recognize any standout features to tell him for certain where he was. After passing into the mountains, it could be difficult to figure out his location. One mountainous area looks like any other when you don't know the terrain. And if the pilot had poor visibility—that would be trouble. If his visibility was good, if he flew plenty high—mountains wouldn't be a factor. But if Gamber didn't have supplemental oxygen on board—which is plausible since neither Mustonen nor Munn were found with oxygen masks—he couldn't fly too high, at least for very long.

Flying east into the mountains, Gamber and crew would mostly be concerned with keeping on course and staying away from cumulo-granite. Sometime soon after leaving the foothills behind, they would become aware of rising terrain. The lieutenant had to trust his altimeter while all cadet eyes watched the ground, monitoring their pilotage and dead reckoning.

If he followed the terrain as Alaskan bush pilots do, Gamber might have deflected from the South Fork San Joaquin when Evolution Valley made its oblique right turn, south and deeper into the mountains. Straight ahead he would have seen the Sierra crest. It must have been cloudy, or maybe only the highest peaks were capped by clouds. Mount Morgan, 13,739 feet, and Mount Tom, 13,649 feet, were ahead, and beyond them were Bishop and Owens Valley.

Flying in and out of cloud strata, wandering off course, is a big danger. Pilots tend to deviate one way or the other when flying in clouds; it happens naturally when visual references are gone. Because a storm was moving in, it would be windy in the mountains, making the AT-7 buck and flex, rise and fall, shuddering in sudden changes of wind velocity and wind direction. Wing icing would be a problem. Well within Darwin Canyon, and staying below the altitude requiring supplemental oxygen, Gamber would have run out of flying room pretty quickly. Making a steep turn to the right, the end would have come in a matter of seconds.

• • •

No matter how hard I tried to put the AT-7 in Darwin Canyon in bad weather—unintentionally carried by flight or intentionally flying eastward over the Sierra—I couldn't make the facts add up unless I left crucial data out of the equation. Contrary to the stormy conditions presumed by army investigators in their 1947 accident report, John Lewis says the AT-7 would have seen clear skies that morning. The big bad storm came later in the day to the mountains and the foothills of the Sierra.

Studying weather maps from November 18 and 19, Lewis extrapolated the storm's leading edge between San Francisco and Lake Tahoe midmorning the day of the crash. "Yet the accident is well to the south of that position at that time. That tells me they were not in the turbulent region of the front at the time they crashed." It would have been windy, but they gratefully wouldn't have been in deep cumulus convection with strong up- and downdrafts.

If bad weather wasn't the reason the AT-7 was in Darwin Canyon, what was? Were they lost? No matter how terrible the weather was, and Lewis convinced me the weather wasn't so bad the crew couldn't see where they were going, Gamber would have deviated over 120 miles due east of Los Banos, his supposed turnaround. In clear weather, that is a complete and absolute navigation failure by pilot and navigators. I don't believe it. No matter how inexperienced Mortenson, Munn, and Mustonen were—they had been at Mather for over a month and undoubtedly knew one end of the compass rose from the other.

The plane crashed due east of its intended route. Odder still, it crashed into northeast-facing Mendel Glacier. The AT-7 couldn't have drifted west to east, from the Central Valley over the Sierra crest, to hit the glacier because the glacier faces the wrong direction for that approach. That's like trying to find a way to drive your car into the back of your house from the street.

CHAPTER 18

East to West:
A More Probable Scenario

Frank Glick, my friend with California's Department of Water Resources, was the first person to plant the idea in my head that Lieutenant Gamber did not fly south to Los Banos. What if Gamber wasn't lost or off course? What if he knew exactly where he was and was trying to get home when disaster struck?

Frank's idea was, "The plane takes off at Mather Field in Sacramento and heads north up the Sacramento Valley toward Corning." This was still the time when everyone believed that Gamber's route was as reported in the news in 2005, after Leo Mustonen was found: from Mather, north to Corning, and then back. It was before I had Colonel Hewitt's route from November 20, 1942, and before I knew about William Bechter's diary.

Frank continued. "The weather gets worse to the north, and is coming in from the west, so the plane turns east to avoid the weather and flies over the Sierra into the rain shadow." Once over the crest, it turns south in better weather and continues down to the Owens Valley and vicinity of Kings Canyon. As John Lewis at the Desert Research Institute suggested to me about such a southern route, Gamber would have been trying to fly *around* the weather. When the lieutenant no longer saw a mass of clouds spilling over the Sierra crest he thought he was south of the storm.

"There, the airplane turns west to go over the Sierra again with the idea of turning north to head back to Mather," completing one big loop. "Unfortunately," Frank said, "the plane hits the mountain while heading west, never making it over the crest." When I asked Frank for a theory about why the AT-7 hit the mountain, he shrugged his shoulders and suggested that, maybe, it was my turn to do some of the work.

Route confusion aside, with some modifications I thought Frank's scenario was a good one. It fit the data much better than the lost and carried by flight version. That scenario relied on the storm catching up to the AT-7, which John Lewis convinced me was not possible. I also liked Lewis's reasoning that, when the crew left Mather the morning of November 18, they took off in acceptable weather without a hint of the big storm to come. And I liked what my crude calculations showed. The Beech 18 can cruise at 150 miles per hour, and the storm that hammered California and Nevada on November 18, 1942, as fast as it was, was traveling at less than 40 miles per hour. The weather map that documented the storm's passing, with observations from meteorologists between Seattle and Los Angeles, says it moved slower than that – a maximum of 13-18 miles per hour.

I appreciated the elegance of Frank's idea in accounting for how bad weather encountered in the north would have deflected flights east. However, his hypothesis didn't account for why five flights had returned the morning of November 18 while two had gone on. Because they behaved differently, I was convinced that Gamber and the second pilot took off that morning and went in a different direction and therefore did not encounter bad weather like the other five. If only we had an idea about that other airplane.

I knew from Glenn Munn's letter that described crossing "the snow capped Rockies at 15000 ft" that bad weather could cause a change in course after a flight began and that crews had no compunction about crossing mountains in good weather. After several years of research, after considering William Bechter's diary and talking to World War II navigators like Donald Satterthwait, Leonard Spivey, and Bill Davis, I was more inclined to think the assignment the lost cadets had for November 18 was not to fly south *or* north but *east*, over the Sierra at Lake Tahoe. Munn had written home to his mother about a similar trip. Others confirmed making trips to Salt Lake City, down Owens Valley, or to Tonopah, about 100 air miles north and east of Bishop.

Donald Satterthwait told me, "All our missions were preplanned in a classroom and we took that plan to the aircraft with us. We got our instructions before we took off." Only if conditions precluded a successful mission would there be a change of plans. Munn proved that in his letter home. Pilots may have been chauffeuring navigation cadets, but they weren't ignorant of the route. Satterthwait said it best. "These pilots were well-trained. The pilot was familiar with the routing the students had." In fact, "He worked as an instructor in the air."

Not only that, "These pilots pretty well knew what was going on with navigation. They could get out and fly back to base without any navigators on board because they flew so much and were familiar with the country." Lieutenant Gamber knew exactly what he was doing. Given all the variables, there could be little possibility that he was lost.

A route that took the AT-7 east, over the Sierra, also helped explain how the plane could crash into a northeast-facing glacier: they were headed home, east to west, over the Sierra Nevada crest when disaster hit. Unlike the carried by flight scenario, this east-to-west scenario didn't require tortured logic to place the AT-7 so far south and east of its supposed route. It also didn't involve the AT-7 doubling back on itself in order to be facing the right direction to collide with Mendel Glacier. It explained why no one reported hearing from the AT-7 anywhere in the Central Valley—searchers were looking in the wrong place. Mather Field's initial queries, the search route used—they were guesses. All assumed that Gamber went one way when he went another. Either the wrong flight plan was filed, the correct one was not found, or extenuating circumstances caused Gamber and crew to change their route soon after taking off. According to Frank Glick's theory and my adaptations of it, the AT-7 hit the glacier while crossing the Sierra crest from east to west. No turns. Straight on.

There are problems with the east-west scenario. I have no way to explain why Gamber would think to transit the Sierra anywhere near where he did. I have no data to suggest what would drive a pilot to cross over Lamarck Col (12,880 feet) into a box canyon of high and jagged peaks when a perfectly good, and lower pass, Piute Pass (11,423 feet), lies three air miles to the north. The canyon of North Fork Bishop Creek that leads up to Piute Pass is a masterfully carved U-shaped glacial canyon. As I saw from my flight with Bishop pilot Steve Ivey, from 15,000 feet up it's very inviting. Easy to see. An obvious route in visual meteorological conditions. Light airplanes fly through Piute Pass all the time these days because it's a visibly lower spot on the Sierra crest, and the terrain west of the pass in Humphreys Basin is gentle. Lamarck Col, on the other hand, is an undistinguishable saddle on a long, high, and sharp ridge, and on the other side is a sliver of a canyon walled in with rock and ice.

Neither Lamarck Col nor Piute Pass are shown on 1942 aeronautical charts. But on the 1942 Mount Whitney aeronautical sectional chart, which the crew would have been using, I found the evidence I needed to place Gamber in the vicinity of Lamarck Col: the 217-degree radio range course between Bishop and Fresno. If the AT-7 was flying southeast down Owens Valley with the intention of crossing the Sierra and returning to the Central Valley, the radio range course would have provided the navigational aid they would need for getting home.

Gamber would know about the 217-degree course. Earlier in the year he had completed his basic flight training at Lemoore Field in a Vultee BT-13, and it's certain he knew about the course from that time and from subsequent trips up and down the Central Valley. Eugene Fletcher told me about his own extensive navigation training during flight school in 1943. "We learned all of the procedures for flying the radio ranges and ADF navigation to pinpoint positions. We were even taught celestial navigation, dead reckoning, and also pilotage using ground reference points. Our training was not as extensive as the navigators, but we had to know all of the procedures because we would fly many times without a navigator."

Factoring in worsening weather for late morning on November 18, 1942, makes the following behavior for Gamber reasonable in my mind: He leaves Mather Field at 7:11 A.M. with three and half hours of fuel and a thirty-minute fuel reserve with good visual meteorological flight conditions. At the same time, five training missions head north, maybe to Sutter Buttes. Leonard Spivey told me "the Buttes" were a popular place to send cadets. Gamber is accompanied partway by another aircraft. They head east toward Lake Tahoe. Gamber continues on across the Sierra to Reno and then flies south toward Bishop in Owens Valley. The second pilot's mission is confined to the Sierra foothills, another common navigation assignment.

Flying their navigation training exercise, Cadets Mortenson, Munn, and Mustonen don't direct their pilot to head farther east to Salt Lake City because that would entail stopping to refuel along the way, as well as refueling at Salt Lake City before returning west and making yet another refueling stop. There are ten hours of daylight in mid-November—not enough for a round-trip flight with navigators untrained in celestial (i.e., nighttime) navigation—which makes Mather to Salt Lake City and back an overnight trip. There is no record of Gamber's AT-7 ever arriving in Salt Lake City.

Once they cross the Sierra Nevada, I see several options for getting Gamber, his crew, and the AT-7 to the crash site. They could have flown east over Lake Tahoe to Reno, southeast to Bishop or farther east and south to Tonopah, and then planned on returning from either destination by way of Lake Tahoe. After he encountered the storm over Lake Tahoe, Gamber would have likely returned south and crossed the Sierra at Bishop, where he knew he could follow the 217-degree radio range course.

Given that the AT-7 could carry 206 gallons of fuel, Michael Kopp, the Seattle-area pilot who owns a Beech 18, told me my idea meant too many miles to Tonopah without stopping to refuel. However, there would be enough fuel "if they had flown to the Reno area, down to Bishop, and back to the Tahoe area to take a look, and then back to the Bishop area. Whether or not they would then have had enough fuel to get back to Mather? Unlikely. It's possible they could have refueled at Bishop and then taken back off to Mather, via Fresno." Or, "If Gamber felt he had enough fuel to at least make it to Fresno," he could have planned to fly there, refuel, and then return to Mather.

I reasoned that Gamber would have been turned back from crossing the Sierra at Lake Tahoe because in late morning the big Pacific storm that dumped rain and snow all over California on November 18 had finally arrived. Gamber wouldn't know where this storm came from because it wasn't in his morning weather forecast, but he'd be confronting it nonetheless. Checking his radio he would confirm the over 3 inches of rain that will come in the next twenty-four hours have begun to fall in Placerville, east of Sacramento. Snow is falling so heavily around Lake Tahoe that roads will soon be closed. As yet unworried by the weather, Gamber is carried by flight because, from personal experience, he knows there are other ways to cross the mountains. In effect, he is looking for the back door before the storm closes in on him for good. He also has to think about his fuel supply, so he retreats to better weather.

Michael Kopp, my Beech 18 pilot friend, had another idea for why Gamber might have chosen to cross the Sierra Nevada east of Bishop. If Gamber was already in the Bishop area and knew there was bad weather to the north, because he had heard about it on his radio, he wouldn't turn around. He would cross at Bishop "because he's familiar with the southern San Joaquin Valley." And in that case, he had enough fuel to do the entire route of Mather–Reno, Reno–Bishop, Bishop–Fresno, and home. Not knowing what the winds aloft were, Kopp thought Gamber could have made the trip in about four hours. That meant cutting into his reserves, but the lieutenant could have stopped in at Fresno if his cadet navigators calculated the need to refuel.

Anyone flying westward over the Sierra Nevada in 1942 in the vicinity of Lamarck Col and Mendel Glacier would have been looking for the only navigation aid shown on their chart, especially in questionable weather. That was the 217-degree radio range course between Bishop and Fresno. It passes rather high in elevation— 12,000 feet at its highest—in the six-mile gap between Mount Tom (13,658 feet) and Mount Morgan (13,758 feet), eleven miles north of Lamarck Col. Glenn Munn wrote home on his Rocky Mountain trip that they flew at 15,000 feet, so I know Gamber would have no trouble in good weather following the 217-degree beam if that was his intent. One other thing, though. The beam was line of sight. If Gamber dropped below the Sierra crest or flew in the shadow of the high peaks he wouldn't pick up the signal.

Eugene Fletcher reinforced and expanded Donald Satterthwait's memory about pilots, agreeing that Gamber would have been well-versed in radio range flying. Importantly, Fletcher had experience, along with ideas, accounting for how the AT-7 could have missed the 217-degree beam. "One of the drawbacks to radio range is that with electrical storms around, the static could become so bad you couldn't hear it and it would be rendered useless."

Another issue with radio range involves fighting bad weather. "It would be much harder to locate and orient yourself on the radio range because of wind drift," said Fletcher. "But you would know if you were flying toward the beam or away from it by listening to the volume on the radio set. You would also know when you crossed the beam, but it becomes harder to line up on that beam with a severe crosswind." Even with the high peaks in front of him, as long as Lieutenant Gamber kept his altitude up and maintained five miles north or south of the beam, the AT-7 would be safe.

• • •

After talking with Beech 18 pilot Michael Kopp, I thought I had a good feel for Gamber's possible route from Mather Field toward his rendezvous with Mendel Glacier. And through the remeniscences of World War II navigators Leonard Spivey, Bill Davis, and Donald Satterthwait, along with B-17 pilot Eugene Fletcher, I had developed an idea of what Gamber might have been thinking while flying above Owens Valley as he piloted the AT-7. But placing him there physically still did not address why he crashed, and answering that question brought me back once again to the weather on November 18, 1942.

When I spoke with Steve Johnson, a meteorologist in Fresno, he was convinced that Gamber couldn't have been lost, that the pilot and crew knew exactly where they were and why. After first learning about the Frozen Airman in 2005, Johnson became obsessed with reconstructing the November 1942 weather. Given how conditions developed the day of the accident, he agreed with John Lewis at the Desert Research Institute that no airplane would have been sent flying in the Central Valley that morning in bad weather.

Johnson manages a Fresno cloud-seeding business called Atmospherics Inc. He didn't use the words "perfect storm" or "storm of the century" in his interpretation of the five-day storm event centered around November 18, but either of those phrasings fits quite well with his description. In Johnson's view, there was a deadly combination of moisture from several subtropical Pacific Ocean typhoons and frigid continental air moving down from Alaska.

In the days prior to November 18, California was a wet, but not snowy, place. Adding to what the newspapers had reported concerning precipitation amounts, Johnson found November 17 data from the south entrance of Yosemite National Park (4,000 feet) that measured rainfall at 3.5 inches. On November 18 the park entrance registered a total of over 7 inches—a record that still stands. Johnson estimates that rain like that in the lower elevations of the Sierra would produce "eight feet or more of snowfall above 10,000 feet."

The moisture from this record-making storm came from a series of Pacific Ocean typhoons, also known as hurricanes in the Atlantic Ocean. Johnson told me that 1942 was a big year for typhoons, with thirty-seven reported rather than the average twenty-one. His interpretation of the November 18 storm is that typhoon moisture was captured by the jet stream (an unknown atmospheric event in 1942) and pumped eastward into California, birthing a new storm by a process Johnson called cyclogenesis.

In Johnson's mind, "They picked the wrong day to cross the Sierra." Storm severity was intense and he is confident that extreme mountain waves and rotors formed east of the Sierra. "Turbulence at the 13,000-foot elevation on November eighteenth would be hard to describe," Johnson said, indicating to me his impression that the AT-7 could have easily been ripped apart. He estimated that wind speed could have been as high as 150 miles per hour near the Sierra crest.

Desert Research Institute atmospheric scientist John Lewis agreed with Johnson's assessment concerning an airplane flying west under those conditions. "I think the accident was weather related but not related directly to the weather near the front. It's related to the larger flow pattern around a cyclonic system. They were flying over a mountain with tremendous, unbearably strong, headwinds with turbulence conditions ahead of the surface front."

•   •   •

To cross from Owens Valley to Fresno, Lieutenant Gamber had to cross the Sierra Nevada in one of its widest and highest spots. This is something a pilot would not attempt in a cavalier fashion. Mountain flying requires skills and knowledge above and beyond what pilots need out of the mountains. With his 709 hours of flight time, Gamber was probably considered by many, including himself, as a highly experienced pilot. In 1942 he probably was. But pilots today think otherwise, as made plain by William Langewiesche's comment about World War II pilots being "people of the ground" and not "people of the air."

Steve Ivey, the Bishop pilot who took me flying over the Sierra, agreed. He spoke about a "confidence gap" in pilots with Gamber's level of experience. The lieutenant had spent the three months prior to the crash accumulating 35 percent of his total flying hours. Given Gamber's brilliant background in sports and academia, Ivey thought the young lieutenant fit the profile of an overconfident pilot, a person with a "can-do" attitude who would continue on against any adversity or challenge. "Of course, that's the kind of guys they wanted back then," Ivey said. "Today, pilots are not encouraged to act that way when they have so few hours of experience."

There's a likelihood that Gamber didn't realize all the dangers of crossing mountain ridges, though he might have felt up to the task. "It is difficult to be able to look out the windshield and say with any certainty whether or not you are higher than the ridge you are approaching," writes Sparky Imeson in *The Shirt Pocket Mountain Flying Guide*. He recommends maintaining a 2,000-foot clearance above mountain ridges. It's preferable to approach ridges at an angle of forty-five degrees, and when crossing multiple ridges a zigzagging course is best. "When the airplane is flown perpendicular to the mountain there is also a possibility of encountering a downdraft that could cause the airplane to impact the mountain." An angled approach permits "a safer retreat with less stress on the aircraft should turbulence or downdrafts be encountered." Experienced mountain flyers also line up their aircraft at least a quarter mile before crossing a ridge, because it's surprisingly difficult to know whether you are at, above, or below the ridge as the plane approaches.

Flying the upwind side of a ridge generally provides an air cushion that gives extra lift up and over. Approaching from the downwind, or lee, side, "the pilot runs the risk of encountering a

downdraft and turbulence," as well as the danger of a mountain wave, Imeson writes.

"The problem in mountainous terrain under wave conditions isn't the mountains, so much as the air which can swat planes against them," according Robert F. Whelan who writes about mountain waves in *Exploring the Monster*. In mountain wave conditions, "The most powerful and dangerous wave systems form when the winds at mountaintop level are strong and [they] strengthen with altitude." No informed pilot intentionally challenges mountain waves or rotors, but these atmospheric phenomena were unknown to pilots in 1942 and even today severely challenge pilots. Imagine how supremely difficult it would be for a pilot living in an era where wave knowledge was unknown.

Whelan writes that flight at intermediate wave altitudes is smoothest, "although a plane will be affected by the rise and fall of wave swells," just like a boat in the ocean, and a pilot's biggest concern would be remaining alert to ground clearances. Flight within breaking waves is "turbulent and unpleasant, and possibly dangerous," and flight in a wave's upper reaches was impossible for aircraft in 1942—it was simply too high.

• • •

In the cockpit of AT-7 number 41-21079, Lieutenant William Gamber is alert, scanning the clear sky in front of him. It is late morning. Westward, clouds obscure the mountains. Bucking a headwind maybe as much as 50 mph, the AT-7 slides south, bounding from one high desert basin to the next until reaching Owens Valley, where the mountains reappear from the clouds. The aircraft experiences bouts of instability intermixed with smooth air. It's very confusing and requires excellent piloting skills to keep the AT-7 on course. They're being blown this way and that like a sheet of paper in the wind. As all pilots are trained to do, Gamber sights down the center of the wide valley, with good clearance between the Sierra Nevada on the right and White Mountains on the left.

At their student desks, Cadets John Mortenson, Glenn Munn, and Leo Mustonen are hard at work plotting their course. The clump of buildings and farmland below must be Bishop, and they compliment each other on hitting their target. They're having a bumpy, uncomfortable, ride but they take it in stride. It could be worse. It could be like their last flight—down to Southern California—flying in clouds so thick the wing tips of the airplane were not visible, hailstones beating against the wings and windshield. And it was so rough when they dropped out of the clouds it rattled their bones.

The sky around the AT-7 is clear. From 12,000 feet up they have an unending and frightening view westward of jagged ridges and pointy peaks that make up the Sierra Nevada. Haze and cloud obscure the higher peaks. Much higher above are some of those weird clouds, the ones that look like stacked playing cards, arching overhead. Each of them is thankful their pilot, Lieutenant Gamber, knows what he's doing, because they'll soon be crossing over those ridges and peaks to their next checkpoint: Fresno.

The AT-7 circles Bishop. Gamber strains his ears through static in his earphones, listening for the 217-degree radio range beam he's using to check the students' course. Picking up the signal, Gamber steers west toward the Sierra Nevada. Static makes the beam bounce all over the place. It's hard to know exactly where it comes from and where it goes. He points his airplane directly at the eastern crest of the mountains, beginning his climb, hoping to pass over the ridge quickly and drop to a lower elevation before the need for supplemental oxygen. He has to keep the AT-7 above the terrain and out of these crazy winds. He rises up and down, the air sloshing him about like he's in a boat on water.

Gamber is going to want maximum power and speed when crossing the mountains. He knows that manifold pressure is essentially how much power the engines are developing and that the supercharged AT-7 Pratt & Whitney engines are rated for 37 inches of manifold pressure at takeoff—7 inches above atmospheric pressure at sea level. But he's lost approximately one inch of manifold pressure per 1,000 feet of altitude gain. At his current altitude he therefore has 30 percent less power than at takeoff and essentially 30 percent less speed, and who knows how many percent less ability to get out of the way if anything dangerous or life-threatening comes his way.

At least the plane burns less fuel with less manifold pressure, and fuel burn is beginning to worry Gamber. The AT-7 has been fighting some heavy winds for 130 miles since leaving Lake Tahoe, and he's just had the cadets calculate fuel consumption again and check their figures against one another. They're telling him they could squeak by and make it all the way back to Mather Field, but Gamber knows it's prudent to refuel soon. That means Fresno. Well, OK. They can do that. Even if it means returning home later than planned.

Gamber rides the air currents, watching his altimeter go up, then down, then up again. Then down. Sometimes it feels as if they are making no forward progress, surfing on currents of air. It puzzles him in an engineering sense but not enough to pull out his slide rule. There are more pressing issues. Like flying the airplane.

The terrain is rising quickly and Gamber struggles to keep the AT-7 at least 2,000 feet above ground level, but his altimeter keeps dropping. Below is broad Bishop Creek canyon, its forest quickly giving way to widely spaced pine trees, a smattering of lakes, and then bare rock. Gamber keeps his nose up. The ridge forming the eastern crest of the Sierra Nevada is dead ahead. He scans the skyline. Though the mountains around him are clear, some of the higher peaks have hints of clouds obscuring them and he can see huge cumulus buildups in the Central Valley beyond.

In the rear of the aircraft, Mortenson, Munn, and Mustonen can't see what's happening in the cockpit. From the port and starboard windows, mountains rise steeply. The boys are bouncing around. It's a white-knuckle ride. They all look forward to getting over the mountains, hoping the jostling will soon be over.

Gamber tries keeping his plane pegged at 15,000 feet but it's a losing battle. One of those updrafts from above Bishop would be nice right about now. The aircraft's wings are flexing. The twin engines whine. Everything is bouncing and rattling around inside. It's a noisier than usual flight. The terrain rises higher and higher. To compensate, the pilot unconsciously lifts his nose and chin. He needs all the lift he can coax out of his airplane. Ahead is the ridge. Closer. Closer. Big, imposing mountains covered in ice beyond. Hard to say for sure right now if they're higher. It's high and exposed up here. Rocks and ice. Not a sign of anything green and living below.

At the crest, Gamber gives whatever throttle he has left. "Oh boy!" he shouts involuntarily, willing the plane higher. They cross. There is a great lifting sensation and then a terrible sinking. Reflexively, Gamber pulls back the yoke. He has no more throttle to give. Keep the nose up. Keep the nose up. It won't lift! Before the thought can work its way through his mind, Gamber knows he's in a downdraft. A deep and dangerous downdraft. He has no throttle left to give. No throttle. No lift.

Dead ahead, that other mountain. A bowl of ice leading to a wall of ice. In a matter of a few seconds it's too late to do anything. He's being pushed down and has just enough time to recognize he lacks any ability to maneuver the airplane. Then, time doesn't matter.

One wing dips slightly and scrapes rock, throwing the entire aircraft off balance. Gamber reacts as quickly as he can but no human being can act as fast as an airplane traveling 150 miles an hour. They never know what they hit, never feel the impact.

The AT-7 careens out of control, bouncing and cartwheeling across rock and ice, the wings ripped from the fuselage, everything disintegrating piece by piece, tumbling, tumbling, tumbling. Over and over, turning around and around. The four occupants of the airplane are tossed about. The main body of the aircraft collides with a canyon wall. Everything explodes outward with a loud screeching and grinding of metal and rock. The four boys are ejected and fly one final flight. Two from the main cabin come to earth close together, mangled but still human. The other two are shredded by the impact.

The airplane's engines, mostly whole, slide and skip down the glacier's surface. So do various pieces of sheet metal, tubing, a rubber tire, pieces of wing, and components. It only takes a moment to happen.

Then, it's quiet again—the empty quiet when there are no ears to listen. Time begins to pass again and snow falls. Soft, white, pure snow, filling all the spaces between rocks and the bumps on top of and between rocks. By the following morning everything is covered under several inches of snow.

Did it ever happen?

CHAPTER 19

Please Remember Me

This story began for me in October of 2005 when climbers discovered the remains of Leo Mustonen emerging from Mendel Glacier in Sequoia and Kings Canyon National Parks. My involvement extended through a magazine article I wrote for *Sierra Heritage* published in early 2006. It continued through several more years of research, reading, interviews, and cogitation, culminating with the twelve months required to write *Final Flight*. In the middle of this my friend Michele Hinatsu and I found the remains of Glenn Munn. As of publication of *Final Flight*, two families of the crew missing from 1942 have found closure. There are still two families who wait.

The central mystery of this story for me has always been, what really happened on November 18, 1942, when the Beech 18 AT-7 Navigator number 41-21079 piloted by Second Lieutenant William Gamber and carrying navigation cadets John Melvin Mortenson, Ernest Glenn Munn, and Leo Mustonen crashed into Mendel Glacier? Were they lost, as so many people thought for so long, or was there another reason? After reading an aeronautical map from 1942 and talking with pilots, meteorologists, climatologists, atmospheric scientists, and men who trained to fly and navigate in the same era as the missing crew, I'm certain I found my answer to what happened the day four young men died.

I don't believe they were lost. The pilot and crew were on a training mission and knew exactly where they were. The AT-7 was returning home, trying to fly around a huge and unexpected Pacific storm. While attempting to cross the Sierra Nevada in what appeared to be clear weather, the aircraft was caught in the downdraft of a mountain wave, which caused the plane to smash into Mendel Glacier.

According to reports sent to Washington DC by Mather Field base commander Colonel Hewitt, search parties were dispatched immediately after learning of Gamber's failure to return on time. That may have been accurate, administratively, but until the big storm passed the following day, no airplanes left Mather Field. On November 19, William Bechter wrote in his diary, "We flew a special search today, patrolling the eastern foothills as far south as Visalia in a vain attempt to locate the lost plane." The following day came another search during the morning, "this time along the western coast range south to Coalinga." Six days later, flying south, Bechter's plane heard by radio that a different airplane wreck had been sighted near Coalinga, and they swung by to assist in locating it. "We used up so much gas we had to land & refuel at Lemoore Airport."

As days turned to weeks, desultory hunting for the missing AT-7 by the army, forest rangers, hunters, county sheriffs, and others expanded to include not only the Central Valley but the Sierra Nevada and Coast Range foothills across a widening swath of California. I don't think they knew where to look; they just were looking. Daily teletype updates from Mather Field to Army Air Forces headquarters in Washington DC continued. Every message ended the same: "AT-7 41-21079 MISSING SINCE 1911Z NOV 18 NOT YET FOUND SEARCH BEING CONTINUED," until December 14 when all searching was terminated.

• • •

At one point during our interview, William Langewiesche abruptly asked me, "What's the end result of all this? These guys crashed." He was questioning my purpose in writing a book about something that, in 1942, was a common occurrence. People flew. Aircraft crashed. People died. It was war.

At one time I would have asked the same question. But the deeper I became involved with the story, the less simple and commonplace it became. I learned a lot too—about airplanes, family histories, glaciers, weather and climate, and about what my country thinks about its war dead. I learned what *closure* and *sacrifice* really mean and that we all bear a responsibility to live our lives with honesty and integrity in order to honor the greatest gift to freedom a soldier can make.

Those boys who marched to war and never came home live through us, and everything about us is lived because of them. We are tied to the past as surely as we look to the future.

What were these young men fighting for in 1942, these small-town boys from Ohio, Minnesota, and Idaho? What thoughts did they have about war in Europe or Asia? Did they know the politics that separated communist from fascist from anarchist from nationalist from monarchist? Did they know the history? Did they know the violence of political belief? Had they seen the corpses that lined the roads to Shanghai or inhabited the charnel houses of Europe's concentration camps? I don't think so. All of that was hidden from general view until after the war—until after so many boys gave up their lives.

They knew one thing very well. The United States of America had been attacked. Everything was at stake. Not only their country but their way of life and everything they had been taught and raised to believe. These boys wanted to fight. After completing navigator training at Mather Field in December 1942, William Bechter wrote in his diary of his greatest fear: that his grades were so good his commander might ask him to stay behind as an instructor. "I think, however, I have talked him out of the idea; my choice was either ferry command [plane transport] or combat flying."

Bechter's friend Leonard Spivey was the same. Remaining behind as an instructor was strictly voluntary. All of twenty-one years of age, Spivey was solicited for a teaching assignment. He declined, saying, "I want to be assigned to a combat unit!" There were many others like him, heedless to the dangers they would face.

Eugene Fletcher told me, "Once we got overseas and into combat, the danger became very real, especially after the first baptism of fire. We tried to gloss it over for the home folks, but it was real in our minds. The glamour of flying was gone and we were just doing our jobs. But this made us just work harder to be the best. The pilots, really, because this was their command and they were responsible for the lives of nine other men. It was a sobering responsibility, especially when the number of missions to fly kept going up." At the beginning they needed to complete twenty-five missions. By the time Fletcher finished in 1944, the mission total had been upped to thirty-five—with most flight crews never making it past fifteen. "I have been told and have read that our Eighth Air Force had the highest rate of casualties of any [air] unit in World War II," he told me.

What were they thinking about, then, these young men, these boys so early out of their second decade? Fletcher says they were living in "the moment." When H. G. Wells wrote, "We must not allow the clock and the calendar to blind us to the fact that each moment of life is a miracle and mystery," maybe he understood the lives of a foot soldier in time of war or of a World War II B-17 Flying Fortress bomber crew over Europe. No thought to the past nor the future. Everything is now. The philosophers had their view; soldiers lived it.

And when the war was over, those who survived went back to their lives. "When we were flying missions we didn't give too much thought to what we would do later on in life," Eugene Fletcher told me. It was enough to do your job and be alive. When it was all over, "A lot of my friends went back to college and went on to become doctors, lawyers, accountants, and almost every occupation."

Plenty never made it home. I think of Leonard Spivey's comment at Memorial Day ceremonies in 2008, in Margraten, Netherlands. Spivey's B-17 was shot down in 1943 near Rosenberg, Holland, by flak and fighter aircraft. But he was lucky. As navigator, he had been in a better position to get out when the plane starting going down. Not so Arthur Everett, a waist gunner on board. "He was only nineteen or twenty when he lost his precious young life."

Spivey was captured and spent the remainder of the war at Stalag Luft III, in Sagan (now Zagan in Poland), 100 miles southeast of Berlin. This is the POW camp made famous in *The Great Escape*. But his duty and responsibility to his crewmates wasn't over, even after he came home. Sergeant Jones was another waist gunner killed when the B-17 broke up in the air. "I wrote to his mother telling all I could about how he lost his life when we were shot down. It was a very sad letter that I had to write. She had written me and said that her son was an only child. And there she was, mother and father, with their one and only gone." Spivey says he will never forget Jones and the other three in the crew who didn't make it back.

Dying in battle was their most remote thought. "This was a war and we were ready to fight," Eugene Fletcher told me. "Our main thoughts were, where do I want to fight? Do I want to be in a foxhole? Do I want to be on water? Or do I want to be in the air?"

Had Gamber, Mortenson, Munn, and Mustonen lived through their training they might have perished over Europe or in the skies over the Pacific. Casualties were certainly high enough for that to have happened. Or, they might have been in that coterie of bomber crews that survived. We'll never know.

"We had a lot of training accidents in World War II," Leonard Spivey told me. "This was because of the pressure and the rush to train and prepare pilots and aircrews. That was the priority."

From his perspective both as an Air Force pilot with over 10,000 hours experience and an Air Force Accident Board leader and investigator, retired lieutenant colonel Tom Betts agrees. There were high accident rates during the war because "the volume of flight training was unprecedented. Experience of instructor pilots was extremely low—most were second or first lieutenants with minimal qualifications themselves." Betts compared a World War II instructor pilot in 1943 to a teenage car driver of today in qualification skills. "Their equipment was poor and dangerous in a lot of circumstances," he said, "using navigation equipment that today would be considered poorer than emergency equipment."

World War II military pilots got their wings with much lower qualification standards compared to today. "Most were barely high-school graduates," said Betts, "with limited engineering or math skills." In contrast, "Today, all military pilots must pass comprehensive prequalification testing and must have four-year degrees—most in math or engineering."

However, as tens of thousands of pilots, navigators, and bombardiers proved repeatedly between 1941 and 1945, "They did what they had to do and accomplished a phenomenal aviation contribution to the war," said Betts. Despite the priority of churning crews out as quickly as possible, the service personnel who served during the war were bright and talented. By way of example, Betts cites his own father. "My dad was a student pilot during 1942 and flew B-25s out of North Africa and Italy during World War II, earning the Distinguished Flying Cross, Air Medal, and Purple Heart before being shot down and severely injured. He went on to a full career as a TWA DC-3 pilot, Lockheed Constellation pilot, B-707, L-1011, and B-747 pilot."

Betts has thought a lot about aircraft mishaps, especially those involving weather and mountains. "All pilots should know that they, and their aircraft, have specific limitations due to weather." During the early history of aviation, weather was found to be the cause of most accidents. After mid-World War II, the study of aviation mishaps had matured and weather was found to be a "major factor" but rarely "the cause" of accidents. "Weather forecasting, pilot use of forecasts, weather monitoring, and minimum weather requirements were usually found to be more root causes than the actual weather itself."

• • •

My thoughts turn continually to William Gamber, John Melvin Mortenson, Ernest Glenn Munn, Leo Mustonen, and their generation—my parents' generation. I don't think I will ever be able to forget these young men. Neither can I ever forget to look for meaning in their lives and their deaths. One thing I know for certain is that it isn't difficult to total up the costs of war. In a speech given March 24, 1968, Robert F. Kennedy said, "Here, while the moon shines, men are dying on the other side of earth. Which of them might have written a great poem? Which of them would have cured cancer? Which of them might have played in a World Series or given us the gift of laughter from a stage or helped build a bridge or a university? Which of them might have taught a child to read? It is our responsibility to let those men live."

We can let William Gamber, John Melvin Mortenson, Ernest Glenn Munn, and Leo Mustonen live by never forgetting their stories.

References

Much of what appears in *Final Flight* comes from interviews, usually multiple and, whenever possible, conducted in person. Those people are cited in the text. Archival material was slim. The following materials were invaluable in providing me with background information, insight, and inspiration.

Books and Manuscripts

Abbott, Mike, and Liz Kailey. 2007. *Jeppesen Guided Flight Discovery, Private Pilot*. Englewood, CO: Jeppesen.

Ball, Larry A. 1995. *The Immortal Twin Beech*. Indianapolis: Ball Publications.

Bibel, George, 2008. *Beyond the Black Box: The Forensics of Airplane Crashes*. Baltimore: Johns Hopkins University Press.

Browning, Peter. 1986. *Place Names of the Sierra Nevada*. Berkeley: Wilderness Press.

Buck, Robert N. 1998. *Weather Flying*. 4th ed. New York: McGraw-Hill.

Craig, Paul A. 1997. *Light Airplane Navigation Essentials*. New York: McGraw-Hill.

Delorme Mapping Company, 1988. *California Atlas & Gazetteer*. 2nd ed. Freeport, ME.

Dilsaver, Lary M., and William C. Tweed. 1990. *Challenge of the Big Trees*. Three Rivers, CA: Sequoia Natural History Association.

References

Elder, Lauren, with Shirley Streshinsky. 1978. *And I Alone Survived*. New York: Fawcett Crest.

Farabee, Charles R. "Butch," Jr. 2005. *Death, Daring, & Disaster*. New York: Taylor Trade.

Faust, Drew Gilpin. 2006. *This Republic of Suffering*. New York: Alfred A. Knopf.

Fletcher, Eugene. 1992. *Mister: The Training of an Aviation Cadet in World War II*. Seattle: University of Washington Press.

Farquhar, Francis P. 1969. *History of the Sierra Nevada*. Berkeley: University of California Press.

Gillespie, Alan Reed. 1982. "Quaternary Glaciation and Tectonism in the Southeastern Sierra Nevada, Inyo County, California." PhD dissertation, California Institute of Technology.

Guyton, Bill. 1998. *Glaciers of California*. Berkeley: University of California Press.

Hambrey, Michael, and Jürg Alean. 1992. *Glaciers*. London: Cambridge University Press.

Harris, Mark. 2008. *Grave Matters*. New York: Scribner.

Hill, Mary. 1975. *Geology of the Sierra Nevada*. Berkeley: University of California Press.

Huning, James R. 1978. *Hot, Dry, Wet, Cold and Windy*. Yosemite National Park: Yosemite Natural History Association.

Imeson, Sparky. 2003. *The Shirt Pocket Mountain Flying Guide*. Jackson, WY: Aurora Publications.

Langewiesche, William. 1999. *Inside the Sky: A Meditation on Flight*. New York: Vintage Departures.

Langewiesche, Wolfgang. 1972. *Stick and Rudder*. New York: McGraw Hill.

Leslie, Edward E. 1988. *Desperate Journeys, Abandoned Souls*. Boston: Houghton Mifflin.

Lowe, Jeff. 1996. *Ice World*. Seattle: The Mountaineers Books.

Macha, G. Pat, and Don Jordan. 2002. *Aircraft Wrecks in the Mountains and Deserts of California, 1909-2002*. 3rd ed. Lake Forest, CA: Info Net Publishing.

McAfee, Norman, ed. 2004. *The Gospel According to RFK*. Boulder, CO: Westview Press.

Miller, Edrick J. 1981. *The SAAAB Story: The History of the Santa Ana Army Air Base*. Santa Ana, CA: Costa Mesa Historical Society.

Mireles, Anthony J. 2006. *Fatal Army Air Forces Aviation Accidents in the United States, 1941–1945*. Jefferson, NC: McFarland & Company.

Moore, James G. 2000. *Exploring the Highest Sierra*. Stanford, CA: Stanford University Press.

Murchie, Guy. 1954. *Song of the Sky*. Boston: Houghton Mifflin.

Moynier, John, and Claud Fiddler. 2002. *Climbing California's High Sierra*. 2nd ed. Guildford, CT: Falcon Press.

Nozel, Mark. 2005. "Discovery on Mount Mendel." Unpublished ms.

Parmerter, Robert K. 2004. *Beech 18: A Civil and Military History*. Tullahoma, TN: Twin Beech 18 Staggerwing Museum Foundation Inc.

Pearson, Michael Parker. 2000. *The Archaeology of Death and Burial*. College Station: Texas A&M University Press.

Pelletier, Alain J. 1995. *Beech Aircraft and their Predecessors*. Annapolis, MD: Naval Institute Press.

Robinson, Doug. 1996. *A Night on the Ground, a Day in the Open*. La Crescenta, CA: Mountain N' Air Books.

Robinson, John W. 1980. *Mt. Goddard, High Sierra Hiking Guide #10*. Berkeley: Wilderness Press.

Saint-Exupéry, Antoine de. 1945. *Wind, Sand and Stars*. New York: Bantam.

Sledge, Michael. 2007. *Soldier Dead: How We Recover, Identify, Bury, and Honor Our Military Fallen*. New York: Columbia University Press.

Swanborough, Gordon, and Peter M. Bowers. 1976. *United States Navy Aircraft since 1911.* 2nd ed. Annapolis, MD: Naval Institute Press.

Sweeting, C. G. 1984. *Combat Flying Clothing.* Washington DC: Smithsonian Institution Press.

———. 1989. *Combat Flying Equipment.* Washington DC: Smithsonian Institution Press.

Tweed, William C. Forthcoming. *An Uncertain Path: A Search for the Future of National Parks.* Berkeley, CA: University of California Press.

Voge, Hervey H., and Andrew J. Smatko, eds. 1972. *Mountaineers Guide to the High Sierra.* San Francisco: Sierra Club.

Waldron, Tony. 2001. *Shadows in the Soil: Human Bones and Archeology.* Charleston, SC: Arcadia Publishing Inc.

Whelan, Robert F. 2000. *Exploring the Monster: Mountain Lee Waves; The Aerial Elevator.* Niceville, FL: Wind Canyon Books.

Periodicals

Anonymous. 2006. "Buried in Ice." *Military Officer* (June): 71.

Bowie, E. H. 1942. "Climatological Data, California Section." *U.S. Department of Commerce, Weather Bureau* 46, no. 11 (November): 120–32.

Clark, Douglas H., Malcolm M. Clark, and Alan R. Gillespie. 1994. "Debris-Covered Glaciers in the Sierra Nevada, California, and Their Implications for Snowline Reconstructions." *Quaternary Research* 41, no. 2: 139–53.

Grubisic, Vanda, and John M. Lewis. 2004. "Sierra Wave Project Revisited 50 Years Later." *American Meteorological Society* (August): 1127–42.

Johnson, David P. 1975. "The Mystique of Mendel." *Summit* (March–April): 30–32.

Koch, R. W. 1979. "The Secret of Mendel Glacier." *Air Progress Aviation Review* (Winter): 32–33.

Ridgeway, Rick. 1975. "A Tale of Two Couloirs." *Summit* (April): 3–19.

Snyder, J.J. "Dargue's Destiny." 1993. *American Aviation Historical Society*. (Summer). 82–102.

Tresniowski, Alex. 2006. "Frozen in Time." *People*. March 27.

Wurtele, Morton G. 1970. "Meteorological Conditions Surrounding the Paradise Airline Crash of 1 March 1964." *Journal of Applied Meteorology* 9: 787–95.

Newspapers and Television

Barbassa, Juliana. 2005. "Experts Know Name of Frozen Airman of 1942." *Salt Lake Tribune*. November 28.

Barber, Mike. 2006. "After 64 Years, a Mystery Is Laid to Rest." *Seattle Post-Intelligencer*. May 20.

Brainerd Daily Dispatch. 1948. "Remove Bodies of Airmen from Icy Mountain." September 11.

Chawkins, Steve. 2005. "Hope Survives 63 years." *Los Angeles Times*. November 2.

———. 2006. "Body of Airman Found in Sierra Glacier Identified." *Los Angeles Times*. February 2.

Council Bluffs Nonpareil. 1947. "Army Mountain Troops Win Victory Over the Elements." September 11.

Enkoji, M. S. 2006. "Frozen Airman's Identity Solved; He's Going Home." *Sacramento Bee*. March 10.

Gima, Craig. 2005. "Isle Team Leads Effort to Identify WWII Vet." *Honolulu Star Bulletin*. November 12.

Grossi, Mark. 2005. "Dental Records Don't Help ID Airman. *Fresno Bee*. November 10.

———. 2005. "Mystery of Mount Mendel." *Fresno Bee*. November 13.

Inyo Independent. 1948. "Army Mountaineers Hunt Glacier for Bodies Lost in 1942." September 10.

———. 1948. "Searchers Recover Bodies of Airmen." September 17.

Inyo Register. 1948. "Army Mountaineers Hunt Glacier for Bodies Lost in 1942." September 9.

———. 1948. "Searchers Recover Bodies of Airmen." September 16.

Iowa City Press-Citizen. 1948. "Four Bodies Found Years after Crash." September 11.

Fresno Bee. 1942. "Weather Report." November 18.

———. 1942. "Snow Closes Two More Highways in Sierras." November 19.

———. 1947. "Plane, Bones Are Sighted in High Sierra." September 25.

———. 1947. "Soldiers Trek to Glacier Where Airplane Crashed." September 26.

———. 1947. "Searchers Seek to Identify Sierra Plane Victim." September 29.

Kakesako, Gregg K. 2006. "Burial Pending for 1942 Aviator. *Honolulu Star Bulletin*. March 8.

KFSN-TV/DT. 2005. "World War II Airman Found Frozen in Glacier." October 18.

Long Beach Press-Telegram. 1947. "Climbers Due Back with Four Bodies." September 11.

———. 1948. "Army Climbers Quit Body Search." September 9.

McAvoy, Audrey. 2005. "Cold Case: Scientists Try to Identify Frozen Airman." Associated Press, November 15.

Miles, Donna. 2006. "ID of World War II Airman Sends Important Message to Today's Troops." American Forces Information Service. March 9.

Modesto Bee. 1942. "Sunday Rainfall in Modesto Area Totals .35 Inch." November 16.

Mountain Democrat. 1942. "Rainfall." November 19.

———. 1942. "Trace of Missing Army Plane Is Sought in County." December 3.

———. 1942. "Plane Search Fruitless." December 10.

———. 1943. Recreationists May Help Find Plane Missing Near Omo Ranch. June 3.

Nevada State Journal. 1942. "Storm Conditions Continue in State." November 19.

Oakland Tribune. 1942. "Army Plane and Four Men Missing." November 19.

———. 1942. "Search Abandoned for Lost Training Plane." December 16.

———. 1947. "Army Searchers Still on Glacier." September 10.

———. 1947. "Army to Investigate Glacier Plane Wreck." September 25.

———. 1947. "New 'Pararescue' Team Will Be Assigned Hamilton Field." December 12.

———. 1948. "Plane Seekers Descend Peak." September 9.

Reno Evening Gazette. 1942. "Winter Weather Closes Roads." November 18.

———. 1942. "Five-Day Storm Reaches across Northern Nevada." November 19.

San Mateo Times. 1947. "Pilots Dead 5 Years Found." October 2.

Unknown. 1948. "Air Crash Victims, Dug from Glacier, Arrive at S.F." September 13. Clipping in author's possession.

Wilson, Michael. 2006. "Military Lab Puts Name on a Long-Lost Airman." *New York Times*. March 24.

Online Sources

Anonymous. N.d. "The Lost Lockheed T-33 David Sleeves 1957."
Aviation-History.com.

Anonymous. 2006. "Frozen WWII Airman Laid to Rest." CNN.com,
March 24.

Gutierrez, Thelma. 2006. "Investigators Closing in on Identity of WWII
Airman. CNN.com, November 1.

Gutierrez, Thelma, and Dree De Clamecy. 2006. "Frozen WWII Airman
identified." CNN.com, February 3.

Smith, Mary, and Barbara Freer. "World War II Navigators." Stalag Luft
1 Online. www.merkki.com/navigators%20of%20usaaf%20in%20wor
ld%20war%20II.htm.

Stowe, Mike. www.accident-report.com.

Weir, Gordon W. "Navigating through World War II." www.
arizonahandbook.com/8thAF.htm.

Government Sources

Raub, William, C. Suzanne Brown, and Austin Post. 2006. *Inventory
of Glaciers in the Sierra Nevada, California.* Open-File Report 2006-
1239. Reston, VA: U.S. Department of the Interior, U.S. Geological
Survey. http://pubs.usgs.gov/of/2006/1239.

Sequoia National Park. 2005. "Supplemental Case Incident Report for
SAR 77: Mendel Glacier." Unpublished report in Sequoia and Kings
Canyon National Parks archive.

———. 2007. "Supplemental Case Incident Report for SAR 58:
Mendel*Glacier*. Unpublished report in Sequoia and Kings Canyon
National Parks archive.

U.S. Army Air Forces. 1942. "Report of Aircraft Accident." In author's
possession.

———. 1947. "Report of Major Accident." In author's possession.

————.1945 [revised]. *Pilot's Flight Operating Instructions of AT-7, AT-7C, SNB-2, SNB2-C Airplanes*. Publication number AN 01-90KA-1. In author's possession.

————. N.d. "Pilot Training Manual for the Flying Fortress B-17." In author's possession.

U.S. Coast and Geodetic Survey. 1941. San Francisco Sectional Aeronautical Chart. Washington DC: U.S. Coast and Geodetic Survey.

————. 2008. *San Francisco Sectional Aeronautical Chart*. Washington DC: U.S. Coast and Geodetic Survey.

Acknowledgments

If in reading this story you are inspired to make the trek to Mendel Glacier, there is something important I ask of you. First, bear in mind that the glacier is in a national park. Any airplane wreckage you might see must remain where it is. Second, please remember that as long as William Gamber and John Mortenson remain buried somewhere in Mendel Glacier, the glacier is as sacrosanct as any other cemetery. If you discover human remains, leave them undisturbed where they are. Mark the site in some way, take a GPS reading if you can, and report your discovery to Sequoia and Kings Canyon National Parks. Alternatively, inform the backcountry ranger at McClure Meadow in Evolution Valley or contact the Inyo County Sheriff's Office.

As for me, the story of *Final Flight* will not end until Gamber and Mortenson are found. This may be never, since the men surely lie beneath not only glacial ice but are deeply covered by a field of rock, talus, and scree. However, I will continue to make periodic visits to Mendel Glacier until both boys are brought home or the time comes when I am no longer physically able to make the trip. I consider this to be the least I can do to honor the memories of William R. Gamber, John Melvin Mortenson, Ernest Glenn Munn, and Leo A. Mustonen and to repay their families for their kindness and support while writing this book.

There are many people who have given me help and support along the way. Thank you, first, to my parents.

I am grateful to Roslyn Bullas at Wilderness Press for recognizing the value of this project. The editing work of Julie Van Pelt made this a much better book. *Final Flight* began in 2005 as "Secret of the

Ice Man," a magazine article for *Sierra Heritage*. Thank you to Bob Evans, managing editor.

Gregg Fauth and Bill Tweed with Sequoia and Kings Canyon National Parks provided valuable insight and information. I'm indebted to Gregg for not only suggesting the title of this book but for our many decades of hiking and climbing in the Range of Light. Also at Sequoia and Kings Canyon National Parks—Ward Eldredge, Tom Burge, Debbie Brenchley, Jenny Matsumoto, George Durkee, Paige Meier, Malinee Crapsy, Annie Esperanza, Jim Gould, and Ned Kelleher—thank you.

A mentor and longtime friend, Rich Stowell, with Naturalists at Large, first introduced me to the Sierra Nevada at Camp Wolverton in 1965. He fostered my appreciation of the Sierra and developed my interest in national parks and the Park Service. There is no way I can repay him for his influence upon my life.

Michele Hinatsu is a great hiking companion. It's a pleasure to find someone who will look at a map of the Sierra and say, "Wherever you want to go is fine with me!" She hiked with me to the glacier many times, listened to my theories, offered her own, and helped figure out what likely happened on November 18, 1942.

Thanks also to Steve Ivey, Michael Kopp, and Dick Shipley, who took me for rides in their airplanes and reviewed many chapters for accuracy; to Marge Carpenter, whose amazing work as a researcher and genealogist was instrumental in finding people; and to John Taylor at UC Berkeley, professor and Camp Wolverton alum, for tracking down the aeronautical charts so instrumental in providing what I needed to crack the mystery of why Lieutenant Gamber's AT-7 was flying anywhere near Lamarck Col. Taigh Ramey, proprietor of Vintage Aircraft, provided valuable information, documents, and insight about the Beech 18. U.S. Air Force retired lieutenant colonel Tom Betts, from Camp Wolverton and with decades of flying experience, helped with interpreting crash data and reviewed crucial chapters dealing with airplanes and flight. Mike Robbins, also of Camp Wolverton, was a great reader, reviewer, and sounding board through every phase of *Final Flight*.

Leonard Spivey and Bill Davis were ever giving of their time, their knowledge, and encouragement. Don Bechter shared the journal of his big brother, William Bechter, Leonard and Bill's best friend. Also, Donald J. Satterthwait and Judge James McCartney shared their memories of navigator training. Eugene Fletcher was unstinting in his assistance about pilot training, encouraging me to keep looking. Each of these World War II vets offered suggestions, discovered errors, and made corrections, all of which improved *Final Flight*. Immeasurable thanks are due to the staff at the Joint POW-MIA Accounting Command (JPAC).

Gary Gershzohn, with four decades of airline pilot experience, and Dawn Meekhof reviewed the entire book and contributed strong advice. So did Douglas Drenkow, Alice Goldberg, Sergeant Major Joseph R. Menard Jr., Chief Warrant Officer Thomas "Sandy" Sandbakken from Camp Wolverton, Michael Sledge, David B. Williams, and Doug Zeyer. Any mistakes that squeaked past their fine eyes are, of course, mine.

Robert Michael Pyle was a wonderful sounding board for ideas about writing and writing philosophy. For good all around help with the writing profession, thanks to Eric Blehm and members of my Seattle writers' group.

Pat Macha was immensely helpful and sharing of his time. Frank Glick was the first to come up with a viable theory of what happened to Lieutenant Gamber and his crew. Google Earth helped me in visualizing the possible routes flown by Gamber. Jim Meadowcroft shared his memories of combat. Jim and Bronwyn Buntine provided space for me to read, review, edit, and rewrite.

Figuring out the weather for November 18, 1942, was a huge problem. Larry Dunn at NOAA in Salt Lake City was a great resource. Stan Czyzyk, science officer at NOAA's weather forecast office in Las Vegas, reviewed and commented on my weather chapter. I deeply appreciate the assistance provided to me by Laura Edwards, John Lewis, and Hal Klieforth at the Desert Research Institute in Reno, and Steve Johnson.

At the *Fresno Bee*, Mark Grossi helped keep the *Final Flight* story alive over several years with thoughtful and complete coverage. This is also true of Pat May with the *San Jose Mercury-News* and Bill Morlin with the *Spokane Register*. At the Fresno County Coroner's Office, Drs. David Hadden, Venu Gopal, and Michael Chambliss listened to my theories of bodies in flight and offered their own interpretations. And I deeply appreciate Michael Nozel for making available to me "Discovery on Mount Mendel," his unpublished account of finding Leo Mustonen.

At the U.S. Forest Service in Bishop, California, John Louth and Mike Hilton were helpful with locating aerial photos of Mendel Glacier. For insights into Sierra Nevada glacial geology, thanks to Hassan Basagic at Portland State University and Douglas Clark at Western Washington University, who both showed me what ice and rock can really do.

Librarians and archivists are some of the best people in the world. You call them up, ask them questions, and they treat you like their closest friend. Nancy Roberts and John McBride at Tri-State University in Angola, Indiana, helped me put together the story of Bill Gamber's college years. Thanks to Bailey Diers with the University of Minnesota archives and David Aase at the Saint Cloud State College Alumni Association in Minnesota for helping fill in some blanks in Leo Mustonen's college career. Anna Shay and Nancy Lyle with the University of Idaho alumni office were helpful with John Mortenson's college years. Penni L. Cyr, librarian/media generalist with Moscow High School, helped track down Mortenson's high-school records. At the Bancroft Library in Berkeley, Susan Snyder and her colleagues were instrumental in filling in the gaps.

I am deeply indebted to the Gamber, Mortenson, Munn, Mustonen, Sulzbacher, and Lewis families and friends. In particular I want to express my extreme gratitude to Bill Ralston, Phyllis Wickstrom, Nancy Ralston Calvert, and Sally Ann Ralston Lane for sharing the Gamber family photos and scrapbooks with me; also, Barbara and Perry Adams, the late Richard Christian, and Pauline Jones for their memories of Bill Gamber. Thank you to Carol Benson and the late Ruth Mortenson for sharing John Mortenson's photograph and letter. Thank you to Jeanne Munn Pyle, Sara Munn Zeyer, and Lois Munn Shriver for making their big brother's letters and photographs available to me; and to Glenn Munn's nieces and nephews—Patty Beck, Debbie Beall Hessler, Scott Shriver, Jim Shriver, Gabe Shriver, and Cindy Davis. Leane Ross and Ona Lee Mustonen shared the few remaining photos of their Uncle Leo.

Marjorie Freeman shared her recollections of Mrs. Anna Mustonen. Julia Volpigno Sulzbacher and Barbara Sulzbacher-LaCroix made Roy Sulzbacher's photos from his two 1948 expeditions to Mendel Glacier available to me. Julianne Lewis and Lauri Lewis Woods shared Robert A. Lewis's map and photographs of Mendel Glacier.

For inspiration, I want to thank the staff at Camp Wolverton, a Boy Scout camp in Sequoia and Kings Canyon National Parks, and Margaret Hill Stowell. She taught me that loving the Sierra Nevada is not enough without someone in your life who loves you just as much. Therefore, I know this book would never have been written without the love and support of Jennie Goldberg.

And finally, my thanks to the Sierra Nevada, the best friend a boy ever had.

About the Author

Peter Stekel lives in Seattle. He has hiked in the Sierra Nevada—mostly Sequoia and Kings Canyon National Parks—since he was twelve years old. That is a long time. But not long enough. He is also the author of *The Flower Lover* and *Best Hikes Near Seattle*.

More photos can be found at www.FinalFlightTheBook.com. You will also find links to videos Stekel shot at the glacier, newspaper stories, television programs, book reviews, a schedule of personal appearances, and other things of interest to readers of *Final Flight*. Stekel's blog, documenting his research, is also at the site.